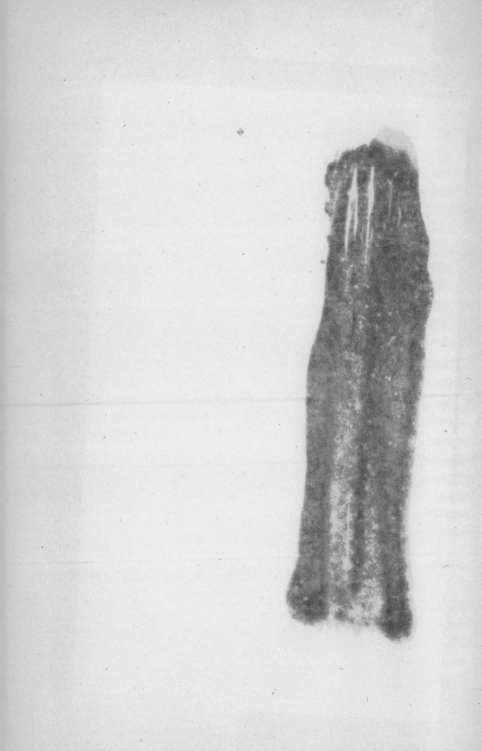

THE HUMAN TRADITION

by the same author

SIX EXISTENTIALIST THINKERS

THE
HUMAN TRADITION

by

H. J. BLACKHAM

ROUTLEDGE & KEGAN PAUL LTD
Broadway House, 68–74 Carter Lane
London

First published in 1953
by Routledge & Kegan Paul Ltd
Broadway House, 68–74 Carter Lane
London E.C.4
Printed in Great Britain
by Western Printing Services Ltd
Bristol

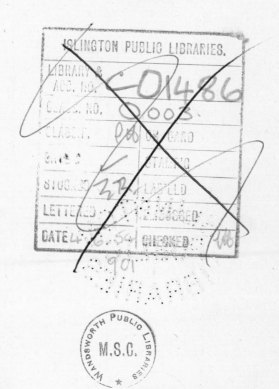

PREFACE

EVERY generation in the West for the last four hundred years and more has been engaged in debate on large and fateful questions of the time. During the latter half of this period the questions at issue have raised the human question, *tout court*; and to-day our part in world politics can hardly be separated from our conception of human nature and destiny. The ideological violence of the present phase in human affairs recalls the worst of the past. Like Burke, many see in the contemporary revolutionary struggle a renewal of the religious wars of the sixteenth century and of the clash of ideals and interests between Athens and Sparta some 1,950 years before that. The parallel is irresistible and, however much it distorts the run of real events, could be instructive if it served only to bring home to men of strong and opposed convictions that it is possible, and even necessary, to respect and to learn from one another. To restore the possibility of communication across the great divide that seals East from West is a long-term problem to which direct argument at the present time contributes nothing, or worse than nothing. The real present-time contribution comes from the attempt to make the alternative ideology in the West equal to its job, able to inspire and guide thought and action in dealing with the actual problems. Part of this attempt, however, is a searching examination of the rejected alternatives. For the primary justification of any comprehensive point of view is in an open and adequate declaration of the reasons why it is necessary to reject established alternatives, of what precisely it is that is rejected, and of the consequences that follow from the rejection. There is no trustworthy authority in any preferred alternative that pretends to be able to do what its rivals can do. On the other hand, an alternative which springs from the human tradition, is oriented on actual problems, and defines itself in ample disclosure of its rejections and their consequences, has done all that can be done formally to justify both itself and its rivals. Unless one looks out on the world from some such position it is hardly possible to discern anything clearly.

What are the present broad alternatives? Marxism by its practical success and bid for dominion has certainly established itself as one. Christianity, of all the historical religions, has been longest in close contact with secular cultural development, and in its counter-revolutionary role has shown itself adaptable and adventurous, able to survive and even to expand. Whether it can regain a grip on civilization and control its momentum and its direction, or will remain only to buoy the castaway, is in question. It is the best equipped of all the surviving religious traditions to play an effective modern role. Its test is, perhaps, the final test for all mankind of that type of tradition. There is also a surviving liberal humanist tradition amongst those who did not go the marxist way and do not share the Christian faith. No doubt this general position accounts for a multitude of people, but it can emerge as a definite alternative only if those who have it in their bones are capable of learning and doing a great deal. To stand by principle is not enough. A real alternative of this kind must be able to use the human tradition and the human situation to inspire a will to civilization and inform a vision of it.

All three alternatives are still in the making. The following pages are written from a humanist point of view as a modest contribution to the spirit and to the argument of the fundamental debate.

CONTENTS

PART ONE

Chapter I

THE HUMANIST TRADITION

1. THE RENAISSANCE AND BEFORE

I

SOMETHING which is treasured and handed down from generation to generation is central in the consciousness of those by
whom it is received and transmitted, and there can be nothing
doubtful about its character and continuity. A tradition is not a problem nor a quest. Therefore, looking for the humanist tradition
requires some justification to begin with, since there is no historical
continuity to establish it without question. Let a few reasons suffice
to justify the pains of inquiry.

There are people in the world today who are called and call
themselves humanists, and it would be very strange if their outlook
and attitude were without precedent or affinity. In the Augustan age
of the eighteenth century there was a conscious cultural affinity with
an original Augustan age in Roman letters; peak looked back to
peak, and in the intervening abyss was the lost obscurity of the Dark
Ages and the gothick gloom of Christendom. On the other hand, it
is said that Christianity alone solved the problems of human fate and
thought which defeated classical philosophy and religion, and rescued
the world from the sterility, morbidity, and pessimism which Greek
rationalism and humanism produced in it; that Christianity not only
saved the souls of sinners but also worked out the cultural and social
salvation of a bankrupt inheritance; that the recovered humanism of
the modern epoch has once again proved its impotence, and that
Christianity has once again the historical opportunity to prove its
power of cultural salvation. There is enough in these opposed views
to indicate that the truth is complicated and that between past and

3

present there is not only continuity but possibly also some resemblance which might throw light on our prospects.

The inquiry that would establish and possess a humanist tradition and learn from it must begin by ridding itself of the possessive lust and itch. Nothing could be easier than a walk through history, on the main roads or the bypaths, affixing the humanist label to satisfactory and less satisfactory persons, parties, and doctrines, and collecting an inheritance in that way. We should gain nothing by it, save more contempt for our opponents and more of theirs for us. Like a jackdaw one may love to rummage amongst the remnants of the works of pre-socratic thinkers and pick out and hold up some bright saying that reflects the solar light of modern rationalism. Jackdaws are like that, and nothing will stop their behaving that way. If we are to learn anything from the inquiry, we have to see what kind of humanist tradition was established in earlier times, and to understand how and why it was interrupted.

The *locus classicus* in Greek literature for a humanist ideal of life is the funeral oration of Pericles in Thucydides; this idealizes the consummation of a long political and cultural development. Athens is the school of Hellas, conscious of enjoying a way of life more liberal and humane and creative than the Spartan regime; and Hellas is conscious of an enlightenment and culture that separates her from the barbarians. This consciousness of an aristocratic quality of life, a many-sided devotion to excellence, rooted in the body and its exercised perfections, and in the city with its public life, its past glory and adventurous future, is a self-confident humanist response to the sufficiency of things. Hellenic clarity and zest (they had no professional priesthood) had rationalized and humanized and overlaid the dumb operational fertility cults with the articulate and visible splendour of a divine commonwealth of superior beings who peopled their imagination in company with the legendary figures of their Heroic Age. These clear images and plastic forms, these epic, idyllic, and tragic stories, made the most human of religions, so human that it hardly served the purpose of religion at all, so human that it taught the moral that out of the body there was no salvation, none of the excellence, the achievement, the delight of this world, nothing but a pale shadow of what had been. The complete inversion of this view which came to prevail, the view that the body in this sublunary world is a prison from which it is the whole business of the soul to get out in order to return to its divine origin, shows the violent contrast

4

between the mentality of classical and of late antiquity by which all scholars are struck. Why did the humanism of Periclean Athens not prevail?

The conversion from rationalism and humanism to mysticism and the occult which became widespread and universal in late antiquity has been described as a 'failure of nerve'. Loss of human self-confidence is the fairly simple central phenomenon; the cause is complex. The humanism of Periclean Athens was bound up with the polity and perished when the city was crushed and lost her independence. Greece became a ruin, one of the most insignificant provinces of the Roman Empire. But Greek culture had been spread throughout the Mediterranean world and the Near East. Why did it not nurse a vital humanism? Why did not the Hellenistic States refound on a greater scale, and develop, the humanism of Athens? Why did not Rome? One may trace the physical, psychological, and moral causes of the failure of Athens as empire-builder, and it does not cease to be an instructive story, but that does not account for the failure of Hellenism which survived the fall of Athens. Or is it true that Hellenism did fail, since Athens, being dead, yet speaks and all have learned from her, the school of Hellas in her own day and thereafter of the whole world? Did not the culture of which Athens was the fountainhead have a resurrection or a renaissance and become glorified by the adoration of generation after generation whose own efforts she inspired? All this is true, and accepted; yet Hellenism did fail, and might not have prevailed again at the Renaissance and have inspired modern humanism if something else had not been added which fortified a mortal weakness.

The literary treatment of the Olympic deities, so human, so exuberant, produced a high-spirited show. It was magnificent but it was not religion; it was not a religious handling of the problems of existence and fate, and the philosophy which attempted to take its place had no religious tradition to work on, nothing like the religious ideas of the Jews, capable of interpreting and moulding and being interpreted and moulded by their historical experience. For the Greeks, religion if it was not poetry was a problem (theology was their invention) or a political instrument (at Plato's worst); it was not, as with the Jews, the ground of their consciousness, the medium of their development. That might have been all to the good, but Greek philosophy also failed to follow the clue to science. It became a realm of ideas, dissociated from active life, not initiating and not corrected and developed by experience. In the end, oriental religion swallowed up both Greek science and Greek philosophy, because science failed to get its empirical foothold, and philosophy, for all its brilliance, failed to get its grip on human existence. The key notions of Greek religion, 'Know thyself' and 'Nothing too much', have a characteristic humanistic ring, until one hears them in their context and discovers their ironic, pessimistic, superstitious undertones: that one shall know oneself to be a mere man, and not tempt the gods by any venture too aspiring. The levelling justice of the gods, the equality of fate, is a depressing, superstitious faith, not the sovereign sweetness of humanist moderation, nor a high-hearted nor chastened trust in the king of kings and the righteous government of the world. Greek religion was in its lack of faith, robust or tempered, a dismal void which the howling winds of demonology and the dizzy vortices of astrology and theosophy filled resistlessly, making havoc of the sane constructions of the Greek mind, which was always sounder, more zestful and tempered, than its religious notions expressed or warranted. When one thinks of the Greeks, it is not this undertone of superstitious pessimism that one has in mind but the classic moderation of their enduring humanist constructions seen in their native sunlight, under the pure empyrean before the vapours and violent light, the electric and vitreous shams and shimmers of the technic and pyrotechnic stage of Greek religion. In Plato, justice is not a levelling fate but an integral harmony in the soul and in the republic—and in the cosmos. In Aristotle, moderation is not a superstitious fear of action but a sensitive measurement of the quality of action. Epicurus dealt with the problem of fate and human helplessness with truly Greek clarity and simplicity, disentangling himself from the assumptions and conventions, social and religious, which made the problems, and gently restoring human confidence and tranquillity by founding it directly upon the immediate sufficiency of friendship and natural pleasures: there was nothing else, neither to hope for nor to fear. This was all true humanism in temper, but it was not total; it was salvage work amongst the ruins, the political ruins of Athens.

The destruction of the polity in which Athenian humanism was rooted would not in itself have been fatal; it could have been far otherwise. If Greek science had stumbled further along the road of empirical discovery, and Greek philosophy had reflected upon the lucky sequence of steps and elaborated a conscious method, it would have been otherwise. The separation of head and hand is perhaps a sufficient reason for this failure. If Greek philosophy had studied the empirical foundations of politics and initiated and controlled social change, instead of seeking the perfect constitution and thinking in terms of final law, it would have been otherwise. But without science and industrialism a dynamic society is only conceivable in terms of military conquest and colonial expansion, and with the establishment and consolidation of the Roman world these reached a term. Rome herself outgrew her republican constitution, and Cicero, who idealized it, appealed for a change of heart when there was hardly an alternative to Caesarism except bold administrative invention. *Libertas*, which was for Cicero a form of social order, survived for Tacitus as only a form of personal character, the resolution to maintain one's personal integrity and moral independence in defiance of tyrants. Altogether, the ancient world came to put great strain on personal character, for lack of the service of developed institutions and techniques. Human confidence broke down under the strain, or fortified itself by the drastic discipline of stoicism or the quiet withdrawal of Epicurus. The 'failure of nerve' was a cultural failure. 'Greek rationalism wasted away as a fire burns itself out for want of fuel. While science ended in fruitless logomachies and soulless compilations, the religious will to believe got fresh vitality.' (Nilsson, *Greek Piety*.)

From the vantage ground of today it is easy to look back and watch the ranging Greek intellect pass over its quarry, hunting by sight and not by scent. They narrowly missed the clue to science and to the rational control of social development. Are we so sure, then, that the line of later events which have given us science and industry and social democracy is the line of true human progress which the ancient world failed to find? The answer must be yes, but the question should not be misunderstood. Undoubtedly, the ancient world encouraged and idealized the attainment of excellence in many forms of human achievement, and produced unsurpassable examples. Undoubtedly, the art of living was valued and taught and led many into the enjoyment of a blessedness as great as any mankind can ever aspire to. Undoubtedly, in the political field 'they created the habit, which our civilization has never either wholly lost or wholly mastered, of thinking things out beforehand'. (Sinclair, *Greek Political Thought*.) This was humanism, and its exemplars made a humanist tradition. But it was not humanism conscious and sure of itself, prevailing over the minds and forming the purposes and claiming the dedication of men, humanism as the demiurge of man's world; and in so far as it was not, men were bound to look elsewhere for their wisdom and their preservation and to form their lives on a different pattern. The humanism of the ancient world was meteoric or blessedly self-possessed, exhibited all the splendour or the grace of which the human spirit is capable, but it was like the brilliant guess or the lucky discovery or the bright and happy nature; it was never able to create the conditions of its own success, because it failed fully and firmly to grasp its own principles, and therefore men had no confidence in it. Men have no confidence in it yet, and for the same reason; but we have gone further along the road towards the possibility of that confidence, far enough to appreciate profoundly the achievement and the failure of the ancient world.

Look again at the achievement, and, again, the nerve of it is in Periclean Athens (indeed, Thucydides, aware of the tragic dilemmas of human action, yet intelligently intent on difficult achievement, is the ganglion of Greek humanism). The key words for moderation and justice, which in moral philosophy meant the harmony of the soul or the city and in religion might be nearer to fatalism and superstitious fear, had another aspect, namely, the conservatism of Sparta and of the established families in Athens, the moral argument which preserved the *status quo* and forbade Athens to fulfil her aspirations. The significance of Pericles is in his open-eyed assertion of an active ideal, against the prevailing standards, knowing its risks, sensing its inexorable logic, but trusting human character and with confidence in the liberal and creative quality of the Athenian mission. The fate of humanism was bound up with that venture, and no human enterprise ever came to grief more disastrously. Even in the ancient world Athens was politically insignificant, and by her political and military exertions alone would hardly have been heard of; she had eloquent writers to magnify her exploits, says St. Augustine. But Greece was a laboratory, and Thucydides was trying to teach from experience the possibility of controlling human affairs by empirical methods. The moral Plato drew from the same lesson was a distrust of men, a confirmation of conservative wisdom, a leaf from the book of Sparta on which to rewrite the maxims of the past; and after the failure of Sparta and her humiliating defeat at Leuctra, Plato's inquest in the *Laws* finds the reason in her lack of humanism, and he despairs of Greece—but his own last work is the tragedy of Plato. In the third book of the *Ethics*, in his tentative and confused analysis of purpose,

8

Aristotle shows the groping stage in the attempt to understand the principles of empirical control, or, rather, the failure to recognize the importance and the possibilities of the matter at all. Like the others, he was preoccupied with the perfect constitution, the final body of laws, by which men would be ruled and disciplined and put in the way of attaining their final good—which for the *élite* was in intellectual contemplation. Metaphysical misunderstanding of the universe reinforced conservatism. The Periclean rocket faded out and was forgotten. It was a dead culture that Alexander carried round the world.[1]

The speculative Greek preoccupation with perfect laws and absolute ends was matched and beaten in a practical fashion by the Roman establishment of their dominion. The benefits of the *pax Romana* were widely appreciated, the wide field of security, order, and intercourse had not been enjoyed under any other regime. There were settled social expectations and social functions. It was in the main a rule of law, although it was a government of men and not of laws. So great a lover of liberty and erudite an historian as Lord Acton is able to say that 'the Roman Empire rendered greater services to the cause of liberty than the Roman Republic', and this was a needed correction of the legend of republican virtue and imperial licence. Under enlightened emperors the government was able and humane, and the enlightened emperors were enlightened by stoic or epicurean wisdom. It was a Rome men came to think of as eternal, with laws that were final. If one excepts the exploitation and corruption and the madmen in the purple and the bloody suppression of such dissidents as the Jews, it seems as fair a scene as mortal man can ever hope to enjoy. The exception is much, and it was a large price to pay for the peace and security which most of the patricians and the plebs in the civil strife of the Republic had preferred to *dignitas* and *libertas*. The conservatism of Cicero's Republic was not able to save itself because it was not capable of the act of development which would have made it master of the situation. Roman law like Greek

---

[1] It would be absurd to slight the achievement. The Alexandriana was the fountain of intellectual culture for centuries, and in its Alexandrian period contributed to science more knowledge than any other age of Greek genius and more than any other people in all antiquity. The failure was as though all the ingenuity and contrivance and scientific advance in Britain during the first half of the eighteenth century should have failed to produce the industrial revolution, as it would have, lacking the intricate set of conditions which were provided in the second half.

intellect belied its own genius, missed the way technically and morally to the confident empirical control of human development, and produced a stasis. There is throughout the ancient world a universal quest for quietude, tranquillity, peace, manifest in the theme and impulse of all their thought, religious, metaphysical, political; a vast stillness that steadily mirrors the soul of that ancient world.

They just missed finding the way to control change, to take the creative initiative, and therefore they lost the condition of any valid and vital humanism, lost the means of self-development, and turned to the esoteric and occult preoccupations of the East. The ideas of Greek science and Greek philosophy were used to elaborate theosophies and astrologies and provide a refuge from blind fate. The humanist when he reads an exposition of even the most refined of these theosophies can be glad that it was Christianity which prevailed, since humanism had failed. Christianity humanized the occult and the supernatural, not entirely but greatly. It humanized the cosmos, and brought God into history, and with the universal mission of the Church it broke the reign of the static and cyclic and introduced a purpose, a certain development of ideas in relation to an historical task: it already contained the promise of the Reformation, or some other revision of its ideas and its mission in the light of the experience into which they would lead. This was the principle of human self-development which humanism had failed to develop out of its own resources, and which none of the other schools or cults or sects which spread themselves about the Roman world had the capacity to develop.

To pitch on Pericles as the embodiment of ancient humanism is not to identify humanism with imperial adventure, nor with the adventurous, nor with the progressive, nor the revolutionary; it is to insist that humanism cannot justify and establish itself without intelligent self-confidence that is inspired by ideals, relies on adequate techniques, and takes responsibility for what it will do; it is not a quest for security but a will to civilization, a generous appeal to the humanity of all men and their desire for achievement and self-fulfilment. Pericles stands for this (does Caesar?) and the power motive is no stronger in him than it is in the quietists, masked by the established ideals. Of course, if Pericles and his successors had succeeded, their achievement would not have lasted for ever; but humanism does not require that its achievements be eternal, so they be achieved. It founds itself on the temporality of all mortal things. The failure of

the Athenian venture made philosophy more abstract and conservative or drove it into sects cultivating individual salvation; and it was
philosophy and its inveterate rival, rhetoric, more practical but not
less conservative, that were the instruments of education. The great
achievements in the arts and in literature, not least the great Hippo-
cratic tradition in the science and art of medicine, remain of course
monuments of the humanism of Greece and Rome, but their
grandeur is the grandeur of ruins, for they were not a substitute for
the inspired and instructed will to human development which the
ancient world nearly but never attained.

Gibbon's judgement, echoing the polemical rationalism of Roman
traditionalists, that Christianity sapped the civic virtues which sustained Roman civilization, and Professor Toynbee's idea that our
modern civilization is 'an almost meaningless repetition of something
that the Greeks and Romans did before us and did supremely well'
(such a beautifully eighteenth-century idea makes him contemporary
with Gibbon) are equally grotesque examples of the antics of brilliant minds distorted by prejudice. A saner view is to be found in
another eighteenth-century historian, and a better humanist. Hume
says he is inclined to think interruptions in the continuity of tradition,
if it were not for the destruction of books and records, are of benefit
to the arts and sciences by breaking the progress of authority.

'Consider the blind submission of the ancient philosophers to the
several masters in each school, and you will be convinced that little
good could be expected from a hundred centuries of such a servile
philosophy. Even the Eclectics, who arose about the age of Augustus,
notwithstanding their professing to choose freely what pleased them
from every different sect, were yet, in the main, as slavish and
dependent as any of their brethren; since they sought for truth, not in
Nature, but in the several schools; where they supposed she must
necessarily be found, though not united in a body, yet dispersed in
parts. Upon the revival of learning, those sects of Stoics and Epicureans, Platonists and Pythagoreans, could never regain any credit
or authority; and, at the same time, by the example of their fall,
kept men from submitting, with such blind deference, to those new
sects, which have attempted to gain an ascendant over them.' (*Of the
Rise and Progress of the Arts and Sciences.*)

Hume, of course, is here using history for the purposes of his constant self-set task of moderating and dissolving faction and sectarian-

ism and dogmatism, for the sake of newly won liberty and toleration, but he is right enough; the mind of antiquity became thought-bound, voyaging about and about on a little land-locked sea.

II

The Europe of the new barbarian kingdoms was even more hag-ridden and intellectually sterile than the Mediterranean Empire, whose cities the barbarian armies had plundered and destroyed. The tough organization and world mission of the Christians and the oppor-tunity which fell to them to convert, civilize, and edify the European nations, introduced a unifying and purposive social drive which, for want of any other, served the interests of all who value human development.

The God of Israel, transcendent and numinous, acted directly in history and in nature, his creation, and is revealed in Jesus Christ as a loving Father who has numbered the hairs on the head of each child and who follows the lost one and bears him back rejoicing. In this divine humanity there is no breach between natural and super-natural, and the source of evil is in the disobedient will, not in nature nor in the body. It was left to Greek sophistication to pose the prob-lems concealed in this simplicity and to ensnare the Christian in a tangle of solutions. Yet it is the concrete simplicity that remains the glory and efficacy of the gospel and the perennial source of its renewal. Augustine, most formative of the Latin Fathers, looks out on a god-made world once enjoyed in its perfection by the first man, made corruptible by his sin, with the consequence that all mankind suffers the miseries of a corruptible body in a corruptible world. It is still a world of glory and beauty, of partial achievements (Athens is 'this ancient and goodly city, the only mother of arts and learned inventions, the glory and lustre of Greece'), but ruined. To the changes and chances of this mortal lot, from which only the philosopher purchases a dubious immunity at the price of his mutilated humanity, the Christian adds the burden of a continuous striving with himself to gain his lost perfection. The effort cannot succeed and the world will never become the home of man, yet victory is promised to the striving and in the end more than the original per-fection will be restored to those that endure. The paradise that is regained is a paradise of bodily perfection ('Corpulence will be cured, but not corporeity', says Aquinas, later). Augustine is not a Christian humanist in the modern sense, but there are elements of Christian humanism in him mixed with elements that are profoundly anti-humanist: preference for the authority of inspired biblical texts against reason and humanity; a human nature infected and incapable of good, requiring a supernatural act of grace and a church with supernatural powers. The strength and the weakness of Christianity at that time, from a humanist point of view, is clearly seen in Chapter 41 of the 18th book of *The City of God*.

Augustine's picture of the philosophical schools and sects differs from Hume's. He does not see enslavement to the master's teaching within the sect. Public opinion tolerates all the winds of doctrine and encourages the able disciple to break with his teacher and set up as arch-dogmatist himself; there is no authority; and what is at issue is the happiness of mankind. In contrast with this deep and dogged disagreement of all the doctors is the happy concord of the canonical authors of the Christian scriptures. This of course, as Augustine sees it, is not the happiness of chance nor even of a common will for truth, it is their common submission to divine instruction. So far, the humanist is all for the winds of doctrine, whatever dust and heat they bring. But Augustine goes on to say, in the most interesting passage, that all this wind is so much sound and fury, it is not harnessed to any social purpose.

'These and millions more of dissensions do the philosophers bandy. And what people, state, kingdom, or city of all the diabolical society has ever brought them to the test, or rejected the one and received the other? Has it not rather given nourishment to all confusion in its very bosom, and upheld the rabble of curious janglers, not about lands, or cases in law, but upon main points of misery and bliss? Wherein if they spake true, they had as good leave to speak false, so fully and so fitly was their society suited to the name of Babylon, which (as we said) signifies confusion. . . . But the people, state, nation, and city of Israel, to whom God's holy laws were left, did not confound with that licentious confusion the false prophets with the true, but all in one consent held and acknowledged the latter for the true authors recording God's testimonies. These were their sages, their poets, their prophets, their teachers of truth and piety.'

On this question of profoundest difference between humanists and their opponents, the question of authority and freedom of opinion, the issue is not quite so simple as humanists are wont to believe. The winds of doctrine in the Graeco-Roman world made the open climate of humanism, unlike the hot-house of priestly cultivation in Israel or in the medieval church, yet, technically, the winds can make a desert and the hot-house can raise useful plants. A complex of vital ideas, developed out of social experience, shaping and directing that experience and being developed by it, was something which the Graeco-Roman world failed to achieve, in philosophy, in religion, in politics. In this, Christianity was technically superior to any of its rivals. The Christian leaders never understood the technique (as Augustine shows), and they attempted to impose on the world of their making a stultifying discipline. Nevertheless, imperfect, and eventually vicious, as their discipline was, it was serviceable, and even necessary.

The subordination of intellectual life to religious life is the great cultural fact of the middle ages. Of course, the destruction of the Roman imperium and the Roman cities by the armies of the barbarians, and the expansion of Islam, left the Christian church in the West with a monopoly of experience and technique in administration and in education; and the hellenism which survived the destruction was fragmentary in the extreme (the works of Boethius being the most important and influential example). This physical fact, which gave the church a clear field and unrivalled authority, has rather obscured the previous fact that in the Roman world Greek philosophy and science had been absorbed into religion, and has led rationalists to think of the tyranny of the church throughout the middle ages as simply the deplorable consequence of the political breakdown of the Roman Empire, and to think of the painful modern attainment of secular and intellectual autonomy as a recovery of ancient humanism, with the important addition of experimental science. But not less important, although far less developed, is the technique of the inspiration and control of a civilization through a body of accepted and developing ideas. The dominance and development of Christianity throughout more than ten centuries in the West, with more than five centuries of totalitarian control, is a supreme example of this control, supreme not in its unqualified success but in its scale, persistence, and complexity. Certainly, recovery of the autonomy of culture is a major interest, indispensable to human development, a requisite of human dignity. The emergence of a dominant complex of ideas capable of superseding Christianity in the direction of civilization is a major interest of equal importance. Christianity is not merely an alien tyranny imprisoning reason; it is a primitive form of the necessary control of human development.

The claim and effort of the Catholic Church to achieve undisputed authority and complete organization in a consecrated Christendom aspiring to world order attained its high-water mark in the early thirteenth century. By that time, the development of European kingdoms and cities, the stocking of libraries, and the organization of studies had gone far enough to provide the means of a centralized Christendom, and not yet far enough to introduce uncontrollable intellectual and political elements. Yet this very culmination coincided with violent social movements associated with heresy and hostile to the Church, and with the European recovery and study of the full works of Aristotle. Innocent III imposed his will on temporal rulers, established the Inquisition, crushed the Albigenses, and founded the University of Paris as the intellectual capital of Christendom, where the mendicant orders detached from national allegiance and devoted to the authoritative tradition of Christian thought and order would teach a curriculum rigorously subordinated to an orthodox theology. Even in the hour of his triumph he was ordering back the tide. The scattered schools of law, arts, and theology were brought together in the new universities under the rule of theology, but it was impossible to maintain the trivium and quadrivium of the arts faculty as ancillary disciplines solely and sufficiently developed for the practical and theoretical uses of the teaching and administrative church. Philosophy, powerfully represented in the fully recovered works of Aristotle, demanded a place, and it could neither be assimilated to theology nor given an independent place with the seven arts without disrupting the unity of the whole scheme. The attempt to control human development by suppressing the autonomy of reason proved futile, and the pretensions of theology to rule all studies had to be abandoned—even within the ecclesiastical scheme, study of the canon law always held its own. This was already clear before the Renaissance.

Classical philosophy, not of course as independent critical studies but in various forms of platonism, stoicism, and aristotelianism, had been a disturbing factor in theology throughout the middle ages. The paramount idea of the Catholic Church was an organic conservation of an authoritative traditional theology without innovation or addition. Doubts and dissensions should be settled by reference to traditional authorities, by councils, or by the common opinion of orthodox teachers. The conservative majority should rule. Augustine, as a teacher of rhetoric and an enthusiastic student of Plato before his conversion, had always after his conversion put Plato first amongst philosophers, as the one who had come nearest to Christianity, in putting man's highest good in love and enjoyment of the philosophical Good, that is, God, and not in the perfection of man's body or mind, or both. This declared affinity of Christianity with platonism was strong in the Christian tradition on the authority of Augustine, and platonism could not be restricted to an apologetic role: its whole bent was a striving for intellectual knowledge of the divine, a theosophy, a religious philosophy, illuminist in character, the reward of those who like Peter venture in faith to walk on the water and are met halfway and upheld. This passionate platonic philosophy, whether intellectualist and hegelian like that of Erigena or illuminist like that of Bonaventura (or Roger Bacon), which insists on going from faith to knowledge, confident of the unity of all knowledge and all being, is in tension with the conservative theology that requires reason to rest in the received verities and traditional formularies of the faith. The achievement of Aquinas was in his reconciliation of the claims of orthodoxy and of reason, relying on the recovered philosophy of Aristotle and accepting his empirical view of knowledge as derived from the senses by the act of intellect and the rules of reasoning. If the received verities of the faith were taken as first principles, reasoning from them by rigorous logic might build a superstructure of higher knowledge in which the human mind, unable to enjoy the intuitive vision enjoyed by the divine mind and by the saints, might participate thus discursively and analogically in the divine knowledge. Aquinas, as confident as the platonists of the unity of being, and more confident than they in the competence of the natural reason, does not attempt to demonstrate the unity of truth in a religious philosophy of the platonic type, but simply defines the relations between the two independent and complementary systems of truth. The spiritual power in Christendom defined the conditions and limits of the office of the temporal power and left to its competence whatever lay within the sphere of its relative autonomy; and theology dealt likewise with philosophy. The introduction of aristotelian logic and metaphysics, concerned with the universal and the necessary, disrupted the traditional hortatory teaching of the faith, concerned with charity and humble devotion rather than with knowledge. The two methods were incongruous and raised many questions and excited much resistance to the pagan philosophy. What had theology, what had a Christian, to do with science? Did the disinterested inquiry and the canons of reasoning exemplified in Aristotle have any independent value and validity for a Christian? Was theology a science? These questions agitated in the thirteenth century had at least an impressive answer from St. Thomas. He tried to show that by purely scientific means, by rigorous deductive reasoning, without any of the divine illumination of the augustinians, the human mind could participate in the divine knowledge by treating revealed truths as first principles, known intuitively to God and to the saints although not to men. Thus the intellectual life which was Aristotle's ideal of human dignity became the religious life which was the Christian's present and supernatural end. His synthesis has outlasted more subtle or more daring systems because it exemplifies *in excelsis* the Catholic genius for co-ordination and definition, the articulation of functions and the creation of order; and there emanates from him a natural humanity and sanity; so that he continues to provide a cheerful and hospitable normality to which men are glad, sooner or later, to return. His doctrine all through is a doctrine of development and fulfilment, of integrity and completion. As a trivial sample, take his treatment of physical pleasure: 'The special object of temperance is healthy pleasure in the sensation of touch.'

Of course Aquinas did not satisfy Christian platonists, who could not be content with reasoning from revealed truths because they wanted to penetrate those truths to their source, to proceed by love and intellectual activity to direct knowledge of and union with God. Nor did he satisfy the serious students of Aristotle in the faculties of arts, who were taking the canons of reasoning seriously, who were showing up the irreconcilable inconsistencies between Aristotle and revealed truths, for whom thomism was pseudo-scientific and revealed truths obscure and outside reason. The disquiet caused by the study of Aristotle and its growing influence was expressed in 1277 by the condemnation of 219 propositions of the aristotelians and by action taken against the chief exponents. But it was clear that religious philosophies in the augustinian tradition and joinery even as craftsmanlike as that of Aquinas were too naïve for the rigorous standards of the now mastered logic. For the first time, Duns Scotus produced not a religious philosophy but a philosophy of religion, founded on a fundamental critique of human knowledge; and William of Occam, in a meticulously argued critique of Scotus's main thesis, sought to show the impossibility of the science of God such as Scotus had conceived possible. His strict logic (like that of more recent successors) swept out of the sky of reason the meta-physical heaven of essences and entities, restricted the scope of deduc-tive reasoning, and demanded unpreoccupied attention to the objects of experience. It was the only way to defend theology from philo-sophy if philosophy was not able to show the truth and intelligibility of revealed doctrine; for then theology remained possibly competent to deal with the problems invincibly beyond the power of reason. Occam's nominalism prevailed against thomists and platonists. It was the triumph of aristotelianism, a triumph of logic which shat-tered, not the Christian faith, but the metaphysics of Aristotle, and made way for the beginnings of modern science.

By the end of the middle ages, before the Renaissance and the Reformation, it was evident that the simple rule of the church as conceived by Innocent III was simply not feasible. There was too much in the world that was too refractory: sovereign rulers, popular movements, and not least the intellectual, and growing, inheritance from the ancient world, which was intrinsically independent of Christian revelation and incapable of being assimilated to it. What was in question was not the Christian faith but its meaning for human life in the world. After all, Christianity was not neo-platonism, it had no necessary contempt for the body and for the world; man might be a *viator* but his sojourn here was long enough to allow of other interests besides his salvation and his supernatural end; the technical training of the professional cleric was too narrow an educa-tion for man. Such was the verdict of many representative figures before the close of the middle ages. The competition from autono-mous interests and studies could not be resisted, like the later compe-tition from science, and the road broadened out to the Christian humanism of the Renaissance.

III

Before all else, the Renaissance was a revival of learning, of which there had been anticipations in the twelfth century, conspicuous in the school of Chartres and in a John of Salisbury. It was not only the recovery of a great deal more of the surviving literature of the classical world but also, and primarily, a new attitude towards the old pagan world. The revival can be seen in its simplest terms as an educational programme, a revolt of the faculty of arts against subordination to the uses and interests of theology. The independent study of Plato at Chartres, and of Aristotle everywhere, with the new effort to acquire the languages, meant new interest, new standards, and new taste in philology and literature which utterly burst the confines of traditional grammar and rhetoric and brought into contempt not only the pedantry but also the elaborated dialectical method of the schools. Within the schools, the troubled career of Peter Ramus, now a forgotten name, exemplifies better than any the attempt to free rhetoric from the technical dialectic of the schoolmen in order to make it a humane and universal discipline. But it is outside the schools in new milieux, in Florence and in Venice, under secular patronage, that the new spirit found free scope and expression. Yet Florence and Venice were rivals and opponents in this field of intellectual activity too. The programme of the platonists in the Academy of Lorenzo the Magnificent was directed against the widespread averroistic aristotelianism, the dogmatic rationalism condemned in 1277, so strong at Padua, the university under the protection of anticlerical Venice, a philosophy founded on the supremacy of the natural reason and belief in the impersonal unity of the intellect, and therefore disbelief in the personal independence and immortality of the soul. The platonists of Florence, interested in the humane values of a personalist culture, used against this professional impersonalist philosophy a philosophy that was in the augustinian tradition of Christian platonism, and the personal immortality of the soul is the dominant motive of their argument. Ficino's platonic philosophy is not so original nor so modern as that of the earlier Nicholas of Cusa, but in his insistence on the native competence of the human intellect and will to attain their consummation in the enjoyment of the true and the good in union with the whole universe, he struck the note of universality ultimately discordant with Christianity, certainly with the Christianity of the Reformation and of the Counter-reformation. These platonists looked towards a universal human religion of the kind to which the eighteenth century aspired, and in practical influence there is a filiation through Socinus and the considerable influence of the writings of the socinians in the seventeenth century.

The response of the aristotelians is seen in Pomponazzi, most distinguished of the teachers at Padua. The argument of his *De immortalite animae* manipulates in the manner of the schools the received opinions of the authorities. Aquinas is used effectively against the current interpretations of Aristotle on the nature of the intellect, and Aristotle is used against Aquinas on the nature and immortality of the soul: the argument is for a personal individual perishable soul, as far as human reason can judge of the truth, although on the authority of the Christian faith one ought to believe quite otherwise. But the humanist interest of Pomponazzi's argument, beyond the rational acuteness of his analysis, is in his realistic appraisal of man's true dignity, standing in its simple sufficiency over against the grandiloquent magnifications of the platonists, and resting in the recognition that the individual is inseparable from the whole human race and is called to participate to the utmost of his ability in the intellectual, the productive, and the practical (moral) life of mankind. Here is a passionate spinozistic philosophy, reworking the aristotelian and stoic themes, with none of the interests of the humanists of the new culture, yet providing a sober and sufficient programme of human civilization to which the ancient world had not risen and to which Christianity had not stooped, and from which the individualism of the humanists was turned away, a theme which needed only the development of historical conceptions to make it a generous and imaginative humanist programme. Pomponazzi's conception of man was suited to a true scientific humanism, congenial to the scientific interests of Padua, and challenging the religious humanism of Florence; but the obstruction of Aristotle's *Physics* had not yet been demolished and cleared away.

The Renaissance of course cannot be understood as simply a revival of learning, the development of independent studies outside the schools of the church and to some extent within them. The revival was also a revival of sculpture and architecture, a digging up of the past, an attentive archaeology with imitation and emulation in view. And the past that was dug up was a humanist past. Pater was essentially right in his essay on Winckelmann, that Greek sculpture is the perfected expression of a delicate pause in human development, the happiest outcome of a generous physical consummation in union with the mind in tranquil self-possession, 'the first naïve, unperplexed recognition of man by himself'. Such a moment, stabilized in its expressive achievements, can ever after be only appreciated by a Winckelmann, never revived by a Michelangelo. Similarly, Geoffrey Scott is essentially right in his thesis that the human body is the centre and standard of classical architecture, its impulse and measure, giving man something that answers to himself, not in the chimerical flights and freaks of his imagination but in the stable needs and delights of his bodily frame. This Greek and Roman humanism, inspired by and founded on the human body, generalized in the forms of its classical achievements, could be adopted and adapted by the powerful minds of the Renaissance artists, but the classical spirit could not be revived: medieval Christian aspiration, medieval decorative opulence, medieval barbarous violence persisted. When the classical movement comes to an end in the formal familiar elegance of established society in the eighteenth century, men do see in their world, with whatever illusion, an image of Rome. It is as near a vain repetition of what had been done supremely well as history is likely to show, yet still it is not the classical spirit that is revived. But it was long enough to dwell on the models of the past. The pioneering movements that have made the modern world do not properly belong to the Renaissance, which contributed a rediscovery of the classical past, a repossession of its autonomous law and order, an original reworking of its themes, and through the reconquest of past achievement created a tradition, that is, a standard by which high achievement could be methodically maintained.

In Machiavelli one sees in another field the attempt to master a contemporary problem by intelligent study of the recorded experience of the past. It is of course a mistake to think that he glorifies the ruthless will to power; he, rather, anticipates Montesquieu, he is looking for the secret that maintains the energy and freedom of a liberal society. The best part of his political thought is a meditation on the conditions of politics as revealed in his diplomatic experience and in his constant reading of history, chiefly Roman history: Livy, Sallust, Polybius, Justin. It is by the checks and balances of the Roman republican constitution and by the limitation of private property that he hopes to promote the activity and secure the liberty of a stable society; and in this he is consciously forming the liberal tradition and standards of political control by formulating the principles of past success, a judicious combination of constitutional and psychological principles.

Montaigne belongs to the latter half of the sixteenth century, younger than the chief figures of the Renaissance and older than the pioneers of modern thought. He is apart from any of the active centres and is far too individual to be representative, yet his witness

21

is invaluable, for in his candid and copious reflection he revolves again and again the world of classical antiquity and the world of the middle ages and reveals fully the view of an unprofessional man of his time on these two great phases of human experience. He has an eye for whatever confirms man in his humanity and for whatever estranges him from himself, for perfection is 'to know how to enjoy loyally one's being'. Man aspires to be divine, but he comes nearest to it when he is content to be truly human. When he sets out to embrace the divine intellectually or spiritually by systems of philosophy or by 'supercelestial opinions' he actually exhibits subterranean behaviour, the extravagances of an Archimedes or a Diogenes or of those whose whole life is one sustained effort to enjoy the incorruptible pleasure that is the final end of Christian desire. Men try to raise themselves above the human condition, and it is an absurdity. 'They want to get outside themselves and escape from being men; it is mad: instead of transforming themselves into angels, they transform themselves into beasts; instead of raising themselves up, they throw themselves down. These transcendental humours frighten me, like high and inaccessible places; and nothing is more troublesome for me to digest in the life of Socrates than his ecstasies and his talk of his daemon . . . and of our sciences, those seem to me more earthly and low which are high flown. . . . The finest lives are, to my mind, those that put themselves alongside the common and human model, with order but without miracle, without extravagance.' (III, 13.) The doctrinal knowledge of the professional scholar is both uncertain and outside himself. Knowledge is priceless if a man knows how to use it to make his life supremely human. To be a Christian is to be more than ordinarily just, charitable, kind. To be too much engaged with speculation, with spiritual exercises, with studies, with disciplines, is vicious folly: 'when I walk alone in a fine orchard, if my thoughts are sometimes preoccupied with other things, some other part of the time, I bring them back to the walk, to the orchard, to the sweetness of the solitude, and to myself'. To understand science and apply it to the needs of ordinary life and the exigencies of affairs is great, in antiquity or in the modern time, but to value oneself upon learning and disengage oneself from public and practical concerns and despise them is sottish. Nature is often more productive of true intellectual excellence than the arts. 'We know how to say: "Cicero says thus; Those are Plato's morals; These are Aristotle's very words"; but we ourselves, what do we say? What

22

are our judgements? What do we do? A parrot would talk as well.'
Thus Montaigne runs on, all the time reviewing past and present,
judging the opinions and practices of schools and systems from the
independent point of view of a humanized lay intelligence, and in
particular castigating the preoccupation of the ancient world with
moral philosophy and of the medieval world with theology and
of his contemporaries with the classics. It is worth noticing that
although Montaigne's favourite reading is in the histories of the
classical authors, and especially Plutarch, he never once mentions
Thucydides and presumably had no idea of the humanist ideal of
Periclean Athens, so that he is always only reading their reflection on
and remedies for their sickness, and is misled by them to prefer the
Spartan to the Athenian ideal, never seizing them in the moment of
their health. A preoccupation with moral philosophy, a preoccupation with theology, these are the preoccupations of those in whom
life has broken down, in whom the springs and wards of natural
activity are impaired; it is the business of a liberal education to evoke
ardent responses, to encourage high-spirited endeavour. 'A mind
inhabited by philosophy ought, by its health, to make the body
healthy also: it ought to make its inward serenity shine through to
the outside; it ought to form on its model the exterior bearing, and
therefore arm it with a gracious pride, with an active and pleasing
demeanour, and with a contented and cheerful countenance. The
most evident sign of wisdom is a constant rejoicing; its state is like
the things above the moon, ever clear, always bright.' (I, 25.)
Emerson has been given the modern affinity to Montaigne, and there
is no need to gainsay it, but it is Hume who uses his scepticism, more
philosophically, to the same positive humanist purpose, namely, to
restore native confidence in nature and in reason by gently dis-
engaging and drawing down the bedevilled mind (not least the
rationalist mind) from its mad abstractions.

The Renaissance was certainly not anti-Christian, although there
were anti-Christian features and tendencies, a little less widespread
than in the eighteenth century. What was at issue was the relation
of the Christian gospel to human culture. The medieval church had
not been able to do with nor without pagan thought. Christian
ethics and its text-books throughout the middle ages had been
founded on stoicism. Christian theology had been developed with
the aid of platonism or of Aristotle. Yet Christian thought had not
been able definitively to absorb these alien systems of which it tried

to make use mainly for apologetic purposes; they fell apart, and in the Renaissance the sources of classical thought broke loose altogether as independent studies. The Renaissance was a revival of platonism and of stoicism, not hostile to Christianity and indeed seeking reconciliation with the Christian life, yet nevertheless developing and demonstrating the essential independence of these doctrines, and tending to promote natural religion rather than Christianity.

The Reformers made use of the new learning to return to firsthand direct study of the Bible and of the Fathers, cutting out the traditional commentaries and theological disputations of the schoolmen. When Erasmus was inclined to make an exception in favour of Aquinas, Colet would not hear of it. 'If he had not been exceedingly arrogant, he would not with such rashness and such pride have defined everything; and unless his spirit had been somewhat worldly, he would not so have contaminated the whole teaching of Christ with his profane philosophy.' Further study brought Erasmus to share this profound antipathy. But the mild influence of those Christian humanists who wanted to see Christian teaching governed by simplicity, humanity, and common sense could not be felt in the heat of the burning zeal of the chief Reformers who wanted a Biblical theology that owed nothing to humanity.

Both the middle ages and the Renaissance had humanized God and divinized man, bringing them together naturally and inevitably in the hierarchy of being. The Reformers separated man and God by an abyss which only God could cross, if and when and how he would. This arbitrariness separated Christianity in principle from any possible metaphysics, rooted it in original sin, and associated it inseparably with the historical Biblical revelation and salvation by faith. Such themes had exercised Duns Scotus and Occam in the late middle ages, but it was the Reformers who transferred them from the realm of philosophical analysis and made them the whole meaning of Christian theology embracing the whole life of man and the human polity under the absolute rule of the sole revealed truth. What the Catholic Church had failed to do for the whole of Christendom in the thirteenth century, the Lutherans and Calvinists or other sectarians set out to do for the polities under their dispensation or the communities they sought to create in the sixteenth and seventeenth centuries. Or, rather, lutheran quietism, calvinistic 'rule of the saints', or whatever other pretensions and aims were peculiar to the different sects, took the place of the hierarchy of the church and the unity of all christendom in faith, learning, piety, and order; forms of doctrine and discipline which had various effects on the fortunes and the temper and the ideals of the nations.

Thus the attempt to inspire and control human development by the complex of ideas and ideals developed out of the historical experience and thought of the Jews was checked and confused at the Renaissance by the full recovery of the independent ideas and ideals of Greece and the new orientations to which they gave rise: and at the same time it was powerfully renewed by the full recovery of Jewish Biblical thought and the intransigent Christian application of it to social life.

Chapter 2

THE HUMANIST TRADITION

2. THE ENLIGHTENMENT AND AFTER

I

THE new learning of the Renaissance was followed by the new philosophy of the Enlightenment: the new learning was not the Renaissance, nor was the new philosophy the Enlightenment; both were the primary formative interests and activities of their periods. The characteristic philosophy of the Renaissance was platonism, of which there were many representatives from Cusa to Campanella, religious philosophies, universalist, drawing all humanity into immortal participation in the divine life, expressing the accented sense of the grandeur of man and the awakened thirst for all knowledge, and for fame. The new philosophy was quite different in temper and in technique.

The other main movement in the period of the Enlightenment is towards a secular order of society. The great schism in Christendom at the Reformation, sealed at the Council of Trent, and irremediably embroiled in politics, brought the Christendom of the middle ages to a definitive end. The faith of the Augsburg Confession is Catholic enough, Calvin is a doctor of the church, owning Augustine and Aquinas as his masters, Henry VIII and Elizabeth wanted as little as possible to change anything in doctrine or practice, yet the old order, the consecrated society, is finished. The Renaissance had roused new interests and activities to fill this life between first and last things, and had exalted the active ideal above the celibate priestly contemplative ideal; the unquestioned medieval primacy of the spiritual was challenged with the challenge to the authority and tradition of the Roman Church. Milton strives to reconcile his unbridled renaissance lust for learning and beauty (and for fame), and his grandiose vision of the destiny of humanity exalted by learning, with his puritanical zeal for the worship and service of God, by seeing in all knowledge the knowledge of God, in all learning the repair by the grace of God of our ruined state. Castellio, the one-time friend of Calvin, has the same idea and the same ideal. Calvin himself, bred in humanist learning, rigorous in logic and austere in discipline, exclusively and ruthlessly Biblical in his theology, reviving the prophetic tradition of Judaism against the priestliness of Rome, is generally regarded as the arch-monster of anti-humanism—and so he is. He confesses that those who have thought that the sovereign good would be not to have been born, and short of that to die very soon, have made as good a judgement as anybody can who is without the light of true religion; but Christians must recognize that even life on earth is the good gift of God for which we should be grateful, since although it is not happy nor desirable in itself it is the occasion and means of salvation for the faithful; for the pagan, unless he deceives himself, it is despair; for the Christian, it is hope and salvation; he must therefore despise it as worthless in comparison with the eternal life for which he strives, and thank God for being able to live and strive in it for the hope of salvation; and thus he is armed for his struggle in the world, to bear witness to God in history. It is this application of the gospel to the promotion of cultural and social tasks, with the sense of God acting in history, through sects and through persons, that is the ethos of Protestantism, and it breaks decisively with the Roman tradition. The archipelago of new theocracies is not less fanatical than the continent from which the cataclysm has torn them, but the islanders are more progressive and more exposed to genial influences which transform the climate in which their descendants live.

The new philosophy and the new secular outlook on man and society are first seen in the concern for method and for natural law and natural religion, the quest for certainty and universality.

II

Bacon and Descartes, so different in method and interests, yet both concentrating upon method and both interested in promoting the development of the sciences, are the prime inaugurators of the new philosophy, breaking decisively with the classical philosophies. The preoccupation of the ancient world with moral philosophy and of the middle ages with theology had developed logical techniques for the purpose of victory in debate not for adding to knowledge, and the Renaissance had merely revived and espoused the ancient sects. Disgust with the verbose inconclusive warfare of sects and schools, and consequent contempt for ancient philosophy, induced men to look for other ways. 'Truth,' wrote Leonardo da Vinci, 'even if it deals with a petty and inferior thing, infinitely surpasses uncertain opinions on the most sublime and elevated problems.' There was a tradition of collecting facts, natural histories, and of manipulating nature, alchemy. Bacon would have the whole world set to work to multiply collections and manipulations, systematically reducing the accumulated facts to order, formulating and verifying laws, and building up knowledge and power. Such a method promised both certainty and progress, hitherto lacking. He contrasted the progress of the mechanical arts with the multiplication of opinions, which varied without any increase of knowledge. To grasp and generalize the principle of success in the practical arts was to open the way to universal progress. Bacon contributed nothing to any of the sciences and was far from elaborating an adequate theory of scientific method, yet he was and remained the inspired founder of modern empirical science because he had the vision and the courage to prophesy its success. Voltaire at the beginning of the eighteenth century noted after his visit to England that the most remarkable and the best of all Bacon's works, the *Novum Organum*, was then the least read and the most useless, because it was the scaffolding with which the new philosophy had been built. The *Novum Organum* was, rather, the manifesto of the new movement. Bacon calls for confidence, for greatness of mind, in an immense enterprise, nothing less than the 'endeavour to establish and extend the power and dominion of the human race itself over the universe'. If it be feared that such power would be misused, 'the same may be said of all earthly goods; of wit, courage, strength, beauty, wealth, light itself, and the rest. Only let the human race recover that right over nature which belongs to it by divine bequest, and let power be given it; the exercise thereof will be governed by sound reason and true religion.' Immense as this ambition is, it is achieved not by raising a pyramid to the pride of man, but by laying a foundation in the human understanding. 'I am building in the human understanding a true model of the world, such as it is in fact, not such as a man's own reason would have it to be; a thing which cannot be done without a very diligent dissection and anatomy of the world.' He was not founding one more sect nor producing one more speculative philosophy, but setting mankind their co-operative never-finished task and encouraging them to set aside their fatalism, their apathy and indolence, and lack of confidence in themselves, and all the other chief obstructions in the way of finding and following the one untried path to success in natural philosophy: 'experience has not yet learned her letters'. The chief ground of hope was that the ways which had been taken in the past could be seen to have been mistaken and hopeless: 'from a closer and purer league between these two faculties, the experimental and the rational (such as has never yet been made), much may be hoped'. Bacon had the insight to put his finger on the one fruitful principle and to announce the greatest conclusions. For that, the beginning of the recovery of self-confidence on the human plane, he deserves the place he has in the humanist tradition, the place given him, for example, by D'Alembert in the influential *Discours préliminaire de l'encyclopédie*, who attributes to him the main design of their encyclopaedia and acknowledges him as their master.

Descartes also turns his back on the ancient philosophy. Brought up, as he says, at one of the most celebrated Jesuit schools in Europe, and avidly reading all that he could lay hands on, he could not find anywhere 'clear and assured knowledge of all that is useful in life'. The clarity and certainty of mathematics alone attracted and held him, and he wondered why so little had been built on so firm a foundation, since the moral philosophy which the ancients had extended on such a magnificent scale was founded on mud and sand by comparison. He began with a firm foundation in clear and indubitable ideas, with a method, a mathematician's critique of ideas, on which he constructed a beautiful system of metaphysics and of physics. It is the beginning of modern philosophy, the first original system since Plato, still a starting-point to return to, a fruitful text for meditation and commentary. Although Descartes was an original mathematician who contributed to the development of mathematics and although he was fully aware of the importance of experimental work and had the highest opinion of Bacon's method as the last word on the way of making useful experiments, he did not himself find the way to the mathematical treatment of experimental physics which from Galileo (or Archimedes) to Newton and since has proved the high road of achievement in that science. His physics is a closed abstract metaphysical system, not a body of verified predictive laws;

his method is not the empirical method which the genius of the Enlightenment took infinite pains to apply on all fronts. Nevertheless, his philosophy is of the greatest historical importance: it is a break with platonism, a new starting-point. Formally, Descartes's philosophy supports Christianity, and was intended to, but only in the sense that he assumed that there could be no inconsistency between the truth of philosophy and the truth of revelation, as Aquinas had assumed it. No specifically Christian dogma has any place in his system; revealed truths, like the evidences of the senses, are not doubted, they are put within brackets. Belief in the existence of God is an integral part of the structure, but the philosophy is not directed towards God; it is an explicit rejection of platonic religious philosophy; it is devoted to building up a methodical knowledge, clear and certain, which aims at human ends and excludes theological perspectives. The complete absence of anti-Christian intention or bias makes the shift in the focus of interest, the secularization of thought, if less dramatic, more revealing, more clearly inevitable.

The *Novum Organum* was published in 1620. Within the next thirty years, Galileo, Descartes, Grotius, and Hobbes had published the works which show so clearly the difference between the humanism of the Renaissance and the rationalism of the Enlightenment, the new learning and the new philosophy. It is above all a break with the past, an attempt to find a new beginning in rational principles, clear, universal, certain, as the foundation of unity and progress in knowledge and the bond of social union. The formation of intellectual circles and the voluminous correspondence of the new philosophers show an unprecedented collective intellectual endeavour oriented towards the new knowledge, and anticipate the scientific academies and scientific journals soon to be founded. At the end of the century, Fontenelle, secretary of the Académie des Sciences, looks back over the stupendous achievement in mathematics and physics and attempts to characterize this scientific movement which is only beginning. It is not the systematic development of some general principle from which all start; it is a work of scattered piecemeal discoveries, dependent one on another, one thing throwing light on another, assimilating the unknown to the known, until the general principle is discovered which brings all together systematically. That is, it is a cultural achievement, the work of organization and method, not the superiority of modern intelligence. Modern man, Fontenelle reflects, is no more intelligent than primitive man, but he has become conscious of the way in which knowledge develops and he can apply that principle to its continuous advancement.

III

The secularization of thinking on political and social questions developed out of medieval clerical theories of natural law inherited from classical sources (mainly Aristotle and Roman law). The medieval papacy tended to push its claims to the extravagant extreme, to establish itself in theory as the earthly regent of a theocracy. But the orthodox doctrine was more moderate: the temporal government enjoyed relative autonomy, but if it did not rule for the natural ends of government rebellion might be justifiable and disobedience even obligatory, and of course the ruler whose rule was inconsistent with the law of God (the Bible and the church) was liable to excommunication. Different forms of government were recognized both in theory and practice, and, although the principle of authority was divinely ordained, actual political authority was strictly conditional, not absolute. Aquinas is regarded (rightly) as a liberal, and has been called 'the first Whig'. Hooker, following Aquinas and like him founding himself on the Bible, Roman jurisprudence, Aristotle, and the stoics, used the conception of natural law ('the law which human nature knoweth itself in reason universally bound unto . . . comprehendeth all those things which men by the light of their natural understanding evidently know, or at leastwise may know, to be beseeming or unbeseeming, virtuous or vicious, good or evil for them to do') to justify the polity and the policy of the established Anglican Church under Elizabeth. Natural law, with the universal human reason that was its correlative, justified both revolt against papal tyranny and rejection of the calvinist idea that scripture was the sole rule of Christian conduct and institutions. Scripture was indispensable for the revelation of supernatural knowledge necessary for salvation, but it was limited to that end and did not supersede, on the contrary it presupposed, natural knowledge. The English people formed both a commonwealth and, since they professed the Christian faith, also a church, as the base of a triangle may be considered either as base or as side. The invisible church of the saints did not and could not be made to coincide with the national church that comprehended all the people of a Christian commonwealth, and there was no scriptural obligation to adopt the Genevan institutions which had been invented for so chimerical a purpose. Hooker was not so much an enemy of Calvin and Geneva as of the purposes of the puritan party in the English church, returned out of exile and burning to build the New Jerusalem in England's green and pleasant land. He read the omens and tried to build against the deluge, the tumult of sects that threatened to destroy all established order, dignity, place, and learning, and to institute the regimen and regimentation of narrow-minded zealots, founding themselves exclusively on scripture, or, even worse, threatened to let loose anarchical mobs of plundering fanatics full of scriptural warrant for crazy social ideas. In place of this, and of Rome, he would have the rule of law, natural law, to maintain the uniformity of Christendom, all sovereign rulers being sworn to it as some were 'to maintain the liberties, laws, and received customs of the country where they reign'.

The abiding interest of Hooker's work (apart from its being the first considerable philosophical argument in the language, and apart from its formative influence upon the predominant temper of the Anglican Church) is in its boundary position, cherishing the Catholic ideals and confronting the new radical ideas in the conservatively empirical spirit of Burke confronting the abstract radical ideas of 1789. The radical ideas of the calvinists were revolutionary in their dealing with established institutions, reactionary in their return to a primitive theological absolute, applying scriptural notions to the whole conduct of human life, personal and social. Yet these ideas, reactionary and monstrously anti-humanist as they were, contributed not a little, directly and indirectly, both to the tough quality of English achievement and also to the eventual triumph of the liberal-democratic complex of ideas and sentiment. In Hooker's day, puritanism coalesced with the passionate protestant nationalism under the leadership of the queen. Its later triumph in the civil war, and subsequent failure, breached the monolithic structure of the Tudor state; alternatives had to be admitted and accommodated. Moreover, the sects had contributed something to the spirit and the method of democracy which could not be forgotten. And the proved failure of the heroic calvinist ideal, in Geneva, in the English Commonwealth, and in New England, strengthened the idea of the secular state. One hundred years after Hooker, Locke, making repeated appreciative references to him ('the judicious Hooker'), uses the idea of natural law and the social contract to construct the theory of the civil authority as the trustee of the people responsible for the preservation of their natural rights; and by natural rights is meant the civil liberties of the individual, a natural right to the preservation and enjoyment of life, liberty, and estate, a new conception that had no place in ancient constitutions. Central in the body of civil liberties is liberty of conscience, religious liberty, a product of the war of sects, persecution, the failure of puritans to control society by scriptural texts, and of Hooker's comprehensive Christian commonwealth to gain the suffrage of all.

When Augustine contrasted the uniformity of the canonical scriptures and their accepted authority with the vain clamour of the philosophical schools, none of them geared to any settled social policy, he left out of account that the early church swarmed with bitterly antagonistic sects and that the Catholic Church had been created only by the power of the empire, under which definition and discipline had been imposed and the element of persecution introduced, of which he himself elaborated the influential theory. Without authority, discipline, and constraint, no great human achievement is possible, and the church is not rightly to be blamed for authority and discipline, only for arbitrariness and abominable excesses. It is the inappropriateness of the ideas by which the church has attempted to control human development, and clerical resistance to their correction by experience, that has identified human progress with emancipation from clerical authority. The persecutions came to a head in the struggles of the sixteenth and seventeenth centuries. The eighteenth century, the Age of Reason, the noontide of the Enlightenment, although not cloudless, shows the clear sky of toleration. The battle was won by a convergence of forces, fighting for different interests.

In the first place, the intransigence of the sects, and of catholic minorities rallied and strengthened by the Counter-reformation, compelled ultimate recognition or extermination, and ruled out the latitudinarian policy of comprehension (exemplified in the Elizabethan settlement), a policy of moderation and toleration but not sensitive to the claims of the individual conscience. The sects themselves tended to be mutually intolerant and intolerant of dissidents within their ranks: the truth which constituted the sect was the absolute, not sincerity of conscience, and what the sects claimed from the state was not freedom of conscience but the natural right of a minority to preservation, in which they based their arguments on natural law. The sects, for the most part, did not want a secular state, were indeed horrified by the idea; even the age-old idea that the state must be supported by a single established religion was too secular for them; their only true version of the only true religion embraced the state so closely that it died in their arms. The trial of territorialism, of comprehension, of presbyterian government, proved their impossibility as permanent settlements and induced a change of mind. And the arguments which helped to induce the change were shaped in the sixteenth century from conclusions hewed by events out of bruised minds. When Geneva burned Servetus, Castellio marshalled the Christian arguments in a remonstrance against persecution. Like Hooker, he insists that the knowledge which comes from revelation, like the knowledge which comes from the senses, presupposes the office of reason. Like Hooker, he regards reason as itself a divine principle, the equal of revelation. The Bible has to be interpreted according to reason and humanity; it is full of enigmas and should never be construed and acted on in any sense that is contrary to our reasonable and ethical convictions. The truths necessary for salvation are few, simple, and certain, but the points of doctrine for the sake of which persecution is resorted to are the most controverted, the most dubious and irresolvable. A man's character and conduct are the tests, because they are the fruits of the inwardness of his beliefs and because they are the conditions of his attaining knowledge of the divine. His integrity, his loyalty to his own sincere convictions, cannot be tampered with, even if he is in error, without destroying the man: 'to force conscience is worse than cruelly to kill a man'. The church does not gain by maintaining or increasing its number by constraint; it loses; like the fool who has a little wine in a barrel and fills it up with water, he spoils what he had. The suppression of heresy does not avoid sedition but provokes it. In a Christian view, it is not heretics that are the wolves, but their persecutors.

Such views, with their radical implications of a new order, were not much heard during the struggles of the sixteenth century, but in the next century they gained ground and came to prevail. Roger Williams applied them, in the interests of a pure church, 'a gathered church', to the dilemmas of the New England puritans attempting to found a commonwealth on the Genevan model; and he concluded for the separation of church and state. History proved, he argued, that good administration did not require the Christian faith, and the anti-Christian might well be as sound and competent in his office as any Christian in the world; the only difference between the two as magistrates was in their inward motivations and view of things; their authority was precisely the same and had no relevance to men's religious beliefs and practices. It was the secularization of the state on the security of this view, and because of the difficulty of maintaining a territorial or a comprehensive solution, that came eventually to prevail throughout the United States.

The tendency towards toleration and recognition of the rights of conscience was also promoted by the considerable influence of liberal Christians, deriving from Renaissance Italy as well as from Erasmus of Rotterdam, and it was their temper which moulded the toleration of the eighteenth century, rather than that of zealous but spiritually minded puritans like Roger Williams. Most influential of the liberals were the socinians. From the middle of the sixteenth century, in Italy and in Basle, then in Poland, for a time the haven of religious refugees, and afterwards in Holland, the headquarters of religious thinkers in exile, socinianism was a humanist reaction to Calvin and worked as an anti-calvinist virus. Socinianism embodied the principle of free religious inquiry directed to the Bible interpreted by reason for the sake of knowing the truth about salvation, on the assumption that it was plain and intelligible and centred in the ethical. It therefore ignored the disputatious and defied authoritative dogmas which overruled common sense or moral sense. The doctrines of the trinity, of atonement, of original sin, of justification by faith, of everlasting punishment, of predestination were challenged by the socinians, not in the name of rationalism but on the unquestioned assumption of the primacy of God, the literal inspiration of the Bible, and the divine authority and ethical mission of Christ. The socinian spirit was congenial to the Latitudinarian party in the Anglican Church, and socinian books, published in Holland, strongly influenced Anglican theologians throughout the second half of the seventeenth century. Locke was for six years in exile in Holland and was familiar with their circle and their views. No Christian thinkers were more opposed to the party spirit, the ambition of dominion, and the ideal of authority and uniformity: their ideals challenged the spirit and policy of the Elizabethan settlement, of Laud, of the Presbyterians, and of the Restoration parliament, not in rejection of Christianity nor in despair of unity but in the confidence that Christianity was reasonable and that trust in reason and individualism would bring unity where dogmatism and authoritarianism had proved futile and fissile.

This ideal involved abandonment of the idea of a Christian commonwealth, Presbyterian or Anglican, Calvin's or Hooker's, the remnant of the idea of Christendom, and entailed the institution of the church as a voluntary society, or rather a congeries of voluntary societies according to their several persuasions. Locke came to this conclusion, like Roger Williams, although he hoped that the reasonableness of Christianity and the comprehensiveness of the Anglican establishment would bring the great majority into the national church; those whose conscience kept them out should be tolerated in so far as the preservation of the public peace did not require their restraint or constraint. In Locke converged all the current streams of liberal influence, the Cambridge platonists with whom he was intimate, the liberal Dutch calvinists and remonstrants, socinians, quakers, students of the works of Erasmus and of Castellio, and others whom he met and knew and lived with in exile in Holland. From him flowed an immense influence on the larger issues of civil liberty, issues dramatically defined and declared a hundred years later in the Declaration of the Rights of Man and some years previously in the preamble to the Declaration of Independence which was its model. In these declarations, society is recognized as founded upon the sovereignty of the law of Nature, the title of the individual to liberties which can be only preserved and enlarged by the institutions of society. Reason, transcendent in its universality, immanent in the individual, is the rule of law in nature, man, and society.

The manifestos of 1776 and 1789 were associated with the political triumph of the ideas expressed, and Locke's writings were associated (because he himself was identified) with the Glorious Revolution of 1688. Locke's principles became the principles of the Whig party, but the Revolution was more than a party triumph, for it expressed a national acceptance of irreversible historical changes and a national resolution to avoid both civil war and political absolutism by distributing the elements of power and accommodating different opinions. This was the unwritten constitution which became the boast of the English in the eighteenth century and was glorified by British achievements on the strength of it. That is to say, these ideas of civil and religious liberty were developed in an historical context over a hundred years and more of national history and became a national tradition.

The theory of church and state which came thus to prevail at the end of the seventeenth century in England was fashioned in a context of Christian presuppositions and by Christian thinkers. The most powerful anti-Christian thinker, Hobbes, had argued for political absolutism, the losing cause of high monarchists and high-churchmen; although his argument was essentially radical, utilitarian, and for the sake of individualism. The champions of natural theology had not yet gained a wide hearing. The platonism of the Renaissance had influenced the socinians and was evident in Lord Herbert of Cherbury who, in spite of his addiction to the sordid and barbarous ideals of the age of Froissart, was a serious student and thinker and developed the Renaissance idea of a few simple and evident truths common to all religions, mainly that there is a Supreme Being who ought to be worshipped by a life of virtue for which there are rewards and punishments in a future state. The science which was so notably developed in the seventeenth century was the work of deeply religious men and its results were enthusiastically propagated by clerics; the fight against ignorance and superstition they represented as a crusade as true as any war upon the Turks. The new science helped in the universities to release theology from entanglement with the relics of aristotelian scholasticism, for it revealed a rationally ordered universe whose study was an alternative road to God. All these influences (Hobbes and his critics, ideas of natural theology, science) directly or indirectly contributed to the climate of opinion and characteristic ideas of the eighteenth century, of which Locke's philosophy was the English core.

IV

The common sense, complacency, and cheerfulness so characteristic of the Age of Reason floated in a medium of awe; they were stayed on contemplation of the sublimities of the great chain of being, all things linked by universal law, expressing the mind of God, acknowledged by reason, 'The God within the mind'. Man who in the state of nature enjoyed life, liberty, and the fruits of his labour, and was entitled to resist encroachment and attack, being required to preserve the life with which he was endowed, in the state of society had a more extensive enjoyment of these human rights, and under lawful government his title to preservation prevailed. Within his own being, reason preserved and reinforced the natural harmony between self-love and social dispositions. Within the universal frame of nature, the rule of universal law could not be broken, neither in the motions of the atoms nor in the promptings of instinct. There was, therefore, in right reason founded on acknowledged law a sufficient guide and a principle of universal consent and union, which no other pretended rules or rights, traditions or authorities, should be suffered to obscure and eclipse. The widespread desire to laicize Christianity, to reduce it to fundamentals, to take it out of the arena of contending sects, went so far as almost to identify it with natural religion. Pope's *The Universal Prayer*, condemned as the freethinker's hymn, is a paraphrase of the Lord's Prayer set in the context of an earth-wide natural cult with a creed of simple, open-minded dependence. In a universe so bound and kept by law and reason, trust is well-founded, and happiness is assured to those who live by law and reason; in Jefferson's phrase, we are to enjoy happiness here and greater happiness hereafter. Revelation sealed what everything conspired to teach us. As an obscure writer schooled in the philosophies of this time has put it: 'the dictates of natural and revealed religion, and the dictates of right reason and the principles of utility, suggest the same rule of life and coalesce in their instruction; that rational and refined self-interest, and the truths or principles of religion, natural and revealed, point to one and the same course of life, to the culture of the same private and public affections, the discharge of the same social obligations and duties; or, what is the same thing, the pursuit of the same end, namely, the happiness of mankind'. The will of God is understood to be the greatest happiness of the greatest number. To move further from Calvin than this would be to begin to return to him.

Different as the new mathematical physics was from the physics of antiquity, the general conception of the universe was remarkably similar; the idea of harmony repeated in the cosmos, in society, and in the microcosm man, the universal rule of reason, and the concept of natural law are in the tradition of classical thought. Indeed, the polished surface of the eighteenth century reflects the old Roman world in more than in literature and in philosophy, brings it back as in a cyclic return such as the stoics believed in. This is a consummation of the Renaissance. After the revolution in France, when the new republic was endangered by the hostility of the powers (in which the Pope conspicuously shared), fervent nationalism attached itself with religious enthusiasm to the philosophic ideas of the intellectuals, and there was a determined attempt, supported by the government for some years, to replace 'absurd dogmas' with 'the religion of Socrates and of Marcus Aurelius and of Cicero', which it was confidently expected would very soon be the religion of the world. 'Theophilanthropy' and philosophic freethought and civic cults enjoyed official support until abolished by the First Consul, who hoped to control the consciences of men by means of controlling the Pope. The significance of these rationalist cults, ardently patriotic and ardently philosophic, is seen in the judgement of Gibbon that Christianity had undermined the virtue of the Roman world, the judgement that Christianity had brought in the dark ages, kept man in ignorance and servitude, and that it had taken centuries for men to rise again to the Roman level. In the eighteenth century men felt that they had at last become emancipated and enlightened enough to compete on equal terms with the choice and brightest spirits of antiquity.

Eighteenth-century civilization, reflected in its thought, is like the baroque style of an earlier period: elemental strife in the grain of things, irregularity, discord, are recognized and represented, but they are overcome and contribute only liveliness to the harmony of the whole. They are feints and conceits, of decorative value and dramatic interest, not the real cleavages and distortions that fascinate and trouble a later age.

V

If the polished surface of eighteenth-century civilization reflects the old Roman world, it is illusion to see only vain repetition of what the Greeks and Romans did supremely well; there stirs beneath the surface the origins of a new world. Especially at four points do the lines indicate the shape of things to come.

(1) Speculative thinking based upon natural law concentrated attention upon the individual or upon the majority or upon the whole society and reduced the importance of the sovereign, the social *élite*, the hierarchy of traditional social order. However tender towards the interests of property owners Locke or Bentham might be, the exigencies and tendencies of their thinking were unmistakably egalitarian; such thinking opened the way not merely to a society founded upon interest and opinion, upon the citizen, but, beyond that, to a society founded upon useful work, the kind of transvaluation of values registered in the *Parable* of Saint-Simon.

(2) A psychology and a society founded upon self-interest, presumed to be in harmony with the public interest, implied a moral

ideal very different from the ascetic ideal of a society dominated by a church or from the aristocratic ideal of chivalry. Hume says that men of sense despise monkish virtues because they have none of the utility of the virtues which serve personal and social well-being: sensible men are not hare-brained enthusiasts who want to figure in the calendar after they are dead, they want to enjoy a genial social life whilst they are alive. Such contempt for the saints with un-ashamed appetite for the world is a new norm for a virtuous man. But what is really new is the recognition that a society which has emancipated itself from the repressive regime of priest and king must be founded on self-interest because only happy men are naturally beneficent; minimal government requires spontaneous social loyalties rising from the real satisfaction of felt interests and upholding with public spirit the social order that provides such private good: that is the basic justification for preoccupation with eudemonism in eighteenth-century ethics. A free society must be founded on men's own judgement of their interests. The marvellous accord of self-interest with the public interest, which is an article of social faith in eighteenth-century thought, is the basic psychological truth of the social order (and of educational theory) if it is stated conditionally, and not made an axiom of the divine economy, with Bishop Butler, or of political economy, with Mandeville. Bentham, like Hobbes, begins with a juridical theory according to which law and punishment bring about an artificial identity of interests in society, other-wise in conflict; with the development of the new political economy, the utilitarians adopted the principle of the natural harmony of interests through the exchange of the market. The basic complex truth about man and society is over-simplified or made an article of faith or confused with independent laws, but it is central in the new social thinking as it had not been at any time before.

(3) The new thinking about man and society, whether it started with speculative theories, as with Hobbes or Locke, or with a practi-cal principle, as with Bentham, was attempting to do for social philosophy what Newton had done for natural philosophy. This attempt to make a science of politics or of law was not in the interest of academic study, it was in the interest of policy and reform. Locke's principles formed the Whig party and policy, Bentham's founded the utilitarians and philosophical radicals, Hume's and Burke's contributed to the philosophy of the Tories. These great schools of thought, which furnished the intellectual and moral

resources for a strong and convinced party in the country working on the destiny of the nation, took the place in the life and preoccupations of men which had been held by the schools of moral philosophy in the ancient world and of theology since that time. Theological and ecclesiastical issues were not eliminated, but they tended to become marginal or to be subordinated to other interests. But the great difference between the new schools of social and political thought and the old schools of moral philosophy or of theology was that the new schools of thought were developed out of present social experience and bore directly on it again in the policies they promoted. In this essential respect of the unity of thought and action they were close to the successful natural sciences whether or not they imitated them in language or techniques. Of course the parties tended to become doctrinaire, not least the most empirical of them, the utilitarians; they developed their principles out of experience, but the theory then became superior and indifferent to experience. In so far as this happened they lost the virtue which made them superior to old-fashioned philosophies and theologies.

(4) The ingenuity and contrivance of men eagerly interested in the new arts and sciences was already widespread in the early eighteenth century, although not yet ready to bear fruit in the decisive inventions of the industrial revolution, because in technology as in science one thing leads to another and the main obstacles were not yet removed.

Bentham began as a man of practical ideas looking for a patron, a man of ingenious schemes and projects hoping to interest an enlightened despot, a man of the eighteenth century. He learned by experience that the aristocratic class was an oligarchy, a closed corporation like the law and the church, hostile to change, opposed in principle to the general interest; and yielding to the influence of the radical ideas of the French Revolution and of the American Revolution, he became a democrat looking to majority rule, a man of the nineteenth century.

VI

The Enlightenment, an age that rationalized phenomena and posited law everywhere, gave increasing attention to the particular and to the individual both in science and in art; the idolatry given to mathematics did not prevent a new devotion to history, and the master passion for analysis and reduction was the obsession of minds anxious to get to the bottom of things, not blind to their multiplicity and their dynamism. With its faith in reason, it was the age that dramatically put reason in question, that bred and debated Pascal and Hume. Arising from the enthusiasm and vision excited by new methods confirmed by new achievements, the splendid intellectual energy of these generations spent itself in a profusion of programmes, issuing not in scepticism and disillusionment (following all that came to light in the quest for universality and certainty) but in a better-informed idea of the nature of our human part in the world. The Enlightenment is the great epoch of the humanist tradition, not because of doctrinal scepticism, atheism, materialism, but because men learned to abandon the platonic aspiration to think the thoughts of God and to establish theocratic forms of society, and began to appreciate the creative character of the human role in nature, and to see that knowledge, art, morals, society, were human inventions as much as discoveries and applications of law, and that to perfect and use those inventions within human limits according to the characteristic mode of each was the enlightened way to seek the divine, whatever might be the origin and destiny of man.

VII

The nineteenth century was an age of historical scholarship, prodigiously developed, and the historical point of view stands over against that of the analytical rationalist. Historical thinking finds its norms within experience: the human mind is studied in what it has done, not in the cartesian introspective intuition of its essence; historical and comparative study of human institutions promotes a consciousness of their development and of their empirical character and organic connections, and guides the next step from within by what has been learned from the past. Rationalist analysis finds its norms outside experience: human nature is defined, and human institutions are criticized or reconstructed by reference to an absolute universal conception. Helvétius said to Montesquieu, criticizing his approach in the *Esprit des Lois*, 'I only know two kinds of government: the good ones and the bad ones; the former have not yet entered an appearance'. And Sieyès expressed the same rationalist view: 'Too many have busied themselves in combining servile ideas always in accordance with events. Political science is not the science of what is, but of what ought to be.'

Hume's position is interesting in relation to these confused issues. A friend of moderation, as he says, he was anxious to take the wind out of the sails of both the main contending opinions, the speculative enthusiasts and the high monarchists. His critique of reason ('reason is and ought to be the slave of the passions') controverted the traditional view and ruled out natural law as the *a priori* of political thought and obligation. In place of it he derived settled principles of social and political order from the settled uniformity of human dispositions as found in experience. He hoped on this basis to construct a political science out of history, a body of axioms that would 'remain true to the latest posterity' and be the foundation of a constitution that would be fool-proof and knave-proof, transmitting laws capable of providing good government 'to the latest posterity'.

In spite of its empirical foundation and method, looking only to experience, Hume's theory was as chimerical as the speculative theory it opposed, since it was generalized from a very limited experience both of human behaviour and of human institutions, and once established it was as rationalist and confident as the *a priori* theories. His historical thinking, like Montesquieu's, is haunted by the classical conception of a sum of laws, founded on experience and sufficient, which should never be altered save with a trembling hand. Hence his dislike of parties, which for chimerical ends threaten the peace of natural government founded on political science. Especially is he unable, as he says, to understand parties founded on abstract speculative principle, known only to modern times, 'the most extraordinary and unaccountable phenomenon that has yet appeared in human affairs'. He is referring to religious controversies, and he tries to account for them by the persecuting power of priests when they are outside civil control, and, more interesting, by the keenness in dispute of ancient philosophy which was taken up by Christianity. 'Sects of philosophy, in the ancient world, were more zealous than parties of religion; but in modern times, parties of religion are more furious and enraged than the most cruel factions that ever arose from interest and ambition.' It is because such speculative differences do not affect conduct (as he thinks) that he finds these enraged party controversies so hard to understand. He sees normal human dispositions and interests providing, with the help of history, the norms of a political science for a permanent political order. He does not see a great party founded on interest and guided by a controversial school of thought initiating and controlling social change.

43

Burke, when the revolution had broken out, saw that '*It is a revolution of doctrine and theoretic dogma*', with little resemblance to former political revolutions, doctrine and theory that had a general appeal that crossed frontiers and formed parties everywhere. It revived on a political plane two centuries of religious wars not long ceased. It resembled the Peloponnesian war between the ideas and interests of Athens and of Sparta: 'the interest in opinions (merely as opinions, and without any experimental reference to their effects) when once they take strong hold of the mind, become the most operative of all interests, and indeed very often supersede every other'. Against the mere opinions of the French theoreticians which had gained such a hold in England on 'the whole race of half-bred speculators—all the Atheists, Deists, and Socinians—all those who hate the clergy and envy the nobility', Burke posed the weight of history. The function of historical thinking was to make one conscious of the whole in which one takes one's place and plays one's part, to make one sensible of and responsive to its true genius, ready to preserve and value it, and willing to alter it only to make it more like itself. Burke boasted that the English had not materially changed since the fourteenth century. 'We know that *we* have made no discoveries, and we think that no discoveries are to be made, in morality; nor many in the great principles of government, nor in the ideas of liberty, which were understood long before we were born, altogether as well as they will be after the grave has heaped its mould upon our presumption, and the silent tomb shall have imposed its law on our pert loquacity.'

Burke's historical empiricism avoids the dangers of a philosophy of history but hardly escapes falling into a mere unreasoning traditionalism. The nineteenth century was to venture into the philosophy of history on the grand scale, with tremendous consequences. Bodin in the second half of the sixteenth century had made a notable beginning, but it was Vico more than 150 years later who really attempted the 'new science', who saw all things without exception as historically conditioned, and constructed the lines of a history of civilization, an order of development seen from a human point of view and putting religion as one thing amongst others, instead of subordinating all things to religion. The nineteenth century rediscovered Vico.

The combination of historical thinking with rationalism was the great feat of Hegel, the attempt to see by philosophic insight that the real world is as it ought to be, not, as the eighteenth century tried to see it, in contemplation of a vast and finished system, but by using a logic of development. The middle term between the individual and the absolute was not an abstract universal like natural law but a concrete universal, the spirit of a people, the nation, the race, humanity, class: it was in these historical terms that the characteristic thinking of the century was done. In science it was the century of biology rather than of physics, of dynamic philosophies of nature. In literature the Romantic school was dominant.

The influence of Hegel was immense, throughout Europe, in America, and in Britain; and it was through the hegelian schools that Hegel's philosophy became real. The British hegelians broke the long monopoly of the utilitarians in British thought, and a philosophy which insisted on the reality and exalted the status of the whole and admitted the individual only as individual-in-the-whole, and which preached public service, self-realization through self-renunciation, instead of enlightened self-interest, was not only congenial to a rising generation of socialists but also, by replacing the atomic view of society with an organic ideal, bred socialists, whether its academic exponents liked it or not. In Europe, the liberalism of Croce gained historical depth and passionate faith from its hegelian source; it was liberalism not as an economic doctrine but as a liberating religion, a call to the mind and to all human energies. In America, Hegel stimulated amongst others the young Dewey, destined to become the exponent and spokesman of a philosophy more characteristic of American democracy, a philosopher as representative as Locke had been in England.

Of course it was through Marx that hegelianism gained its most sensational influence, although it was only one of the main formative influences that went to the making of marxism. As scientific socialism in the place of utopian socialism and as a critique of liberal economic doctrine, marxism shifted historical and political thinking from its concentration on the citizen and his opinions and parties, or on the nation or race, or on humanity, and fixed attention on the set of interests embodied in a social class defined by its relations to the instruments of economic production; this was the clue to the understanding of laws, literatures, morals, politics, philosophies; this was the master-key that unlocked all the chambers and opened access to all the secrets of the great palace of history; above all, this insight into the dynamics of culture, the general laws of human development, made men aware of their destiny and enabled them to live and act intelligently, adapting themselves and altering their world in the direction of its necessary change. Marxism instituted the closest relation between the school of thought and the party, the unity of thought and action; and in this case the party was inseparable from an historical class, ultimately identifiable with humanity itself; and the school of thought was scientific and historical understanding of man by himself.

The adoption by the benthamites of the *laisser-faire* principles of Adam Smith's political economy to deal with the problems of the new industrial age insensibly transformed the original principle of the utilitarians, which had imposed a large and important role on governments. The complications introduced into the economic theory by the principles of Malthus and of Ricardo again brought in the question of government and divided the utilitarians into the Manchester School and the Westminster School, the one exerting with Cobden an immense influence for two generations on the dominant trends of thought and policy and raising Britain to the pinnacle of prestige and power, the other developing principles and policies of which the Fabians were heirs. It would be hard to exaggerate the influence of both schools on law, on the theory and practice of democracy, on administration and local government, and on imperial policy.

Other heirs of the utilitarians were the pragmatists at Harvard at the end of the century who, accepting the greatest happiness of the greatest number as the ethical basis of democracy, transformed the other doctrines and methods of the school by their being more deeply versed in history, in biological and psychological science, and in logical analysis. They therefore freed the point of view from its attachment to over-simplified rigid dogmas and prejudices, and propagated it in American culture as a liberal and fertile discipline for the critical use of ideas in the promotion and control both of research and of policy. They opposed all forms of dogmatism, without hostility to religion, and both rugged individualism and ruthless collectivism, in the name of creative individual freedom and the relative status of all ideas, concepts, laws. Their influence in the fields of education, law, religion, and other social disciplines and activities has been incalculably great.

VIII

Throughout the nineteenth century, one of the most influential ideas, comparable to that of natural law in the eighteenth, was the idea of progress. It was an idea encouraged both by scientific and by historical thinking. Bacon looked forward to the progress of knowledge by methodical and organized advance, as something new which would become a dominant characteristic of humanity. Once the obstacles to the practical application of new knowledge and methods in the arts and industries had been overcome, one invention led to another as one discovery had led to another, and social life was more changed in a hundred years than it had been in all the previous centuries of Western civilization: progress was easily thought of as industrial development and measured by the use of mechanical inventions. The historians gave the idea larger scope. It had been developed by Voltaire and by Turgot and Condorcet, and with no less enthusiasm by Guizot, who devoted to it his lectures of 1828, treating it as the soul of civilization, defined as the 'perfecting of society and humanity'. It is the liberal faith in the principle of increasing enlightenment, emancipation, and prosperity, and it is the hegelian metaphysical principle of necessary development—there is an evolution of humanity towards unity and self-realization. Even Christian thought, in that it had its mission and its faith in the providence of God, had a belief in historical process and a standard of progress. The enlightened despot of the eighteenth century, respectful of natural law and employer of men of ideas, became the progressive government of the nineteenth century, promoting popular education, free enterprise, and equality of opportunity.

The idea has not lacked serious critics, who have called attention to the decline and fall of civilizations as no less characteristic than their development: the civilization which embodies the idea of progress may be itself doomed and due to decline. The critique is complicated by different evaluations of progress. For Toynbee, there is progress in the death of a civilization that gives birth to a higher religion. For Nietzsche, or for Georges Sorel, the ideals of the progressives are the final symptoms of extreme decadence. And Herder stands at the end of the age of Enlightenment, a rebuke and reminder to all rash rationalists; the human is the historical and the humanist like the anthropologist has no prejudices. Evidently progress is an idea which needs to defend itself. It raises the profoundest questions of history, that is, of human existence. But nineteenth-century historians, whether rationalists, idealists, materialists, or Christians, wrote their history with the idea of controlling human development.

IX

Pater, writing of Pico della Mirandola, concludes, 'the essence of humanism is that belief . . . that nothing which has ever interested living men and women can wholly lose its vitality—no language they have spoken, nor oracle beside which they have hushed their voices, no dream which has once been entertained by actual human minds, nothing about which they have ever been passionate, or expended time and zeal'. On this view, the humanist tradition is the human tradition. On this view, nothing is alien to the humanist; he may be as much interested in Sparta as in Athens, in Calvin's Geneva as in Lorenzo's Florence, in Hitler's Germany as in the welfare state. To be this kind of humanist is to be infinitely interested, infinitely tolerant, to take all points of view without exclusion of any. This omnipartial interest of man in mankind, the universal sympathy of a literary celibate who espouses no cause and founds no interest of his own, takes its place in the academy of learning with all formal studies. It presupposes an established liberal society in which ultimate questions are not raised, or not forced, and vital decisions are not required. If the interests of disinterested culture are threatened, if the standpoint of the spectator is made untenable, this kind of humanism is eclipsed and exposed. Such a humanism was the glory and the shame of the German universities. Jean-Paul Sartre, bitterly disillusioned with this kind of humanism because three generations of Frenchmen had been bred in it and had been so evidently unfitted by it to play their part in history, wishes to refound humanism on a dogmatic basis, on a metaphysic of man, on man's total knowledge of himself, and therefore on his free and instructed individual decisions. Erich Fromm, standing in the aristotelian humanist ethical tradition, wishes to found a humanist art of living on a more adequate empirical science of man than the rationalists have made use of. The marxists have founded their humanism on a metaphysic of history, and on the necessary decisions determined by the historical situation. All such humanist views and programmes propose an active development of human life, social and personal, in the light of ideas and ideals of man and of the human situation, historical and cosmic. That is justified, a lesson to be learned from the failure of Greek humanism and from the progress initiated by the Enlightenment. But an abstract metaphysic of man or of history can never furnish the required idea and ideal: such rationalism is chronically anti-humanist. And psychology, even if it is empirical and if it penetrates to the dynamics of behaviour and the profundities of man (an immense advance on some of the old thin and threadbare rationalist assumptions and fictions), is only one element in the total complex of general ideas fit to inspire and instruct a universal project of man.

Man has become a problem to himself, says Max Scheler. Man has no nature, what he has is history, says Ortega y Gasset. In truth, these are not new discoveries, but as an outcome of the great quest for certainty and universality on which the Enlightenment set out they are brittle conclusions with which to shape the future. With all the depth and richness of his historical knowledge and the elaborate refinement of his science, man has still to pick up in voyaging the primitive art of navigation and to find the fixed points by which to steer? That would be so if it were left to his will and his imagination to initiate everything. But it is not so, because the universal project of man is already rough-hewn in historical shape. What is the contemporary consciousness of one world and the striving for world order, institutionalized in the United Nations and its subsidiary agencies, but man's project for human life on earth? It is the project of a universal civilization founded on the principles of science and of democracy, as the tremendous upshot of all history. It may be that it was Christian liberal statesmanship which contributed most to the establishment of these international institutions after the two world wars. It may be that marxists have no confidence in them and regard them as characteristic of a certain stage of capitalist imperialism. It may be that religious faiths and social theories are irrelevant to the practical interests of the U.N., and in particular that evolutionary humanism has been explicitly rejected as an unacceptable and unnecessary ideology for its purposes; and that even the Universal Declaration of Human Rights adopted by the General Assembly in 1948 was a declaration of agreement about the rights and of disagreement about the grounds on which they were to be upheld. It may be that many are disillusioned with the U.N., and some with contemporary civilization, and have turned to short-term or to long-term views and aims, to pleasure or to salvation. It may be that the institutions, procedures, and principles of the U.N. repeat on a world scale and with sovereign nations the mistakes of earlier rationalists who based rules for society on a simple abstract man and ignored the rationality of real men. It may be that this universal project of man which has taken historical shape, even if it be finally established on earth, does not answer the insistent questions, does not make man less a problem to himself, does not give him a nature and the satisfactions of that nature, does not touch his cosmic situation.

All this, and more of the same kind, is true and in point. What is more to the point, however, is the primacy and pressure of the world situation as the condition of the historical future of man. Desire to avoid world war in fear of its consequences is a weak ligament to bind mankind together, but until now there has been not even that, and it is organic and tougher than the ligatures of the U.N. Negative and treacherous as it is, as unlovely as a foetus, it is nevertheless the beginning of genuine common interest, the human interest as such. It would hardly be possible to say this if the reason why war has become universally feared, instead of being grasped still as the decisive instrument of policy, were not also a reason for hope: the same science which threatens war promises peace; everyone stands to gain more by the collaboration through science and democracy than in any other way. Of course this is not literally true, but it is so much more true than it ever was that it makes a new situation. Science and democracy as principal means of a universal civilization are man-making on a scale no religion or philosophy ever was. For some, this is a common human tradition in the making, a common civilization with universal standards, beginning tentatively with this cold-war dread of war. For others, this is the abolition of man and of the human tradition, mankind turned into sand, 'small, soft, round, infinite sand' (Nietzsche). Man, however, is not made by science and democracy, instead of by religion, instead of by personal choice and decision: the alternatives are false. Science and democracy, as standards and methods, as the most formative achievements of Europe, are not simply techniques nor simply historical achievements; they are also ideals. As historical achievements, they are not the work of any one party or school of thought or tradition or nation; the credit is unequally shared, but shared. As ideals (the standards they imply, the uses to which they are put), they divide East and West as bitterly as Christian ideas and ideals divided Christendom in the sixteenth century; and they also divide, along multiple lines, people in the

West. There is a human tradition in the making, and it concerns the uses of science and of democracy more than anything else.

At this point in history, then, the initiative is, so to speak, in the situation rather than in the will and imagination of men. That is why at this time ideas and ideals are so urgently called for, to second this initiative, to shape the rough-hewn universal project of man. Such ideas and ideals cannot be new, and are not arbitrary; they, too, have taken shape, rough shape; they, too, come out of the past with the momentum and the trend which the pressures of history and creative human responses have given them. These two realities, the historical situation and the historical ideas and ideals which work upon it and on which it works, are producing the future, as always. Here in this interaction is the body of human reality, of human presence in the world, history. It is not the whole of human reality, unless its requirements are ignored; as health is not the most precious value unless it is lost.

Chapter 3

THE USE OF IDEAS

I

Astatement is not long before the world, says Whitehead somewhere, before it begins to disclose ambiguity. Philosophy begins with linguistic analysis, or, some would say, philosophy is linguistic analysis. It is always relevant to ask of a statement, what does it mean? is it true? and these questions require the disclosure of how it was arrived at and of what use is to be made of it. Statements have to be owned, and owned by candid people, before they are entitled to the intellectual respect due to the impersonal status of science. The more cautious will not admit that two and two make four until they are assured of what use is to be made of the admission. Whitehead's point is the starting-point of the platonic dialectic, the probe of inquiry which pushes about amongst the opinions to which a statement gives rise, and exposes the underlying concatenation which entails that nobody can raise one question without raising all; the unity of all being, seized in the ultimate intellectual vision, meanwhile teases the rational grasp not by what slips through the fingers but by what becomes something else in the very hand. It is not in the realm of logic that such vexations occur, nor can they happen in the realm of experience; it is in the twilight between the two that notions turn into their contraries, and antinomies and other monsters appear. Our minds are founded on the principle of identity and on the axiom 'once true, always true'. What happens according to established expectations does not start a question nor inhibit action. If there is a difference, we look for a difference to make the difference. We have an idea what it might be, and try that out; or in a very serious case we have to revise our ideal scheme of what is. Without ideas, animals learn by experience; the inborn mechanisms of be-

52

haviour are modified and conditioned by each new context of relevant experience and become adapted to quite a range of events. The distinctive human success with ideas is by invention and intervention, by contrivance rather than by adaptation; it is an active, aggressive role. But it does not inaugurate a victorious campaign of conquest. In making himself master of his animal situation, man dissolves all the firm familiar lines and finds that he has broken through into a world of imagination; he is no longer dealing with what simply is, but with what might be, what perhaps ought to be, not simply in the world of encountered events but within himself as well. Everything is in question. How profoundly and permanently everything is in question, especially how deep a question man is to himself, has never been recognized widely and steadily before our time in a spirit not of scepticism but of responsibility. Ideas have dissolved the firmament of our ancestors, and ideas must reconstitute the inheritance of man. That, however, requires an appropriate hold on our certainties, an appropriate use of ideas.

II

The use of ideas in the methodologies of the sciences is of special importance, but it is special and it is under the constant scrutiny of philosophers of science. One may say that it is responsible, even exceptionally responsible, if one speaks strictly of the construction of scientific knowledge and not of its propagation nor of its uses. The use of ideas at a more general level is of vast importance, and if it is to be responsible requires a discipline of its own. The use of ideas at this level can be seen only on an historical scale. Take, for example, a body of ideas which enables a people to see and to seize themselves, their history, their destiny. Israel is not merely a number of tribes occupying and cultivating Canaan. It is a chosen people brought up out of captivity in Egypt by a strong hand and given a promised land, a good land, a land flowing with milk and honey. Such ideas have a long history; they are brought out in their explicitness and stamped in by events. When the ten northern tribes are scattered and eventually the remnant of a remnant returns from captivity in Babylon to rebuild Jerusalem, no longer a nation, all the transformation of the ideas of the covenant in the light of their experience is in the making, the simple theology of a desert tribe develops into the most remarkable of historical faiths: weaned of corn and wine, the chosen people embrace their utter dependence upon the strong hand that brought them out of Egypt and has nigh destroyed them for their disobedience; the obedience required is a thorough inward transformation of which no man is capable, and for this therefore their dependence is also absolute; they can only wait for a salvation that is inward and outward and will be what it will be; all their virtue and all their vitality are concentrated in the waiting, the dependence, the openness. The imagination of Jesus and his people's reception of him are conditioned by these ideas which in oral obscurity had promoted their experience in its aggressive phase and which can be seen in the literary record to have been modified and intensified by their experience in its suffering phase. The continuity of the same body of ideas, dominating experience and subject to it, transforming experience through action and through interpretation and being transformed by it, is the secret of the persistence and the influence of this extraordinary people; and this same body of ideas was generalized and further developed in the Christian church. The intense, sustained, and cultivated waiting upon God, which was the outcome of reflection upon the original ideas in the light of the historical experience they had fermented, created amongst an elect few of the remnant a frame of mind and a set of will ready to seize on the identified response of God to Israel's need of salvation. Concentration upon the person and teaching of Jesus as the identified response of God initiated an experience which developed the original ideas of Judaism, producing the Christian mission and the Christian church. Through the ascendancy of the church these traditional ideas created a new Israel not after the flesh. Policy, institutions, and experience were moulded and interpreted by these ideas throughout centuries. Partly the results of this monopoly, partly the challenge of ideas from other sources, have so modified the Christian scheme that today it is a question which is the more remarkable, the continuity or the change. The God of the modern Christian is recognizably the God of Abraham and of Isaac, but the Old Testament has been pushed back amongst other records of the past, and the theocracy, as after its decay the Roman Empire, survives as a ghost.

If one considers the immense historical influence of this body of ideas, and that it has given identity and continuity to a complex culture, a tradition, and if one considers all the vicissitudes in the interaction of these ideas with experience, the elaborate methods of synagogue and church for binding the people by and to these ideas and for adapting the ideas to the concrete case, the repeated breaking loose in heresy and schism and sometimes in rejection of the whole body of ideas as archaic and irrelevant, and if one considers these ideas from the outside as an ideology, and not from the inside as a religion, an historical body of ideas with the function of promoting and controlling human development, if one considers them in this way, one can hardly fail to see the need for an appropriate acknowledged discipline in this all-important comprehensive art of human self-direction. Such a discipline would not be itself concerned simply with the question of the truth of Judaism or of Christianity or of any other world view, a question for theology and philosophy; it would be concerned with the use and abuse of such ideas in promoting and controlling human development. Assuming that the function of ideas is to make our experience consistent and to extend it, and that in doing this ideas are themselves modified and developed, what are the rules for this process, since history shows that it does not simply take care of itself? We are familiar with the use of ideas in sciences in this way, and the rules are well established, but this historical purpose is both sufficiently like and sufficiently unlike the scientific purpose to make it a question whether or not the same rules apply in the same way. Before thinking about the rules, it is necessary to look at this likeness and difference of purpose.

III

The purpose of science is science, more science. The idea as hypothesis is science in the making, and in so far as it is consistent with established science and is not falsified under tests it becomes established science. But the hypothesis in being tested calls attention to a new repeatable feature of the phenomena, and usually it leads to further inquiry. It is in this sense that in science ideas create experience and are themselves developed by the experience they create. But the scientist, as scientist, is not interested in experience, in events, save as they challenge or extend the abstractions of his established science. It is important to distinguish thus, if possible, between the work of constructing science and any and all of the various uses of science: otherwise, science itself becomes ideology, metaphysics, a theory of reality, a life to be lived. In science, then, the development of experience by an idea and of the idea by experience has a precise and simple meaning: the idea proposes to settle a question raised by experience, or by theoretical elaboration, and leads to the expectation of a certain event not observed before; the observation tests the idea and also raises other questions which prompt other hypothetical ideas. The ideal goal of this process has been thought of as the achievement of a complete deductive system, which can be finally elaborated out of its own resources without further reference to experience. At this limit, ideas would no longer develop experience, nor experience ideas; the ideal scheme would be exhaustive knowledge of what could happen, which experience could exemplify but never confirm, contradict, nor extend. Such an ideal is illusory, not only in the sense that it can never be achieved in practice but also in the sense that it mistakenly identifies the structure of logic with the structure of the world. Nevertheless, the purpose of science as science is to construct a map that is as little as possible subject to revision, that is, to further experience, not because it is a self-contained independent system, but because it is a reliable and adequate system of prediction. At this ideal limit, science is not any longer building science, because there is no further experience to be reduced to its mode; it has then not exhausted experience but produced an exhaustive scientific notation of experience.

The purpose of an ideology, on the other hand, is not truth (notations and predictive techniques) but realization. It is a complex of ends and means founded on assumptions about human existence. Like the hypothesis, it derives from experience, it conditions and determines experience, and it is modified and developed by experience, but this is incidental to its career not its whole history as with the hypothetical idea in science; it projects enjoyment of an experience as its goal, not its own test as prediction. An ideology, therefore, can never be scientific in the strict sense. But it has scientific bearings, and its incidental modification and development by experience can be given more attention and be brought under control. An ideology is not scientific, but it may be rational.

The attempt to realize the vision of human life projected by an ideology is a long-term business exceeding the life-span of several generations, and it involves elaborate institutions and traditions as well as the complex body of ideas. The ideas are likely to be dissipated and lost unless they are preserved and developed by an authoritative priesthood or rabbinate or party enjoying high social prestige, and then they inevitably become a jealously guarded vested interest resistant to experience. Even so, they are not likely to maintain real social influence unless they are kept in touch with actual social needs and possibilities. In such circumstances, the development of ideas by experience is likely to mean nothing more than an adjustment of old rules to new cases, for example, relaxing the law of the Sabbath to allow of ocean travel. In this case of the Jews, the total body of rules, bound up with their ideas and assumptions about themselves, stands for their existence as an historical people, their dependence upon God and therefore upon their religious tradition and their religious teachers, and it is the instrument of their purification by the discipline of obedience and observance until the time of their Messianic deliverance and the consummation of their hopes in the promises on which they rely. These ideas and this practice condition their experience, and if the providence on which their whole project of Israel and of man relies seems to be belied by the experience which befalls them, that experience can always be explained (by the religious teacher, it always is explained) as the just consequence of their sin, their inward failure; if they are never so blameless, to the anxious scrutiny of their introspection their suffering may always be the privilege which enables them to transcend the limits of this life, and raises them nearer to God. Thus experience at this level may remain invincibly ambiguous, unable to test an ideology as the crucial experiment tests an hypothesis.[1]

Nevertheless, over a period experience does heavily modify an ideology. It may be modified in its assumptions about human existence, in the ends envisaged, or in the means relied on. Normally, it is the means that are most readily modified by experience. The Protestant Reformation was such a modification, and, even more clearly, the separation of church and state. Experience also modified millenary beliefs. And in the prophetic age of Israel there seems to have been a radical reconstruction of the primitive ideology as a result of national experience. The hardly less radical modification of Christian belief as a result of the modern development of science and of scholarship has been the impact on the ideology of ideas drawn from a separate source of experience, a bringing together of total experience in a consistent body, not a modification of ideas by the

[1] In the pagan classical world, disappointment with the performance of the gods was likely to lead to impulsive destruction of their sacred images and places, the turning to other gods or to the occult, perhaps the breakdown of morale. It is in its marked contrast to this type of belief that one should see the persistence, not unchanged, of a highly developed ideology such as Judaism or Christianity, through the phases of historical experience it influences.

specific experience governed by those ideas. This difference is important for the criticism and control of ideology. It is one thing to reconstruct or to restate Christian belief, with the evidence for it and the ways of arriving at it, in the light of the methods and results of modern science and scholarship, and thereby to raise or to seek to resolve the question whether or not this belief is consistent with ideas established by scientific methods, and therewith to compare the logical status and ultimate validity of Christian and scientific belief. This is the arena of modern apologetics. It is another thing from within the standpoint of Christian belief to seek to learn the lesson of history in order to reproject the city of God, in a new idea of Catholic Christendom or in a revised and developed Protestant idea of God. Both these two things are going on at the present time. They are connected but distinct. One is the attempt to establish theology as reasonable and reliable knowledge; its purpose is scientific. The other is a renewed effort to realize the historical project of man founded on theological knowledge; its purpose is a total achievement. The first pushes theology out into the world to justify itself in the context of all public knowledge. The second, as an outcome of reflection upon the experience into which the ideas have led, seizes the ideas with new insight and develops them by a new and better-informed project of realization, brings them nearer to the needs and possibilities of human living. This does try and test them, but it is not scientific in intention and does not have the simple and public character of scientific verification. In the same way, any other ideology has its inner and outer dialectics, its development by reflection upon what it has produced and its development by relations, controversial and assimilative, with other ideas.

IV

What bearing has this distinction on the judgement of the claims made for an ideology? First, however, there is the rationalist's objection that any and every ideology is a myth, unscientific and irrational, and therefore its claims are not to be taken seriously. Science is enough. There are two conclusive objections to this view.

(1) Science is itself ideological unless it is strictly held that it is wholly and solely concerned with science and ceases to be science so soon as it is used for any purpose whatever that is not the consolidation and extension of science. Therefore science, always a necessary

intellectual activity, can never be a sufficient one. It is necessary to use science, and there are several purposes for which it is useful. Its uses involve ideologies, assumptions about science itself, projects of man. The more man allows the scientific preoccupation to engross him, and science proliferates in specialisms and accumulated research, he risks the enfeeblement of science and of man. This tendency is part of 'the modern theme'. It is science informing and informed by an ideology that is a vital human enterprise.

(2) Science itself in practice is not a wholly impersonal objective procedure. It develops minor ideologies of its own within the various fields of study, and it may itself become an ideology, when others are rejected. The schools and cults which do develop within a science are, of course, unscientific, but there are many reasons why it is inevitable that they should develop. There are, for example, human factors which can be condemned or excused but which can hardly be eliminated like mechanical defects: individual scientists and their colleagues and disciples, for instance, are bound to make extravagant claims for their programmes of research, and to see in them the looked-for solutions not merely of the problems of their own specialty but also the solutions mankind has been waiting for in other fields. Then there are inherent factors which cannot be easily eliminated: the most important is in the nature of science as drastic simplification. There cannot be science except on the assumption that all that is left out for the purpose of schematization can be safely ignored for that purpose. This is all very well in relatively simple fields like physics; it is far from the same situation in highly complex fields like human behaviour. In these fields it is always possible to remodel the science on alternative data by different decisions; and even in physics and in biology this happens, and the views of the new generation which supersede the obsolescent concepts are not necessarily more true: at least, it would be naïve to think that it is solely because of demonstrable truth and error that new views in science gain ground and push out the old, just as it would be naïve to think that new styles in art are of course superior to earlier ones; the analogy is far from exact, but it is not irrelevant. In the human sciences, then, the drastic simplification which is requisite in order to have a science is bound to leave out so much that is or may be of the kind that makes all the difference, that in such sciences there is sure to be great instability and a strong tendency to dogmatism. One has only to think of psychology, of anthropology, of sociology for

examples. These studies have been both fertile and influential, but in each field there have been multiple studies, many of them linked with ideologies. Amongst older names, it is sufficient to recall Bentham, Comte, Spencer, Marx, or nearer our time, Freud, McDougall, Sorel, Pareto, and the roll could be increased by contemporary additions. The point is that it is more scientific to work in these fields within the framework of an ideology consciously elaborated on adequate grounds, public and universal, than to develop *ad hoc* a quasi-ideology on the narrow basis of some aspect of one field.

Particular programmes of research start from their own declared presuppositions and set their own terms and goals, but when it comes to the organization of the science and systematization and assessment of the results of research programmes, an ideology is invented if there is none established to refer to. Research programmes which are fully candid, which specify what they are assuming and what they are looking for and how they are going about it, are fully scientific, as, for example, anthropological field studies, gestalt or behaviourist experiments, or population studies. Attempts at classification may also be scientific, as, for example, character typology or comparative legal studies which classify societies on the basis of their legal institutions on a universal scale of regular evolutionary sequence. All such scientific work is fully open to criticism and establishes itself with those competent to judge, or fails to do so. But to put together the results of such programmes under the concept 'man', or even under the rubrics of semi-autonomous studies, anthropology, psychology, sociology, is to have to go beyond science. In the physical sciences, accurate knowledge of what has happened is reliable ground for knowledge of what will happen. In the sciences of man, it is open to man himself to introduce the difference that will make the difference, and accurate knowledge increases his power to do this purposefully. In this field, therefore, more than in the physical field, knowledge is knowledge of what has been, not knowledge of what is and of what will be and can be. Ideologies are attempts, based on knowledge and will, to stabilize this open future, to give it reliable definition; and they are therefore relevant to these sciences; there is an interdependence which ought to be consciously controlled, and neither denied nor ignored. As for those who would make of science itself an ideology, they are either saying that human beings are wholly and solely concerned with knowledge, with building coherent abstractions from experience, which nobody will use for any other purpose than to perfect these abstractions, or else they are smuggling in half-baked ideologies.

The problem, then, is to make ideologies technically sound, since they cannot be avoided. They cannot be made scientific, for that is a contradiction in terms; but they can be well founded and they can be kept under continuous revision by maintaining the double dialectic, inner and outer, with the experience which they develop and with the alternatives which they exclude. It is on these lines that one can try to answer the question raised, how are the claims made for an ideology to be judged?

Ideologies, with their conceptions of man, of the ends of human striving, and of the means of achieving them, may be merely verbal, as so many theosophies are, or well founded on history and science. The conception of man as a mortal product of biological evolution, the conception of a universal civilization as the goal of effort, to be achieved by the solution of the common political and economic problems of world order and world welfare with which mankind is anyhow faced, using all that can be learned from history and from the relevant sciences to find the way to workable solutions, these are intellectually fair and modest conceptions, as close as possible to rationally ordered human experience and the generalization of human interest. Of course they start an infinitude of questions and leave room for a multitude of refinements and differences. But even in the innocence of such bare generality such an ideology is absolutely divided both from marxism and from Christianity. Christianity cannot leave out, even provisionally for the working purposes of this life, the first and last things of the faith. Marxism cannot admit the generalization of human interest, the possibility of solving political and economic problems by any other means than ultimate conflict à outrance: the will to use other techniques is the rejected utopian ideology, because like the pacifist the deluded idealist is alone in walking into that blind alley, and history is made by the organized interests marching to their destiny on the high road.

Such differences go beyond science. One cannot in strictness say that the modest ideology indicated above is scientific and that Christianity and marxism are not, and judge them on this ground. What one might say at the outset is that the modest ideology makes fewest assumptions, is closest to normal experience. But even this is doubtful and exposed to contention. Nevertheless, the question of congruence with experience is highly relevant to justifiability, and rules out verbal theosophies as qualified ideologies. Those in the running must be able to make out a plausible case as being founded on the facts of human experience. Theoretically, Christians may argue that without faith man will ultimately lapse into animality; marxists may argue that men will defend and seek to expand their economic interests regardless of the social consequences. Such arguments cannot be settled conclusively by the appeal to experience. They go beyond science, and decisions which are founded upon them, or upon the rejection of them, cannot claim to be scientific. They are, more or less informed, acts of will. Their great importance, the human tragedy, is that they tend to make their assumptions come true. That is why the region in which contemporary justification for ideologies is sought and controversies with alternatives are carried on is not stale, flat, and unprofitable, but is of the highest importance to human interests, for although nothing quite conclusive can be attained and an irreducible element of venture remains, there may be great differences in the reasonableness of the claims made, that is to say, great differences in the initial reasonableness of what it is supposed human existence is and ought to be. The lines and methods of controversy shift from one generation to another, which is some indication that argument of this kind is not without effect; ground is lost and won, and victory or defeat may be brought near or pushed off.

The inner dialectic, between the ideology and the experience which it governs, is even more important, for this is the primary means by which an ideology is developed and modified for those who hold it. Criticism and development are to some extent the result of the theoretical organization incidental to exposition and controversy, but the meaning and value of ideas can be understood and appreciated only in reflection upon the results of the actions they initiate. They cannot be proved nor disproved in this way, but there is no other way in which an ideology can be proved, and without this dialectic it is a barren dogmatism, an empty substitute for experience, not the management of experience. If an ideology is incapable, by reason of its structure, of being developed in this way, or if it is not being developed in this way, it is condemned by that fact. A dogmatic ideology which claims to be superior to experience, or one which in practice has been made superior by a party or school, is noxious, and nothing but expediency should stand in the way of its being attacked and destroyed as actively and unreservedly as a pest. On the other hand, any ideology which is being actively developed in this way is worthy of respect.

V

But what does it really mean to develop an ideology in this way? An example might be taken from economic planning. The virtue of an economic plan is in its being fully and reliably informed and in its being flexible. It is governed by social policy (that is, it is a project of what is wanted), but it grows out of conferences, consultations, investigations. The unworkable and the incalculable can never be eliminated from the planned phase, but they are minimized by fulness of accurate information (including predictions). Flexibility allows administrators to take tactical decisions which will maintain the initiative of the plan, and limit the effects of breakdown or partial failure and of untoward accidents, and take full advantage of particular success and of favourable winds. At the end of the planned phase, the result can never be exactly what was planned, but in so far as the events in retrospect look as if they had been planned, the plan is successful. The 'retrospective plan' may not be better than the original in the sense that it accomplishes more than was proposed of what is wanted, but it is better in the sense that it is closer to the possibilities; and all effective development of the governing policy comes from the 'retrospective plan'. This creative learning from experience can come only from success, that is, from a 'retrospective plan', not from failure, the experience of a plan that breaks down in muddle. (The proverbial saying, experience keeps a dear school but fools will learn in no other, makes sense only if it means the primary school which experience keeps. Of the higher grades, it is only true to say that experience keeps the only school in which the wise can profit.)

The example of economic planning can be taken to pieces because it is relatively mechanical. At the other end of the scale exemplifying the same process is the work of the artist, whose original conceptions initiate the work and both prompt and control its advance and are prompted and controlled by the advancing work itself. The dialectic here is too continuous and subtle to be separated into stages and operations, and it is less under direct control. All one can say is that artistic creation is a process of learning from experience, and the funded experience becomes a source of conception and intuition, a source of fertility, and not merely an acquisition of technical skill. Between the extremes of artistic creation and deliberate economic planning are many familiar contemporary examples. The revision of socialist ideas and ideals in Britain after the Labour Party's first period of power is on the full scale of a thorough many-sided re-examination of assumptions, objectives, guiding principles, policies and programmes, stimulated by controversy within the party and with opponents. The traditional diplomacy of the United States has since the war been subjected to analysis and criticism in the light of its consequences and of the changed situation. The original assumptions and aims which went to the making of international institutions and procedures are being revised in the light of the failures of the League and the dilemmas of the United Nations. The ideas and ideals both of protestantism and of catholicism are being examined again in the light of history and the contemporary situation by thinkers bred in these traditions. Influential general ideas that have been shaken by experience, for example, *laisser-faire* or the idea of progress, can only perform again if their appearance is plainly penitent. And of course the whole of contemporary culture in its manifold daily manifestations is a complex continuous criticism and revision of tradition as well as its transmission.

All such revision is painful, and beset by temptations. The natural process is like the swing of a pendulum, and to maintain creative human control requires confident effort founded on mastered technique. The zealous application of the good ideas of yesterday to today's problems makes trouble more troublesome. But infatuation with the necessary ideas of today is no wiser. What is wanted is not new ideas but the completion of old ones. Exemplified crudely, what is wanted from the trade unions is not co-operation and all-out production instead of aggressive wage demands and restrictive practices, what is wanted from the nations is not internationalism instead of self-determination and power-building, what is wanted from the individual is not public service instead of private interest. The trade unions in learning to take responsibility for economic policy and production must not lose the will and power to defend and further the interests of their constituents: they have to do the same old thing, and something else, in a new context, which certainly requires a changed approach, but does not cancel the original requirement. Similarly, the nations remain responsible for their own interests in the new context of closer interdependence and common responsibility, and individuals for theirs in the new context of social welfare. New ideas are as distracting, perhaps ruinous, as new loves, but the choice between old and new is only the headache of folly. All ideas have virtue and legitimacy only in so far as they keep in touch with an experience they govern, and in so far as they do this they are always new and increasingly adequate. The notion of empiricism as mere trial and error, zigzag improvisation, a reaction to facts and events as they are encountered piecemeal, and to dangers as they appear and press home, a stomach for facts with no taste for ideas, such a notion is a vulgar error. More than any other method empiricism makes use of ideas, more than any other course it is undeviating progress. For it presupposes an initial policy based on a thorough study of the complete situation, and it is on that basis that it is a steady persistence of a body of ideas and ideals in touch with an experience they govern and by which they are governed. Least of all is empiricism the kind of learning from experience which turns its back to the future, tragically exemplified in the period between the wars, when statesmen in this country and elsewhere began by returning in their ideas and ideals to conditions which had gone for ever, and followed events, political and economic, at home and abroad, with too little of the right policy too late. In war itself, the tank and the aeroplane, which in the first world war were introduced as ancillary means of carrying out established tactical ideas, became in the second war the foundation of a remodelled strategy, for which the democracies were disastrously unready, being only prepared to begin where the last war had left off.

The short answer, then, to the question raised, what does it really mean to develop an ideology? is that it means using it to take and to keep the initiative with experience, that is to say, continuously to create one's own experience and not to suffer it. This goes far beyond the animal ideal of a well-adjusted individual; it is the distinctively human power of integral living and learning in a creative project. If the original ideas are sufficiently relevant and adequate, intelligent use of them in the systole and diastole of living and learning is the unfailing dynamic of personal venture. What is true of personal life and party policy and philosophic view is true ideally also of the human tradition itself and the shaping of the human interest as such. If the idea of progress has any future it is along these lines that it has to be made good.

VI

Ideas have other main uses, of course, besides the scientific and the ideological. They are used, for example, in speculation, in argument, and in propaganda, in the applications of science and in the popular dissemination of science, in poetry and the images of fiction, and in everyday living.

Speculation is not necessarily idle verbosity. It may be that. The speculative thinker is reporting on a journey he has never made, perhaps one that nobody can ever make. In that case it might seem that he can tell only travellers' tales. Some think so. But a good part of his journey may be genuine enough, and his projections and guesses from the point beyond which he can proceed no further may be skilful and ingenious enough to make conceptually accessible what cannot be reached. The supreme virtue here, as in all intellectual matters, and in others as well, is candour. If he discloses his starting-point and gives his bearings and says just what he is doing, there is no just complaint against him. Pretentiousness, obscurity, mystification, always vulgar or vicious, are here particularly objectionable because the danger of imposition is greater. The venture into possible worlds will always remain one of the major intellectual excitements, and like other human excitements is not to be forbidden because of the risks that are run.

Ideas may be used properly or improperly in argument. Propaganda has a bad name and may be thought to be the improper use of ideas in argument. If by propaganda is meant the appeal past reason or under reason, by use of the principles of applied psychology, then propaganda is not argument at all, and the scholastic logicians named appeals of this type *argumentum ad hominem*, *argumentum ad baculum*, etc., merely to expose their pretensions. But propaganda may mean, originally did mean, the reasoned propagation of ideas, which just is argument. The structure of argument is really the structure of thought; one makes over one's thought to another, and if it is rickety the argument is likely to collapse when somebody tries to take hold of it. Thinking is argument with oneself; a sound argument, critical or constructive, is the revelation of a sound piece of thinking. Again, technical competence and candour are the requisite qualifications. Without competence there can hardly be candour, for one does not really know what one is doing, and may not even know that one does not know. If one is versed in logical form, one knows also that one cannot really make a case without absolute candour, for it must be open to public inspection and test from first to last. It is the nature of argument to invite all-comers to tell me where I am wrong in my thinking. In this sense, argument is always giving assistance or seeking assistance in the continuous co-operative human task of thinking to some purpose.

The use of ideas in applied science is straightforward enough, at least in most of the various branches of technology, where the practical problems and possibilities are fairly definitely indicated, although even here of course the general orientation and objectives of social policy exert constant pressure and influence. In the fields of law, medicine, and education, ideology plays more part: one speaks of the philosophy of law and the philosophy of education, indicating that there are more possibilities than those settled by actual social policies. Educational theories and legal theories are not merely scientific, nor are they usually ideas about means to attain given social ends; they are projects of society, ideologies. The *Republic* is an educational theory. Plato's philosophy can also be regarded as a theory of law.

However, it is in the synthesis and popularization of the sciences that one should recognize the big modern problem, big in scope and scale, but brittle in texture so that it seems past all handling. Indeed, there has been much lusty work in this field, bold pioneer ventures and any number of light-hearted bids. It has not been only the fools who have rushed in. The greatest names in science have led the way. Even the first-rate scientist is likely to talk nonsense when he addresses the general public on findings in his own field, because he has not merely to translate the untranslatable, as in communicating the poetry of another tongue, but to communicate signs which refer to an experience which the general public does not have. The task is impossible, therefore why attempt it? Because (1) a society of which science is the life-blood requires a scientifically educated public, bred in scientific habits of mind and acquainted with scientific language and appreciating the conditions of scientific advance; and (2) because an intelligible map of life is more than ever needed by a society which depends for its material progress on increasing specialization and segregation, and such a map in a scientific age must be a scientific map. The construction of this scientific map of life is a special job, to be competently done only by those who understand its difficulties and its important purpose, and who are therefore governed by an instructed responsibility conspicuously lacking in most of the many scientists who undertake to inform the public about science, not seldom with popular success. It is a co-operative job, and cannot be done otherwise; and it is a job neither of popularizing nor of synthesizing results; it is the creation of a new discipline which will enable people to enter into the sciences and inform their views from the sciences without serious misunderstanding and without impossible conditions of special training—as one may learn, not without apprenticeship, appreciation of the arts without becoming technically skilled. Appreciation of science is the foundation, and appreciation of nature is the constructive achievement in view.

Aristotle defined man as a rational animal, Pascal as a thinking reed, Carlyle as a forked radish. Only the first attempts to be scientific, but the others do not admit to being less true, and they appeal no less to the witness of mankind and stand or fall by public judgement. All three attempt to hit off essential characters of the thing defined; the difference is that the scientific definition attempts to seize an aspect which is always and everywhere relevant, and is the source of all specific characters, whereas the poetic definitions seize aspects which are essentially true but not always and everywhere relevant and not the general source of all specific characters: they have general truth, and are not merely true of a particular man, but not a truth that is always relevant. For that reason, poetic ideas may be more striking and revealing than scientific ideas; they light up with flashes aspects obscured by the steady diffused light of rational abstractions, and they therefore need to be multiplied; poetry piles epithet on epithet, whereas science holds all in the simple pattern of dependence upon the single essential character. (All this is traditional and has to be qualified by the modern abandonment of metaphysics, the abandonment of definition for description, of 'natures' for histories, of essence for existence: man is not a rational animal but a life-history with certain variable and invariable features. Modern scientific theories whether they grow more abstract or more concrete are more flexible and tactical and have a more poetic and dramatic quality, whilst submitting even more strictly to the control of scientific purpose which gives them their justification.)

What is true of the poetic epithet and the rational definition is true also of the complex ideas of science and of literature. The images of fiction may claim a higher truth than history, in virtue of their greater generality, expressing a more complex or concentrated experience. But the contrast here is not really between generalized truth and particular truth; rather, it is between the pale formality of public truth and the vivid free handling of personal vision; and again it is the multiplication and clash of personal views which bring out what scientific history or biography, or photography, cannot catch. But it is stupid to generalize much in this way, since there are so many more common uses for the images of fiction than for the ideas of science. To put it broadly, one may be interested in the reconstruction of what has happened, or in what universally is, or in what might be, or in what never was on land or sea, or in the concrete image for itself of some particular thing which has no reference to anything but itself. If one follows someone like Leonardo, equally interested in the visual and in the scientific or technical aspects of things, one sees him drawing the surface modelling of a limb and then the interior arrangements of structure and function, and in both studying accuracy, truth to the eye; and both allow of or lead on to playing with ideas, remodelling or rearranging what is there, either to please the eye with shape or mass or texture or to stylize muscles with cords to please the mind with analogy and principle. This concern with truth, both particular and general, and with possibility, both abstract and practical, is a concern of both science and arts, and there is no final nor useful separation; all are mixed and interconnected, serving the purpose in hand, the interest in view. But the greater variety of possible types of representation in any of the arts makes a general theory of art more difficult to achieve than a theory of science, although the variety of uses for any of the sciences, apart from the diversity of sciences, makes it doubtful that there can be only one form of science.

Ideas are not used always and only in systems or in the formal pursuit of the arts and the sciences, for they are used every day and all the time in meeting the many small emergencies and minor crises which are the occasions of all our ordinary thinking, when routinized behaviour does not quite suffice. All this habitual behaviour of established routine is itself determined by ideas, which may or may not be adequate. Even strained attention nerved by the desire to observe accurately what is there and equipped with unusual precision and saturated with previous acquaintance will see a good deal that is not there save in the form of preconception, of ideas. This can be studied in Leonardo's anatomical drawings, and it is a commonplace of the history of science, and of the visual arts. This calls attention to the most important of all truths concerning the use of ideas, namely, that ideas may easily substitute themselves for the world, even for oneself, and cut one off from the responsiveness of what is there and from one's own responsiveness, from encounter and its unpredictable and often powerfully determinative results; and this may be done under the highest auspices. On the other hand, ideas may facilitate and fertilize this very thing, two-sided meeting and responsiveness, vital appropriation and vital production, by the highest economy of effort in perception and invention. This nervous mediation of ideas, which puts one in touch with what is there, not least with oneself, is the common ideal in all the several uses of ideas, casual or deliberative.

VII

It remains to say that the history and criticism of ideas is the primary, some would say the secondary, concern of philosophy. Philosophy is a critique of science, of ideology, of speculation, of the map of life, of poetry, of argument, of the conduct of life, a criticism not of any actual example of any of these things but of their possibility and first principles, a critique of techniques, of the use of ideas, not a criticism of life. But philosophy may also be a criticism of life, an actual ideology or speculation or argument, a map of life, a poem. Even in this form, however, it is really an instrument of living; the real criticism of life is the outcome, the expression, of a complete experience, to which philosophy as the critical mastery of ideas brings all that the architect brings to the building. Philosophy, so often the most verbose, abstract, and sterile employment, has supreme responsibility for the use of ideas, and ultimately for the ideas used. Wisdom is the effect of their proper use. Wisdom, the experience created by the proper use of ideas, may express itself in many ways, in personality or in a life lived, for example, or in art. Such an experience, however expressed, is the sole source of a valid criticism of life, and such a criticism of life is the highest achievement of the human spirit.

Chapter 4

HUMANIST ETHICS

I

MORAL knowledge is necessarily the most simple and certain of all knowledge. If I want to attain a certain end I·may be obliged to acquire obscure or technical knowledge, but moral obligation can never require such knowledge. Whatever I am morally obliged to do is always something which I am expected and relied on to do by people whose interests are concerned and who are upheld in their demands by public opinion. As a grown person, I know what I am under moral obligation to do: I can be reminded what it is; I can be made to acknowledge what it is; I cannot properly be taught what it is. That does not mean that this knowledge is obtained by intuition. What I am justifiably counted on to do is known to me by the demand, and by my similar demands and dependence upon others. It is not in any sense a privileged form of knowledge. Although I may know only too plainly what people expect me to do and count on my doing, how do I know that this is what I am obliged to do? And how do I know that I am not obliged to do anything which is not as a matter of fact expected of me in this way?

Such questions imply the notion of moral obligation. I am not long in the world before my will is checked. I soon learn to live and labour under a sense of obligation: I am obliged to others, dependent on their good offices and favours; I am obliged by others, required under penalty to do what they want me to do; I am obliged to employ appropriate means if I want to enjoy chosen ends. I live in a world of law and of laws, which both limit and form my own will. There is nothing obscure about the notion of obligation used in a conditional sense: if I will the end I must will the means; if I want to keep out of prison I must obey the law. But the notion of moral obligation seems to imply an absolute constraint independent of my will and independent of sanctions. Of course it may be a bugaboo, the ghost of early authority that haunts the grown-up mind. An absolute constraint of this kind would impose on me the necessity of willing a certain end. That is absurd. I may be so rigorously determined that I am under the necessity of willing a certain end, but if I am free (and moral obligation implies that I am) I cannot be under such a necessity. Some moral philosophers have been so impressed by the annihilating effect on the person of an absolute obligation imposed on man from outside that they refuse to see the possibility of any moral obligation that does not have its source in a man's own will. On this view, to say that a man ought to will an end which in fact he does not is simply to say that he probably would will it if he knew himself better and saw the situation completely; and if in the light of total knowledge of himself and of the situation he yet did not will it, there would be no possible appeal beyond that final moral fact. On the other hand, other moral philosophers are more impressed by the inexorable demands which press in upon man from the outside with majestic authority, and they find it absurd to suppose that a man's own will on its own petty authority has the competence and right to deal with such demands. On this view, to say that a man ought to will an end which in fact he does not is to say that if he persists in his own will, even though he is not punished, he forfeits his competence, his justification, his title to life; it is to rob him of personal status, to make him guilty and unworthy; it is to deny him the right to choose his ends because he has chosen wrong. That you can make a wrong choice in this sense presupposes that you are not really free to choose, you are under the obligation to make a certain choice; there is a right choice, and it is only in terms of this situation that moral obligation has a meaning.

The narrows which run between these irremovable rocks of human experience make a stormy passage for any moral philosopher before he can move out into open water and choose the coasts he will explore, the inland excursions he will make, the places he will linger in, the harbour where he will bring his voyage to an end.

II

The world itself, human existence as such, seems in the end to impose an absolute obligation. Within a certain scope, human existence is the work of man; beyond that, it has to be accepted unconditionally. Unless it is refused. That choice is always open, and may always be honourable; that is to say, if man is really free to choose, really a personality, there can be no question of a right choice here. One can think of a thousand appropriate reproaches against the man who refuses to live, and he can hardly expect his fellows to approve his act and honour his memory. Nevertheless, there is no experience and there is no argument to justify anyone in saying anything against the man who does refuse life upon a personal choice; least of all is he justified in criticism who has not made a personal choice of his own human existence.

If I do choose to accept human existence, I must accept its ultimate conditions: to accept is to accept the conditions. The necessary conditions are not all apparent, and the decision is always subject to revision in the light of their discovery. But so long as my decision to live is in force it implies my conformity to the necessary conditions. Of course I can hide the conditions from myself, and I can dodge having to assume them by hiding behind the conformity of others. Such conduct is common enough: it is impossible to justify it, and therefore it would be silly to take the trouble to justify not adopting it. If I choose human existence and its necessary conditions, I virtually choose the development and exercise of my powers, with the disciplines that requires, and I choose also the obligations involved in membership of a society, since human existence implies existence in society. Thus acceptance of human existence commits me to acceptance of the particular obligations imposed on me by the society in which I live, the plain unmistakable expectations of me under public sanction which constitute my duties and offences. Without such obligations, there can be no reliable conduct, no human interdependence, and therefore no human achievement. I am bound to this moral order as intimately as to my body. The minimum basic obligations are enforced by legal sanctions; the requirements which are not enforced by legal sanctions may be no less definite, and even more important to the common interest and to human achievement. The moral obligation is the obligation to meet these requirements regardless of sanctions and regardless of inclinations. They come from outside and with the external authority of society, but they are essentially willed by me as willing my human existence, and that is their final authority for me. The proof of their obligation is the proof that I will them in willing my human existence, for I cannot concretely choose my existence without willing society, and that for me must be the historical society in which I find my life.

Thus morality is not a privileged form of knowledge that comes by intuition; it is the most familiar and public and unquestionable knowledge, a knowledge of obligations that are rooted in the will of the person whom they bind. Although he wills them, he can release himself from them only by withdrawing from human existence. The moral law is law but the law of an ideal order, an order in the making. In that sense it is conditional, but if there is to be this type of existence which human existence is, it is absolute. To choose human existence is to recognize and accept, amongst other things, the absoluteness of moral law, to submit to moral obligation.

At bottom, then, there is this simplicity in morality. There are the settled expectations, under public sanction, in the settled relations of life, on which reliable conduct is founded. This rudimentary simplicity is fundamental. Real problems continually obscure it, but like the sun it will remain as long as human existence lasts, and like the sun it will continue, even in obscurity, to serve the daily needs of the just and of the unjust.

III

If morality did have this ingenuous countenance, some moral philosophers would have portrayed it. Some have. Hume says that public opinion is the only competent court in morals. Butler says: 'In all common ordinary cases we see intuitively at first view what is our duty, what is the honest part. This is the ground of the observation, that the first thought is often the best. In these cases doubt and deliberation is itself dishonesty. . . . That which is called considering what is our duty in a particular case, is very often nothing but endeavouring to explain it away.' More recently, Bradley says: 'Point out to a man of simple morals that the case has other sides than the one he instinctively fixes on, and he suspects you wish to corrupt him. And so you probably would if you went on.' Others in their own ways have made the same point, that what we are under an obligation to do is immediately certain to us. Only, for the most part, they have mistakenly thought, like Butler, that it is known intuitively, whereas it is known in the way that what as a matter of fact is legitimately expected of us by others is known, knowledge which can be simply verified by inquiry, and as to which, in case of doubt, not intuition but public opinion is the final court of appeal.

The idea that moral knowledge is not knowledge of simple matters of fact like these, but a superior intuitive sinaitic knowledge, comes from the recognition, which can hardly be avoided, that these actual expectations which are simple matters of fact are not morally ultimate, that they are in some way subject to a superior knowledge of this kind. The idea that there is no higher moral authority than these common expectations and the public opinion which is behind them is not one that will be taken seriously unless it can make its way by removing or avoiding mountainous objections. For ethical theories are looking for a permanent and universal morality.

All those theories which find in nature not merely analogies but also sanctions and principles for morality can be summarily dealt with. These include theories which see in the law of the jungle the law of nature and therefore, on naturalist premises, the law for man, and theories which make a norm of evolutionary trends or find in the self-integrating principle of organism an ideal for man or a sanction for human ideals. Certainly, what happens and will probably happen in nature is relevant to moral ideals, since the conditions of human existence have to be accepted as the basis of what can be done with it, but to found moral obligation on natural principles (as distinct from specifically human principles), however firm, is to abdicate human authority more decisively than by obeying commandments imputed to deity. It is always more convenient to work with the grain of nature, but it is always a possible choice, which may be justified, to work against it or partially against it; still more is it characteristically human inventively to use the nature of things for quite remote purposes. There are limits beyond which it is quixotic to go, there are limits beyond which it is impossible to go, but to simplify the matter by limiting human choice to conformity with nature is a delusive simplification, since it does not do what it pretends, because either it is equivocal, concealing quite different motivations and evaluations, or else it accepts as necessary or as ideal what is simply rudimentary.

Moral evolution as a cultural phenomenon is quite another question, and interests the moral philosopher as indicating the sources of moral progress. Anthropology shows plainly how arbitrary a local moral code is. Only principles that are quite universal can really form and bind the moral conscience. To be completely bound by customary morality is not to be a person at all. In any case, customary morality registers a very low level of human behaviour, and the prime need of man is to rise above it and establish standards which will require behaviour that goes against the grain of customary morality, the morality, for example, of the market, of international relations, of conventional society and conventional religion. Customary morality may be destructive, may keep whole classes of persons in servitude and block their way to self-development. Clearly, all these objections and others like them, which look for a more authoritative source of morality outside the existing moral order and in tension with it, are not to be dismissed as frivolous complaints or academic sophistication.

There are two main regular means by which historically the inadequacy or iniquity of customary morality is progressively corrected. The first of these is as much a matter of fact as the mutual expectations established in customary morality: it is the claims made by groups or classes of persons who are dissatisfied with what is expected of them, and persistently demand a revision of their obligation. They may exert pressure by one method or another, resort to sanctions to enforce their claims. Usually, it is a change in power relations which enables them to demand the moral change, but the political and economic changes are accompanied by agitation, and this working upon public opinion is not separable from them. Although the moral change effected in this way is produced by and registers and expresses a shift in power, it is none the less moral and the new obligations established in this way are none the less obligatory, for the moral order is nothing other than a regulation of interests, an adjustment of interests, a mutuality, that produces enough satisfaction to evoke and command general support. A platonic morality which prescribes human interests is no morality at all, that is to say, the obligations it imposes are factitious and fictitious. The felt actual interests of individuals are the raw material of morality; they are both conditioned by and constrained by customary morality, but unless they are allowed and even encouraged to work on that morality in their turn and reshape it nearer to their needs, that morality will become corrupt and lose its obligation and

76

command, and the society will drift into a revolutionary crisis. No morality can replace and supersede individual felt interests and the claims arising from them, but of course such interests are not in themselves authoritative; they are candidates before public opinion for recognition and acknowledgement, and there are the established procedures by which the readjustment is to be worked out: they may establish themselves by direct action or by preponderance of number in a way that proves intolerable and provokes counter-action. The moral order is not a simple reflection of the order that is established by force and maintained by an existing set of power relations. It is a modification of the enforceable political order, it is what people will accept and acknowledge and respond to, and the regime, however oppressive, is subject to the pressure of dissatisfactions and the erosion of evasions. In so far as the established political order is not supported by a consensus, there will be an irregular moral order fitting more closely the actual needs and feelings of people.

Morality has this secondary historical source in claims which press for recognition, but the claims as such are not moral obligations unless and until they are acknowledged and embodied in the established morality of recognized rights and duties. What constraint, then, is there, other than force, to recognize a claim as having superior moral force to an existing moral obligation? The existing moral obligation has the sacredness and sanction of established human existence, the new claim is disturbing and dangerous. The question opens a new class of considerations, with regard to another source of morality, but this much may be said about it in the present connection, that since morality is essentially a self-sustaining order of mutually satisfying and productive human interdependence, dissatisfaction with it calls for remedy anyhow. Obviously, the remedy cannot always be the giving way to demands for a better deal for certain interests, but persistent serious dissatisfaction does require some remedy, and to that extent weakens the validity of the particular obligations complained of, and thereby carries a threat to the whole moral order which continues to require and to sanction them. Therefore it is everybody's interest and responsibility to find a satisfactory remedy for the grievance. The malcontents threaten to become delinquents, persons who are against society because it does not bring them enough satisfaction to engage their interest and evoke their loyalty.

In saying that morality is essentially a self-sustaining order of mutually satisfying and productive human interdependence, does one not go far beyond the *de facto* moral order and speak in terms of an ethical ideal? If one begins with the *de facto* moral order and insists on the absolute moral obligation of that unless and until it is revised, obviously in most historical cases it will be anything but an edifying self-sustained order of the kind described, and from a later point of view will be very difficult to defend. That is to look at the matter unhistorically in terms of rational abstractions, for even if the actual moral order is unjust by later standards, or is felt to be unjust, as a moral order it is human existence simply; it is to be revised, not abolished: it is to become what it essentially, necessarily, is, a self-sustaining mutually satisfying and productive order of human partnership. Burke puts the matter with an eloquence that is sober truth and not rhetorical mumbo-jumbo, in spite of his invocation of nature. 'It is the first and supreme necessity only, a necessity that is not chosen, but chooses, a necessity paramount to deliberation, that admits no discussion, and demands no evidence, which alone can justify a resort to anarchy. This necessity is no exception to the rule; because this necessity itself is a part too of that moral and physical disposition of things, to which man must be obedient by consent or force: but if that which is only submission to necessity should be made the object of choice, the law is broken, nature is disobeyed, and the rebellious are outlawed, cast forth, and exiled, from this world of reason, and order, and peace, and virtue, and fruitful penitence, into the antagonist world of madness, discord, vice, confusion, and unavailing sorrow.'

Moral obligations, then, are imposed by the *de facto* moral order upheld by all, and are unmistakably plain, but beneficiaries may be challenged by those who feel their interests to be thwarted or oppressed, and a new accommodation made. There is still a third source of morality, and it is more complex. There are, in the first place, established rights and duties, there are, in the second place, claims and offers seeking to be acknowledged and established as rights and duties; in the third place, there may also be dues, not established and not claimed nor offered, yet due to or due from persons or classes of person. How can such dues be recognized, defined, and embodied in actual morality?

Take as an example the treatment of women. They have often been cast for an inferior role and subjected to the social pressure of a body of expectations requiring them to play that role. Their rights

78

and duties were established to reinforce this status and part in society. They may not have claimed emancipation or any improvement of status or recognition of real interests: they may have accepted as their own idea and ideal of themselves the image which the body of surrounding expectations presented them with. It is conceivable that this treatment was not really good for them, that they were not developed by it as persons, that some were destroyed by it. Therefore it is conceivable that the status of equality and the availability of opportunities which they neither enjoyed nor claimed were due to them as persons, independently of rights and claims. It is often said that everyone has the right to the development of his personality. This most modern idea was prominent in the ethical thought of the ancients. Cicero insisted that everyone should hold fast to his own peculiar gifts and sustain his own character: it would be improper for Ajax to behave like Ulysses. But when one speaks of the right to develop and maintain the momentum, style, and ideal proper to oneself let Bentham be heard saying that 'right' is a word unless secured by a law. What is not yet a right, however, may yet be a due.

The determination of what is due to or from persons has been based in the past most often on metaphysical doctrines of man and society. The Rights of Man declared or claimed in the American Revolution and in the French Revolution were founded on the metaphysical notion of natural law, the kind of notion Bentham rejected as unscientific. 'To each according to his needs, from each according to his abilities' is a definition of dues founded upon the promise of abundance vested in the economic machine in the hands of those who would use it to capacity, an abundance that would abandon measures and make justice meaningless; a limiting case that has at least the relevance of calling attention to the relevance of available resources to the determination of dues. In modern societies determination of dues by metaphysical doctrines, religious or rational, has for the most part been superseded by four main processes, which are inseparable in practice and reinforce and develop each other powerfully.

(1) Conflict between powerful sectional interests in a society tends to develop the concept and the sense of the public interest. The public interest is not identified with any sectional claims, nor with conservative resistance to such claims. It is rooted in attachment to order as the first priority and the ultimate common interest, and, with the

recognition and acceptance of deep and persistent differences of interest and opinion, the public learns to conceive of order as orderly development, and to identify its interest with the principles and procedures by which adjustment and reconciliation of interests and opinions are progressively achieved. Public interest is the interest of all in civil liberties, in fair play, in productive efficiency, and, in sum, in allowing and gaining the responsible participation of each in the work, wealth, and welfare of the society.

(2) It is a principle of culture that techniques and disciplines which have been established operationally are developed and refined theoretically, and further development is a product of the interaction of theory and practice. Language is a principal example. This principle is no less true of law and morals. Established usage is described, systematized, analysed, and in the light of the formal principles derived from it there is a tendency to make the system consistent with itself and complete, or it is subjected to criticism as inconsistent, partial, or lacking coherent, justifiable universal principles. Apart from systematic theoretical treatment of this kind, a similar process goes on more vaguely in the public mind: it is felt that the remnant of discrimination against religious belief, in the case of Jews and Roman Catholics, should be abolished, that women should have equal pay, that poor persons should have public assistance in obtaining divorce, that advanced industrial nations owe economic aid to backward peoples. Dues of this kind, which may or may not be claimed, are implicit in the system of rights already firmly established and unchallenged. It is not of course, or not primarily, the schools of moral or of legal philosophy that promote this theoretical development, but the great schools of political and social thought, whigs, utilitarians, radicals, fabians, with their agitation and programmes of reform, but also with their principles and their philosophy.

(3) It is a principle of human development that men become critically conscious of their achievements by comparison with those of their rivals. Our modern consciousness of our society through historical and anthropological studies and the study of comparative institutions, and by the challenge of communism, was very simply anticipated in the rivalry of Athens and Sparta. The standards of the more advanced societies become goals for the more backward. Something a little beyond the most advanced practice is worked out as a theoretical universal declaration of human dues for the whole

world. Historical studies tend perhaps to reinforce tradition, anthropological and comparative studies to weaken the hold of tradition. The result may be to refine tradition, to filter it from prejudices, to help to create a human tradition, cumulative and irreversible, with achieved permanent standards as the foundation of further development.

(4) The main source for the determination of dues which has taken the place of metaphysical doctrines is empirical science. It is possible in many fields by appropriate investigation to establish rational public norms. For example, a satisfactory diet, in terms of certain criteria, can be defined. That may not be what people can actually get, nor what they want to eat, nor what they actually demand; nor does it supersede these things; but it is highly relevant to them and becomes a fundamental factor in public policy. Even more fundamental and far-reaching, it is possible to define, in terms of certain criteria, for children of a defined category, a satisfactory education. Again, it may not be what the child can get, nor what its parents desire and demand for it; and again it does not supersede these things, but they cannot remain unmodified by it. There is sense in saying that a certain diet is due to a child, or a certain education, whatever the child is getting under the law and whatever the parents are giving or wanting to give the child. By the establishment of such rational public norms, people are being taught what it is right and reasonable to want and to demand, and governments are being taught what it is right and reasonable to provide or to enable people to get. And in this way the public interest is enlarged in scope and informed in content; and thus a new context is built up round the old empirical conflict of sectional interests.

The development of the public interest, of a social philosophy, and of a conscious tradition, and the establishment and refinement of rational public norms are interdependent processes which promote each other, but it is through development of the public interest that contributions from the other sources are tested, consolidated, and consistently applied to social improvement; so that the public interest stands in general for this whole complex source of morality.

IV

There are, then, these three main sources of morality, namely, rights, claims, and dues, or established interests, new interests, and the public interest; and at any time the obligations imposed by the first are being modified by new requirements drawn from the other two. There is no reason at all why rights, claims, and dues should not be identical, and this indeed is the moral ideal. But in practice there usually is, and there is likely to be, considerable friction between rights and claims, and it is dues, through the complex of processes represented by the public interest, that are the means of reconciliation. But the process cannot be jumped. It may seem simple and rational to replace both rights and claims by dues. That is the rationalist platonic form of utopianism. It may seem that the pulse of society is in the claims, and that if artificial protection is removed from established rights society will recover a spontaneous vitality and resolve its tensions. That is the anarchist form of utopianism. On the other hand, if claims and dues are left out society is either merely repressive (and that cannot last very long) or else so successful in conditioning the character of its members, so that they want only to do, and want others to do, what they have to do to maintain the society, that personality is virtually destroyed.

Not only is it fatal to try to found society on one source of morality only, it is hardly less disastrous to leave out any one of the three sources. If dues are left out, there are no means of resolving the conflict of rights and claims except by trials of strength: the rational element is left out. If claims are excluded, there are only the purely rational, the immemorial, the obsolescent, the partly rational, without the felt interests and actual needs to pose the problems and give meaning to the social order. If society were founded on claims and dues, without established rights, there would not be a society at all, for it is the historical element, the established rights, that constitutes the society; the other elements are introduced as necessary sources of renewal and development; they presuppose rights and could only supersede them by themselves becoming rights: they are candidates for establishment as rights; claims and dues are obligations in the making, not actual obligations. There can be no actual obligations but those imposed by the actual order.

This statement may seem revolting to the moral consciousness, or at least too tough to digest, for it will ever seem that dues are highly charged with moral obligation, most powerfully represent what ought to be, whereas the established order is heavy with dross, interests established by force and fraud, fortification of the line of least resistance, sanctification of the conventional, and such dreary masses of bricks and mortar of which the city of man is built. The men of tender moral sensibility who feel the pull of obligation most acutely, the men of conscience on whom the fate of man so mightily depends, will be irresistibly magnetized by dues, and will tend to be pulled out of the orbit of rights. Nevertheless, obligation lies first with the *de facto* order. Without it there would be no human existence. Crude, ugly, dilapidated, and inadequate though it is, nothing else provides the necessary shelter. It is this sorry city of man that demands and commands our first loyalty and love. The plans and blueprints have their place and excite their passions, but if we give them our loyalty, 'the law is broken, nature is disobeyed, and the rebellious are outlawed, cast forth, and exiled, from this world of reason, and order, and peace, and virtue, and fruitful penitence, into the antagonistic world of madness, discord, vice, confusion, and un-availing sorrow'. So easily is the best made the enemy of the good, which ruins all.

It is of course not less ruinous to allow the good to be the enemy of the best. The inescapable truth is that the moral order can be nothing less than the total complex of rights, claims, and dues in a dynamic relationship oriented towards identity; and the moral con-sciousness, the moral temper, is the striving for this ideal identity. The public interest, which is so intimately bound up with the complex of processes that lead to the recognition and definition of dues, is primarily founded on the moral order as such, the strongest value, the first priority, and the moral order as such must always be the actual moral order with all its unsatisfactory contents; but this order can only be defended and loyalty to it evoked and held if it includes procedural designs for the perfection of its contents through the assimilation of claims and dues. The public interest is nothing less than the total process constantly maintained in all its several parts. Those whose own particular interests are best represented at any time in the sphere of rights or of claims or of dues are, in the long run, even more vitally interested in the total good which the public interest represents. Nobody, therefore, can have an exclusive interest in any one sphere, even if he considers only his interest in that sphere. The moral order is one and indivisible, and loyalty to the established order, to the sphere of rights, which is the foundation of morals, turns out to be loyalty to the other spheres also since they are necessary to its fulfilment and even to its maintenance.

V

A further word on the status of moral knowledge. Rights (including of course unwritten mutual expectations under public sanction) and claims are simple matters of fact readily ascertained. Knowledge of obligation in regard to rights is ultimately contingent upon an act of choice in willing human existence, and, thereupon, is the recognition that there neither has been nor can be human existence without a settled order of reliable conduct, and that the essence of such an order is the binding character of the actual rules; and the knowledge of obligation in regard to claims is recognition that the absolute obligation of rights is arbitrary unless qualified by provision for the challenge of claims. All this knowledge is as abundantly plain and secure as anything that can ever be known to man.

(Of course one may choose to will a perverted form of human existence. There have been, there will be, those who choose human existence and pervert it. To name the enemies of mankind is seldom, but sometimes, above question in practice. Such persons are far more dangerous than noxious animals, and humanity is as much bound to defend itself from them as it is to sustain and perfect its human character. To destroy the anti-human is bound up with developing the human.)

It is not essentially otherwise with knowledge of dues. The knowledge of obligation in regard to rights is in respect of their being established not in respect of their being dues, but knowledge of the obligation of the moral order as such is knowledge of what is due, of what is required by human existence regardless of actual rights and claims; it is knowledge of the primary public or human interest. The order of rights is an establishment of harmony by force of custom and by force of law. It is arbitrary but necessary, as Hobbes saw; and his recognition is the indispensable foundation of ethics. The order of claims, historically related by established procedures to the order of rights, progressively transforms the enforced harmony into an actual harmony of reconciled interests upheld by consent. The order of dues is independent of force and of wills, an ideal ascertainment of what ought to be, regardless of what is enjoyed and of what is wanted. What kind of knowledge is this, and how is it obtained?

If we reject all metaphysical knowledge of man and of society, we are left with only empirical sources. The main source of the knowledge of dues was given above as empirical investigation of the characteristic facts in the fields of ethical interest, investigation, for example, leading to the knowledge of educational materials and methods by which children of characteristic types are normally stimulated and developed. Recall also Cicero's point that everyone has his own peculiar gifts and proper character, to which he adds that we shall therefore work to best advantage in that role to which we are naturally adapted, and that if circumstances thrust us into an uncongenial part, all we can do is to devote all possible thought, practice, and pains to the elimination of faults, for excellence is beyond us. This is a point which can be investigated, and it has been. Investigations can show what tends to happen. One may in consequence get contrasted pictures: a repressive society breeding undeveloped hooligans, impoverished, unstable, domineering; a free society enabling people to become themselves, exercise their own talents, play their own parts, thus developing resources, encouraging vitality, evoking and holding loyalty. These are emotionally toned pictures: the facts might be otherwise, but they are open to investigation; whatever they may be, there are certain characteristic patterns produced in determinable ways and with determinable consequences. The human sciences, history, anthropology, sociology, psychology, are competent to establish findings of this kind.

Or take the example of economic order. Any economy, taken in the example of some fairly self-sufficient unit, such as a farm, a factory, a household, a nation, may conserve, renew, and develop its resources, consume or distribute its products, in general, maintain itself as a productive instrument increasingly efficiently adapted to its purpose; or it may be plundered, exploited, or it may be allowed to run down, or its products or resources may be hoarded—even the home may be run efficiently in a way that leads to no enjoyment. These are characteristic patterns of behaviour in relation to the resources and instruments by means of which human life is maintained and developed. To study such patterns of behaviour in relation to the functional efficiency of such economies and the functional efficiency of such economies in relation to the total needs and possibilities of human existence is an immense field of knowledge relevant to dues, to human interests as such, the public interest. Civilization itself is an economy.

Or take the difference between a society founded on work and a society founded on wealth or on status; that is to say, between societies in which the chief consideration is given to work or to wealth or to status, for there is no society which is not founded on work. The characters of such societies can be studied, have been studied, and they are not perhaps likely to differ essentially in the future.

These studies are partial, perhaps arbitrary, torn out of context. The proper study of mankind is the total cultural complex of a society developing in time and in a geographical and political environment. The question is, what relevance has any or all of such knowledge to the knowledge of dues, of what ought to be, of human interests as such? Have dues any status at all as knowledge, is there any reality in them to add to the indubitable historicity of rights and claims?

The clue to the answer is context. At certain levels of abstraction, the difference between characteristic patterns of behaviour, say, between plundering an economy and running it productively, is merely a difference in the configuration of events; at another level, it may be the difference between opportunity and habit. But there is no significant level for the ethical question that does not take in human interests as such. In choosing human existence, one does not choose merely one's own life on as favourable terms as one can make, nor merely throw in one's lot with one's group, kith and kin; one chooses human existence as such, the total long-term venture, history and prospect; and it is a choice not merely for myself but for all, that is to say, the will to participate to the full extent of one's powers and opportunities in the realization of the human character of human existence for all. This is not merely an option to which one is invited. To choose or to refuse human existence as such is such an option. But if one does choose to will human existence, to limit that choice to one's own or to that of one's group is arbitrary; it is unreasonable in the sense in which to exploit and destroy the soil is so, to plunder an economy. On the other hand, of course, in immediate practical results it may well be reasonable to prefer one's own good or that of one's group to the larger interest of mankind. To take the point of view of man is to identify oneself with man, a form of self-transcendence to which men are called in virtue of their humanity. This is a religious or metaphysical point of view, or it is entirely vague, unless and until it means something in terms of actual policies and politics. It is an historical consciousness, a product of cultural evolution and social situations. Whereas for the stoics or in the eighteenth century the brotherhood of man was envisaged primarily in terms of universal law or universal religion, today the unity of the world and human responsibility for the future of mankind is a question of organization and of policies. The vision of man, the city of man, the beloved republic, is for us historical not metaphysical, but it involves the self-identification of men with man; without that point of view, there is no vision, there is no humanity. Given that point of view plus all the concreteness of history and of science, there is developing, empirical, never unchallengeable, knowledge of what is due, of human interests.

Ethical knowledge, as knowledge of dues, whether or not established as rights or staked as claims, is formed by the practical success of the policies which it justifies, for its *de jure* character never can give it an absolute authority over the *de facto* order. Knowledge established in this way has all the authority and virtue of empirical knowledge; and it is cumulative and irreversible in this field as in any other. There is no knowledge which mankind needs to protect with more vigilance and jealousy both from dogmatism and from irresponsible challenge.

Chapter 5

ANOTHER LOOK AT EPICURUS

I

FOR many, the philosophy of Epicurus, like Dr. Johnson's patriotism, has seemed to be the last refuge of a scoundrel, communicating a discreet human odour to the hedonist sty. Others have not scrupled to compare him to Christ, for the unusual love and veneration in which he was held by his disciples, his brothers included, and for his easy reception of outcasts and his exaltation of the affections. His person and teaching will always have the interest that attaches to the founders of religions. And the way in which he wears his classical Greek thought with a difference has become an attraction, although until recently he got only contempt for it, the majestic contempt of minds bred in the sumptuous metaphysics of Greece and Germany for the pedestrian poverty of the positivist, the austere contempt of aristocratic conservatives for the light-mindedness of the radical, the angry contempt of religious believers 'long fed on boundless hopes' for the modesty of the naturalist. Looking now after more than two thousand years at the old uplands of Epicurus, one sees that they have weathered less than the aspiring peaks of Plato, and they look nearer and more familiar.

The philosophy of Epicurus is hedonist, but it is not founded on the doctrine that man by his constitution seeks pleasure and avoids pain (psychological hedonism), nor on the doctrine that men ought in reason to seek pleasure as their sovereign good (ethical hedonism). It is the doctrine that being, human being, is pleasure: pleasure is not one of the goods of life, even the supreme good, which ought to be pursued; it is human existence, and it is possessed with human life and not pursued by human life. Pleasure is our inborn well-being. We cannot pursue it because it is with us, but we can flee from it, and we can bury it. There are philosophies which have no faith in life, which teach us how to endure it. So prevalent and influential is this teaching that it has assumed the name philosophy *tout court*. Yet such philosophy, the synonym for resignation, blindly leads us into the pit, teaches us only to renounce the only good there is.

How do we learn to possess the pleasure that is in us, in our human existence? Simply by removing and avoiding what clouds and smothers it, chiefly, physical and moral suffering and fears. Once pain and fear are avoided, all is gained that can be gained, 'since the living creature has not to wander as though in search of something that is missing, and to look for some other thing by which he can fulfil the good of the soul and the good of the body'. There is a natural autarky, a spontaneous well-being and inner contentment, which has only to be preserved and reinforced by knowledge and discipline, wise choice and avoidance. Knowledge is the sovereign remedy for suffering and fear. In our simple primary needs, in our dependence upon the body and in our dependence upon each other, is the source of our life and the source and the rule of our pleasure: all simple things in our own immediate keeping. We can easily get what we absolutely need, we can avoid or endure the pains that flesh is heir to. There is nothing to hope for nor to fear from the gods, there is nothing to fear in death, there is no fate that besets us and lies in wait: our life is in us and its management is in our hands, to be perfected by wise choice and avoidance. This dependence on the body is pleasure in the exercise of the senses, and is cultivated in the arts. This dependence on each other is regulated and cultivated in friendship, which is both spontaneous community in the pleasure of the senses and a fundamental mutual need of help, comfort, and security. Sensation is the root of both life and thought, and trust in sensation is the foundation of certainty and of serenity. Pleasure is not increased by multiplying nor by sophisticating desire. It is that way ruined, for that is to chase pleasure and to run away from the only place where it is hid. In faithful attention to the pleasure which our human existence simply is we find our freedom and our rule, our necessity and our happiness, at the same time.

Such teaching is both simple and subtle, easy to practise and an exacting discipline. A teaching of this temper can work on the tough material of experience, and in this case it can produce character, quality of life, and the serenity it promises. That, after all, is the vulgar test of a philosophy.

II

Several points of doctrine in Epicurus are permanent foundations of the naturalist position in philosophy.

(1) The notion that human existence is itself pleasure, from first till last, and not a mere point of departure for a problematical pursuit of pleasure, is the basic trust in human vitality and in the possibility of maintaining it unimpaired which is the ground of any profitable philosophy. Plato's apology for philosophy (the unexamined life is not a life for man) makes a noble start, but when the life of reason has been fully substituted for the life of nature, the unphilosophical may sometimes suspect that wisdom is another name for folly and that its prescription for life is death. Stoicism, for example, speaks also of autarky as the ideal, and does not mean, as Epicurus does, the spontaneous self-sufficiency in well-being of the autonomous human life secured by knowledge; it means a life cut off from dependence upon desires and fastened to metaphysical faith in the rationality of events. The fundamental philosophic merit of Epicurus is that he does examine human life without destroying it. He knows its tragic fragility, and his tender handling takes care not even to finger the bloom on the fruit. He is single-minded in scrupulous regard from first to last for the entire life-cycle and complete economy of the plant. It is one perfect thing that is studied in its integrity. Therefore when the examination is over, when the fatal philosophic break has been made and everything is put in question, life can be quietly resumed with its totality intact, and is not fretted by any fever of contempt, nor staled nor vulgarized, and does not require any patronage or any cult or any pretence to keep it going. This supreme virtue makes Epicurus a model for any philosophy that is not a professed philosophy of despair.

(2) Philosophy inevitably elaborates and sophisticates. Epicurus is the reminder that what men want from philosophy is a simplification of human living so that it is brought within the reach of all both in understanding and in attainment. 'Vain is the word of a philosopher which does not heal any suffering of man.' And philosophy when it is not vain, when it is seriously addressed to the needs of men, deserves serious study. 'We must not pretend to study philosophy, but study it in reality: for it is not the appearance of health that we need, but real health.' The philosophy of Epicurus and the study devoted to it by his disciples provide a consistent example of

these precepts. And behind these precepts and this example are the protest and action of Epicurus against certain tendencies in Greek culture, universal tendencies, for the culture that should save and serve life always threatens to become an incubus that smothers and devitalizes it, a superstition, a Moloch, and the threat is bound to come true if a learned caste, an *élite*, is allowed to get a stranglehold over the popular elements. Epicureanism is the struggle for cultural vitality, that is to say, for popular enlightenment, against obscurantism and authoritarianism—against dominant aspects of platonism.

(3) In one life one enjoys, or may enjoy, all that can ever be had by such beings as we are. 'Infinite time contains no greater pleasure than limited time, if one measures by reason the limits of pleasure.' There is infinite distraction in the vast variety of possible pleasures, but nothing is to be gained by seeking them, since all the pleasure we can know is to be savoured in our simple existence which is destroyed by distracted pursuits. This enjoyment is immediate and absolute, in the sense that it is possessed without search and is not inferior to any other and is complete. Enjoyment of the physical motion of the body, of the exercise of the senses, of the satisfaction of primary appetites, of the study of nature, of the common pleasure and mutual responsiveness of friends, here is the manageable field for cultivation in the art of living. There is nothing more, and it is enough. Such husbandry is not postponed in any of its phases to some dreamed-of future, is not the privilege of any age or race or class or creed, is the common and excellent life of humanity with which all may satisfy themselves completely before they die.

(4) That the world came into existence without purpose, and that the gods are indifferent to the life of men and have no purpose for them and impose no fate upon them, gives us our human status, neither subordinated nor omnipotent. This purposelessness of the universe makes a climate favourable to our action and our aspiration. There is the underlying foundation of adamant necessity, there are the variable winds of chance, and there is wide-open scope for rational calculation and control; and these three permanent elements constitute an environment ideally suited to the health of the active human spirit. What happens by necessity enters into the conditions of the blessed life, what happens by chance may be the occasion of evil or of good, and all the benefits of civilization are the results of profiting by chance occurrences, for things have discoverable uses which were not purposed but out of which humanity builds its

distinctive life. Epicurus is as opposed to the strict determinism of materialist reduction as he is to religious mythology: he defends the autonomy of man in its integrity, the integrity of experience. What he appreciates is that it is proper to man to take the initiative in dealing with his experience. '. . . he [the prudent man] does not believe that good and evil are given by chance to man for the framing of a blessed life, but that opportunities for great good and great evil are afforded by it. He therefore thinks it better to be unfortunate in reasonable action than to prosper in unreason.'

(5) If trust in the evidence of the senses and in the feeling of pleasure is the rudder by which we steer in science and in morals we do not drift with the current of words off the course of our practical purpose, drawn away by ideas which do not come from experience and have no bearing on experience. Epicurus is a pioneer in the making of the empirical tradition which insists to this day on sensation and practice as the ultimate tests of ideas. In the picturesque language of the logician Peirce: 'The elements of every concept enter into logical thought at the gate of perception and make their exit at the gate of purposive action; and whatever cannot show its passport at both these gates is to be arrested as unauthorized by reason.' This razor cuts away volumes of meaningless verbiage, and rids our minds of the phantom problems that haunt them. Without its skilful use, and it does demand skill, there is hardly any possibility of mental health. Epicurus at the start thoroughly disinfects the mind against this 'first distemper of learning, when men study words, and not matter', not only by making sensation the first test and practical use the last, but also by giving language its place in the natural history of civilization, a capital example of his perception that the discoverable uses of things essential to civilization are accidental to the nature of things. Language was developed by deliberate convention out of sounds spontaneously emitted. Words therefore had no metaphysical status, referred to no entities outside experience; they should be made to mean what we want them to mean, and strictly used in that sense. 'Justice', for example, 'never is anything in itself, but in the dealings of men one with another in any place whatever and at any time it is a kind of compact not to harm or be harmed.' It is no use searching in the socratic manner for the abstract essence of justice which is always and everywhere true; it is not to be defined metaphysically but operationally, as what is of mutual advantage in the dealings of men with one another.

(6) 'Of all the things which wisdom acquires to produce the blessedness of the complete life, far the greatest is the possession of friendship.' This friendship is the perfection of something already at hand, namely, our dependence one on another. In his open-eyed recognition that friendship is both utilitarian and ideal, Epicurus avoids both the two common and pervasive fallacies, materialist reduction and romantic idealization, the scylla and charybdis on which so many are wrecked at the setting out. 'All friendship is desirable in itself, though it starts from the need of help.' Like society, friendship is founded on our necessary interdependence, our need of one another for aid, comfort, and security, but since we share a common nature community of pleasure reinforces our own pleasure, and friendship therefore becomes itself a supervening and supreme pleasure. To neglect the utilitarian ground is to endanger all, as neglect of the root impoverishes the flower. This appreciation of a thing in its integrity, with unfailing attention to the total economy in which it thrives, is the primary principle of this philosophy, and the secret of its success.

(7) One may hunt pleasures with the fastidiousness and the pride of a connoisseur. One may do it in proof of superiority, even superiority to pleasure, to show that one can traffic in pleasures without ever giving oneself away, a proof of arid self-mastery, a refinement on renunciation. One may cultivate pleasure only, in and for itself. Hedonism lends itself to the most sophisticated and even fantastic refinements and elaborations because of its ruthless egoistic directness. This is not the hedonism of Epicurus, for whom pleasure is merely the savour of natural existence without pain, the natural state of a positive existence which lacks nothing, that is to say, which disposes of the easily acquired means of maintaining itself without care or fear. Such an existence being full overflows, transcends itself in its self-sufficiency. It lacks nothing and therefore seeks nothing and is free from preoccupation with itself. Therefore it blesses others by its own condition. This self-affirmation of human existence, which is not the affirmation of one over another but the affirmation of one equally and simply in himself and with others and with all things, is not an acquired merit but the basic natural state of human existence. Such human simplicity, as spontaneous as Wordsworth's daisy, is the effect of knowledge, the highest achievement of philosophy.

(8) Man is mortal. Human existence is temporal throughout. Epicurus shows full and explicit recognition that such beings as we

are must be bound up with such conditions as we know, that the survival of the soul is not a question, because the idea has no meaning, it is not a possibility. 'For it is impossible to imagine it [the soul] with sensation, if it is not in this organism and cannot effect these movements, when what encloses and surrounds it is no longer the same as the surroundings in which it now exists and performs these movements.' But death is no evil. Not only does temporal life allow of complete experience and final satisfaction, which cannot be improved upon by being prolonged to infinity, not only is death nothing to us for ourselves 'since so long as we exist, death is not with us, but when death comes then we do not exist'; after all such reflections have yielded their consolation, there remains this compelling thought: man's mortality, the final extinction which is open to everyone at will, is the only condition on which human life is a choice. Those whom it does not invite to joy and works can take their leave once for all, and without complaint.

(9) All the conditions of human existence, our needs, our dependence upon others, the necessity, chance, and reliable calculations which enter into our constructions of reason and will, these conditions make life an art, for they are the same conditions of disaster and of perfection. The art which avoids the one and chooses the other is a skill within the competence of all, and is certainly not most practised by the most clever.

(10) We provide most securely for the future by not sacrificing to it the present, for it is by present enjoyment that we appease ourselves and please our friends, thereby gaining ourselves and our friends, which is the best we can do to secure the future, for the blessed life is saturated with happy memories and to transmit possession of the past is to guarantee the future.

III

In these doctrines, Epicurus speaks in his own way for all naturalists in philosophy. Such doctrines publish the permanent open secrets of the human condition, and the everlasting wisdom of those who are content with such knowledge. Of course it is not necessary to build everything on so narrow a bottom as pleasure or self-interest. It can be done by an accomplished philosopher, as a farmer if he has the skill can stack all his corn on a cart-wheel. That is what it looks like today, a *tour de force*, although it once seemed to be the scientific way. Epicurus, in any case, is a miniaturist, and he has the passionate simplicity which saves work on that scale from pedantry. His perspective seems to exclude the great totalities of human existence, beyond the scope of pleasure, the tasks and problems of historical civilization, yet his philosophy of personal life was a conscious challenge to his times and founded a movement; and in this it was like the great religions. It is worth comparing the teaching of Epicurus with that of buddhism.

For Epicurus, human existence lacks nothing, once provided with simple necessities; it affirms itself as pleasure in sensation, and is naturally completed within the scope of individual life. For the buddhist, life is suffering, because sensory experience gives the impression of fixed and separate things including individual selves, and men crave and strive on this assumption. For Epicurus, the conditions of human existence are favourable to human interests; for the buddhist, they are wholly unfavourable. Both are pragmatists, concerned in their teaching wholly and solely with the conduct of life, and scornful of everything irrelevant to this concern. Both are concentrated on the question of human happiness. Epicurus affirms sensory experience as the prime reality, and its satisfactions bring him fulfilment and thereby transcendence of individuality in community of pleasures with other self-same individuals. The buddhist rejects sensory experience and the idea of the self rooted in it as the prime illusions which bring suffering and sorrow, and he seeks fulfilment and transcendence by striving through meditation to rid himself of these illusions. Epicurus appreciates death as the negative condition of the human choice of life and as no positive evil. The buddhist appreciates death as the condition which enables the individual to strive for ultimate release from self and suffering. For Epicurus, life is an art, wise choice and avoidance, and without this art it is confusion, pitiful striving, miserable fears. The buddhist devotes himself to unremitting religious discipline as the only way of escape from suffering and sorrow. Both provide for the future not by planning but by the quality of immediate living.

The formal teaching of the two could hardly be more different; the results in temper and manner of life seem more remarkable for resemblance than for difference. But the relations between buddhism and the epicurean type of philosophy are far more intricate and historical than a superficial comparison could suggest. The epicurean system had a counterpart in Indian philosophy in the Charvak system, which like epicureanism was the culmination of a development promoted by schools of naturalist and speculative thinking. Buddhism was powerfully influenced by these schools and was formed with them in opposition to the dominant priestly caste and the authority of the sacred scriptures. Like epicureanism it was a movement of emancipation and popular enlightenment in a time of social dissolution. Like epicureanism it was an ethical movement founded on a materialist metaphysic. The profound difference between them was that one was dominated by the conviction that individual human life was and only could be pain, the other by the conviction that it was and only need be pleasure; with the consequence that the one strove only to escape from having to live, and the other entered into his human inheritance of individual happiness. Both proclaimed the truth to the world. What was at the bottom of this difference (frightening when one considers the immense influence of buddhism)? When all has been said on this point that should be said about historical circumstances and the like, two reflections furnish the theme of an epilogue to such discussions: ideas are the glory and the tragedy of the human race, the real promethean fire to serve or to destroy; life is finally a choice for human beings, and it is lived only by those who choose it.

Chapter 6

MARXISM, PAST AND PRESENT

I

BECAUSE marxism is the dominant form of scientific human-ism in the world today, humanists ought to go to some trouble in making up their minds about it; and, because of its claims and its position in the world, to reject it for any but the strongest reasons would be frivolous. It is no time for refining on differences. Marxists claim that they represent the historical human cause, and reckon against them all who are not wholly with them. Heresy and schism may reasonably be felt to be even more damnable on historical issues of collective human fate than once they were felt to be on questions of the eternal welfare of the individual soul. Therefore there is every reason for seriously examining again and again the marxist case, and it needs no apology. Or rather, because of the patronizing appreciation of elements of marxism by academics and intellectuals who do not take seriously its central tenet of the unity of thought and action, an apology is due to marxists from anyone who undertakes to make a critical examination of it. I will say at the outset therefore that I do appreciate and take as seriously as possible the tremendous issues upon which it is staked.

Marxism claims to be scientific socialism. Its sources are in German philosophy, British political economy, and French socialism, the three chief ideological currents of the nineteenth century which it claims to have continued and completed and to have applied in a way that is not only a scientific technique for realizing historical socialism and liberating the productive energies of industrial society developed by capitalism, but also a scientific interpretation of human nature and destiny. No question of human importance is left out. It is a philosophy of nature and of history informing a programme of revolutionary action fulfilling the destiny of man.

II

The philosophy of nature can be shortly dealt with. It is a form of materialism, the view that nature is primary and given, and mind is a product of natural process and wholly dependent upon material organization. Marxists of course are not mechanistic materialists but biological and historical materialists, and take a dialectical view of natural process: the view that the complex vitality of motion issues in transformations, emergent novelties, the interpenetration and union of opposites, which make over a long enough period a discernible progress. The progress is chequered—long intervals of gradually accumulated change, sudden transformations, 'mutations', set-backs; but the immanent laws of motion imply a necessary development, which has characteristic features, providing clues to detailed study. Such a view of mind and nature is one of the more probable alternatives. For instance, Professor Broad in his *The Mind and its Place in Nature* lists seventeen alternatives as the exhaustive set of possibilities, and an emergent materialism is one of the theories which, he argues, have the greatest probability. There is good reason for holding some such doctrine as dialectical materialism, but there is no philosophical reason for supposing that it destroys the plausibility, and finally disposes, of every alternative. And there is no reason for supposing that it disposes of the epistemological problem in philosophy. Nevertheless, marxists do assume that dialectical materialism disposes once for all of the epistemological question, and indeed brings to an end for all time all metaphysical philosophy and all religion. Any form of theism, of idealism, of agnosticism, of positivism or pure empiricism is put out of court for marxists. Thinkers who expound these views are very severely dealt with in polemics written by marxists for marxists. Marx says somewhere that any polemics worthy of the name should be both brutal and subtle. These polemics fail in only one of these qualifications. However, two things may be said in extenuation of this failure.

(1) The doubts about our knowledge which arise from reflections upon its foundation in systematized sense impressions cannot be resolved by appeals to positive science and to practice (as the marxists claim), because it is reflection upon the presuppositions of

science which raises the question. One can blithely drive in double harness a theoretical scepticism coupled with animal faith, like Hume or Santayana; or one can refine on this by combining agnosticism with rigorous analysis of the synthesized and systematized content of sense presentations, like Kant or present-day logical positivists or phenomenologists. But such intellectual austerity is congenial or tolerable to few and there always remains the bold alternative of overriding the question in the grand manner by treating the world as an object of experience of the same kind as the experiencing mind, like Plato, or Hegel, or Christian theists, or by treating it as an object of labour, material for use and transformation, like marxists and pragmatists. Such philosophies do not answer the question, but they solve it in the only way in which it is capable of being solved, by making assumptions on which it does not arise, or which give it no importance at all. Who says that the assumption of marxists is not the most plausible of all such assumptions? Johnson's refutation of Berkeley must always be contemptible to philosophers and welcome to common sense; and in the end there is no other kind of refutation.

(2) Why, then, don't marxists in their philosophical polemics dispose summarily of the epistemological problem on the dogmatic ground that knowledge is practice and successful practice is its own criterion, instead of engaging in protracted attempts in detail to refute the irrefutable? It is one thing openly to override the question, quite another to pretend that you are answering it. Lenin in his *Materialism and Empirio-criticism* and more recently Maurice Cornforth in his *Science versus Idealism* (which characteristically puts the futility of the argument into the title) bring no new considerations to bear on the subtle questions which are dealt with in the works which they criticize. What they have to say about science is perfectly well known to the philosophers against whom they write, and has nothing to do with the case. Theoretically, marxism is much more effective when it is content with its true philosophical position, overriding the epistemological question—although scattered in the writings of Engels there are perhaps hints of a genuine epistemology. But for practical reasons marxists cannot be content with that: it is necessary for them to discredit and rout every form of agnosticism in philosophy, not because it is incompatible with materialism but because it is compatible with idealism and theism; it offers a foothold to the enemy; it threatens to breach the monolith solidarity of

materialist philosophy which is the ground of all marxist theory and practice. It leaves questions open; it keeps open contacts and continuity with other traditions; whereas marxism shows from the outset its tendency to break abruptly with the past (in spite of its historicism), to bring peremptorily to an end not only religion and philosophy but also in a little time politics and all that belongs to the preliminary phases of history before the fully conscious self-direction of humanity is achieved. Therefore the epistemologists have to be shown to be beaten on their own ground in a sham fight. Although this must be either ignorance or obscurantism, it is understandable. Nobody who wishes to see a justifiable and fruitful view of the world establish itself and gain ground can reasonably complain of the more or less arbitrary treatment of fissile individualists and cavillers. Deplore as one may the philosophical ineptitude of marxist polemics in this field, one should also recognize that if they had been conducted with strict philosophical propriety on the legitimate ground of a justifiable alternative treatment of knowledge, they would, however convincing, have left open in principle the possible choice of a different alternative, and thus have failed to seal the past and open a new epoch: they would not have changed anything.

When all this has been said both in extenuation and in criticism of marxist philosophical polemics, it must be repeated that there is much to be said for marxist philosophy, dialectical materialism, as such. Its shift of emphasis from substance to process, being to becoming, essence to existence, universality to historicity; its abandonment of a block universe for a universe pursuing its adventures, its attention to the many-sidedness of phenomena, the multiple context and reciprocal interaction of causal agents, its decisive use of the test of practice for the elimination of verbal pseudo-problems: all this and more has been abundantly confirmed and used in subsequent developments in philosophy. These hints and ideas which were thrown out by Marx and Engels in the course of their preoccupation with other studies have proved sufficiently precise and fruitful to make them rather than Bergson, or old Hegel from whom they learned so much, the watershed which divides the old from the new in philosophy, although their direct influence on philosophy in the West may have been negligible.

III

If dialectical materialism is the spine of marxism, the limbs by which it moves and takes hold of human life and destiny are the materialist conception of history and the revolutionary strategy and tactics for the present epoch which spring from it. The materialism of Hobbes and of the French writers is a metaphysical materialism. Mind is strictly determined by material events and in theory can be causally explained by reference to such events. But psychologically mind is influenced by pleasure and pain, and in history mind is influenced socially by the issue of laws with annexed penalties, and to a more limited extent by rewards. The business of philosophy is to show the source, authority, and utility of the laws, and the principles which should inform them. It is in this way that human life is rationalized, brought under conscious control and to the perfection of which it is capable. Marxism is not an abstract materialism of this kind; it is historical, and begins with detailed study of the concrete material conditions of life in a given society, the way in which the members of the society get a living and the social organization and cultural content which belong to the mode of production. The factors in this complex influence one another reciprocally, but the *ultimate* causal factors and the essential objects of study are the material conditions of production and the changes which are accumulating there. The philosophic mind can act causally upon history, influencing the making of the laws and obedience to them, but it is a local and limited operation idealizing an existing system of social relations. Material changes accumulating in the economic substratum of that society will eventually do away with both legal and philosophical systems. The attempt of mind to control human life directly, even by the scientific application of philosophically conceived laws to universal motives, is not really scientific because it is not studying and operating with the factors which have ultimate causal efficacy. In the economic sequence of events there is a necessity which *ultimately* always asserts itself. Therefore philosophers who look for the universal grounds of a permanent human order and try to use their prescriptions to produce it can never succeed. Hobbes and Bentham (or Machiavelli) may come closer to the psychological and social facts than Plato, and to that extent have greater practical influence, but their method is still metaphysical, for they take the given facts as permanent and ignore the dynamic process which determines history and will change them; and thus their philosophy does not bring man to an understanding of history, still less to the control of it, but merely to the view of an abstract possibility, or, at best, to the idealization of an existing order. If one wishes to understand and to change the world one must study in detail the historical causes in operation, and these are never primarily ideas, nor are they facts which can be generalized as universal truths about human nature and human society.

This might be exemplified by asking what Marx would have to say about our modern preoccupation with the problem of reconciling the claims of the individual person with the claims of the state: how is the relation between the two to be conceived philosophically as a norm for social policy? I think he would say that this is a vain search for a formula, a formula, whatever it might prove to be, which could enlighten nobody and effect nothing, except to advance the discoverer in his own esteem and deceive the public. Instead of this literary phrase-making, he would say, look at the social relations and conditions which you actually have, and you will see such and such persons enjoying such and such liberties and such and such persons enduring such and such privations. This specification of liberty is a property of this organization of society based on this method of economic production. It is quite unalterable by talking about it and changing our ideas. But political, moral, and ideological changes are in process (of which our talk may be a symptom) as a result of earlier economic change, and the transformation of society which is impending will inevitably mean a new specification of liberty, not determined by our ideas but by the new social relations for economic production. No formula or philosophical prescription can determine the conditions or content of freedom in a society. The conditions and the content are historically given; the changes which are transforming conditions and content are also historically given. We can choose between phrase-making and serious participation in history.

Marx and Engels are all the time making ethical judgements, are all the time concerned with the immeasurable, elaborated, degradation of man by the exploitation of labour; their total vision of history is the most serious call to a devoted life imaginable: yet all the time they contemptuously reject and spit upon ethical ideals, 'the modern mythology with its goddesses of Justice, Freedom, Equality, and Fraternity'. Such ideals have no independent status, no power and no content of their own; their content is determined by the economic facts and their derivatives. In the socialist society there will inevitably be liberty and justice and love, and their content will compare very favourably with their counterparts in the capitalist state. It is a distraction to think in terms of these ideals because they have no absolute content and no causal efficacy. The expansion of productivity does not merely make an expansion of justice and liberty possible, it makes it necessary; but what makes it necessary is the militant action of those who alone can use the productive capacity that has been developed. In the end these ethical concepts will lose their meaning and disappear from consciousness because the conditions which determined their appearance will have been superseded: this is the historical absolute of ethical concepts, when they dissolve in the facts.

Similarly, in spite of abusive language all the time about exploiters, oppressors, robbers, predatory imperialists, and so on (and fierce partisanship for proletarian heroes out of due time like Spartacus), Marx never regards dominant classes and persons in general as opportunists who by a bid for power, a sheer act of will, have established themselves and their interests: they are always necessary agents of a necessary system. When they are displaced in due course by new men, it is solely because the new men have a new competence (in terms of techniques or interests, or both): the old are superseded not primarily as oppressive but as inefficient; the new order is not merely a turn of the wheel in the fortunes of parties, but an historical achievement for humanity. This is different from the older socialist conception of class struggle, as the simple conflict between haves and have-nots exemplified in any slice of history. Marxism certainly includes this simple truth on the psychological side, but translates it from the plane of mere wishes and dreams, and fantasies of will, to the practical level of actual conditions studied in detail, the economic possibilities and pressures, the emergent novelties, the transformation of interests in their content and basis; it is a shift from the subjective to the objective, from human nature to human history, from effects to causes, from ideals to understanding and power; and in place of unending conflicts and meaningless oscillations it puts dialectical process and progressive achievement. How far does this challenging conception of history hold good; in particular, how far does Marx make it good in his own detailed analysis of the capitalist system?

IV

There are six main lines of emphasis having a practical bearing which distinguish Marx's description and analysis of capitalist economics from the classical English political economy.

(1) He insists that *laisser-faire* capitalism is a temporary historical form of production, neither natural, in the sense of founded on natural laws discoverable in the nature of men and the nature of things, nor final, in the sense of ideal. Adam Smith had assumed two systems of economy, the mercantile system and the agricultural system, both of them mistaken political policies; and he had argued that when these were taken away, 'the obvious and simple system of natural liberty establishes itself of its own accord': productivity is maximized and is self-regulating. Marx regarded this liberation as a necessary phase in the expansion of capitalism, not as a discovery of the principles of economics.

(2) There is a significantly different emphasis in Marx's descriptive economics. Earlier economists had assumed that the various forms of dealing were as useful and necessary as production itself. Commerce was, so to speak, the vascular system, as productive industry might be the muscular system, and transport and administration the nervous system, in the whole economy. Marx elaborates the distinction between selling a commodity for money in order to buy and use another commodity needed or desired, and buying a commodity not for its use-value but for its exchange-value, in order to pocket a margin of profit. It is not an odd transaction of this kind to which he draws attention, nor the indefinite multiplication of odd transactions in a whole society, but the exploitation of differential exchange-values as a conscious persistent activity, unlimited and insatiable. Hume had regarded this type of activity as of enormous use in stimulating consumption and production and bringing about cheap goods and cheap money. Marx is not unmindful of its necessary part in the genesis of capitalism, but is thinking also of its distortion and destruction of 'normal' exchange for use—to be paralleled by production for profit instead of for use. The elaboration of this distinction is an anticipation of his distinction between the use-value and the exchange-value of labour as a marketable commodity, which is the master-key that opens capitalism to theoretic understanding and effects its exposure to the masses.

(3) Engels after Marx's death compared Marx's theory of surplus

value as a liberating force with Darwin's theory of evolution. In the marxist view it is the secret of capitalism, the hidden dynamic of capitalist exploitation and expansion. Capitalism poses as freedom, 'the obvious and simple system of natural liberty'. It is built on free contract, and therefore presupposes free men: on the one hand, men free to employ their capital in economic enterprise as they wish, free from medieval monopolies, regulations, and restraint of trade; on the other, men free to offer their labour, not slaves and not serfs, men emancipated from relations of status and free to enter into relations of contract. But capitalism also presupposes that the men who offer their labour are compelled to enter into a necessitous bargain and take what they are given, for they are in competition with one another and have no other means of living, having been expropriated as peasants or as artisans and left with only their labour to sell: because the creation of a proletariat, a protracted and exceedingly harsh expropriation of the masses, is a necessary condition of capitalism. The exchange-value of their labour, under certain conditions, approximates to the minimum necessary for the subsistence of themselves and their families; and the employment of women and children tends to reduce the *total* family income to subsistence level. But the use-value of their labour hired by the capitalist is worth more, at first far more, than the equivalent of its exchange-value. When the worker has contributed the socially necessary labour-time equivalent to his subsistence for a period, he has produced the number of commodities which pay for his labour for that period; the surplus he produces during the remainder of the period is unpaid labour. This surplus value, 'unpaid labour', is appropriated by the capitalist, and it is this lust for the appropriation of surplus value that gives the enormous incentive to capitalist enterprise. In the pages of Marx as nowhere else one feels the struggle for the opportunity to create and appropriate surplus value, the fever, force, and pace of a gigantic, prodigal, protean expansion. The workers, then, having been expropriated are exploited, in the sense that the exchange-value of their labour is well below the exchange-value of its products which remains in the hands of their employers.

This theory of surplus value has been hotly contested, and is generally regarded by non-marxists as an exploded fallacy, a myth. Certainly the classical economists, even assuming the labour theory of value, did not recognize exploitation as inherent in the mere employment of labour in production for profit. Adam Smith, particularly, recognizes and describes many forms and cases of exploitation, mainly through the natural advantages of employers as a class, or through the monopoly of a market. But a free market economy is supposed to minimize exploitation, not to exemplify it on an unprecedent scale. However this may be, Marx's theory, apart from its importance in the history of class agitation, is worked out with subtlety and power and enables him to predict and explain phenomena to which the orthodox school remained blind. In its technical exposition, it is a development of Ricardo's theory, and has no necessary political implications.

(4) The surplus value is not appropriated until the commodities produced by the realization of the use-value of the labour employed are exchanged in the market at the value equivalent to the socially necessary labour-time that has gone into their production: then the surplus value is roughly the proportion of commodities produced by unpaid labour. Since by the necessity of the system there are more commodities produced than labour can buy with the wages paid, there is periodical crisis and stagnation. At the same time the development of new forms of capital expansion is stimulated. The increase of scale and pace produces more catastrophic dislocations, unutilized capital on the one hand and unutilized labour on the other, with nothing to bring them together, since because of the fundamental contradiction of the system it does not pay: there is poverty in plenty.

(5) This situation is temporarily improved by finding overseas markets and fields of investment, which in the sequel involves imperial adventures, the enlargement of monopolies and cartels, wars. These overseas commitments and adventures are not extras, in the sense that home needs have been satisfied and home resources fully utilized, a world market for surplus capital and surplus commodities. The reverse is the case. The satisfaction of basic needs at home and the reduction of socially necessary labour-time in production are neglected because they are unprofitable or less profitable. The system creates impersonal, irrational world forces, hard to understand, impossible to control, of which ultimately all are victims, but by which meanwhile some few profit extremely.

(6) Believing that human nature and behaviour are determined by the material conditions of living, Marx and Engels were bound to study the human effects of capitalist conditions. They noted: the destruction of the common interest which had sustained and regulated earlier small communities satisfying their needs by exchange in

a local market; the separation of hand and brain, enjoyment and work, production and consumption, by the extreme division of labour; the reduction of the worker to an appendage of a machine; the destruction of the home by the pressures and opportunities provided by the employment of women and children; the separation of town and country; the depersonalization of relations which turned personal worth into exchange-value; the transformation of personal powers and moral responsibility into blind world forces. The sum of effects, in their view, added up to a degradation of human life at all levels, historically produced and unintended, but calling for remedy —and providing one.

This view of the capitalist economic system is strikingly different from the classical view: it sees a temporary historical form of production, driven into prodigal expansion of productive capacity by the opportunity to create and appropriate surplus value, but at the same time crippled by the contradiction which prevents it from delivering the goods to the homes of want and from fully utilizing the productive resources it multiplies; a system developing monopoly, imperialism, and increasingly catastrophic dislocations, and creating a mass proletariat whose exploitation, frustration, and degradation are its necessary conditions. It is not less true, nor does it displace the classical view: it is the other side of the picture, more revealing of some things, truer for some purposes and in some respects. Neither view is the true view, neither is merely the distorted view of class interest, although both have been adopted and developed by opposed class interests. Marx's view is both more distorted (because of a certain primitivist bias) and richer in insights (because of his concrete historical thinking). Subsequent history has demonstrated largely, although not yet conclusively, the truth and error of each. Both views are historical, and neither is applicable directly to the system as it stands today, but there are always people who prefer the quaintness of the past.

Academic economists, many of them exceptionally humane men, remained remarkably complacent about the system. They assumed that capital and labour must be fully utilized. Marx tried to show that they could not be. They assumed that adjustments, more or less delayed, more or less harsh, would always put things as right as they could be put; the system was self-regulating. Marx tried to show that things would get worse and induce remedies ultimately more disastrous; the system was self-contradictory. It was not until the chronic large-scale unemployment of the 1930's that economists were jolted out of their long-term complacency and re-examined their assumptions about the full utilization of resources (full employment) as distinct from the rational allocation of resources (assumed to be the real argument for socialism). Lord Keynes in his book *The General Theory of Employment Interest and Money*, published in 1936, addressed to fellow economists although subsidized to make it widely influential, argues that orthodox economic theory is the theory of a special case (like Newton's physical theory) and that a general theory is necessary to understand the facts of the economic order as we find it. His general theory takes account of the intricate relations of the variable factors involved, and gives the picture of an economic system recognizably like our own and considerably different from the model described in the classical theory. He gives an honourable prominence to heretical theories of under-consumption which had persisted ignored in the underworld of economic theory. Marx is mentioned in this connection. In another connection Marx is mentioned with a dislike that suggests fear. Undoubtedly, justice is not done to Marx's view in this revision of orthodox theory. Undoubtedly, on the other hand, Marx does not supply or anticipate the general theory which Keynes sets out to provide. Economics is an extremely intricate and problematical science. Marx made himself technically competent to deal with it in his own way and brought to it an historical vision which shattered its prescribed limits. Although he is dealing with the same facts and using orthodox theory and correcting it, one must say that his theory is different in kind and stands for an independent alternative development. It takes more than economic theory to produce from capitalism a managed economy in a social service state, with the main drives and incentives unimpaired; and it takes more than economic theory to turn a capitalist economy into directly planned community production for community consumption, with outright prohibition of all dealing and all employment of labour for private profit: but there is more of economic theory in the first and more of revolutionary will in the second. Theoretically, the two are alternative solutions of the same problems. But that does not mean that in practice they are historically offered as alternatives.

Marx assumed that the capitalist system was a necessary phase, and a real advance, in the development of the productive power of society. There could be no question of looking for something else.

On the other hand, it could not go on in the hands of the capitalists who had developed it, because their interests were unalterably opposed to its full use and to the distribution of its products according to need or according to work. In their hands the system worked blindly and violently, producing large-scale catastrophic, and unintended, consequences. It had to be understood and brought under control. Fortunately, the necessary social transformation, the transition to socialism, had already been prepared (as always) by history in the womb of the capitalist system itself, and would prove as easy as inevitable. By contrast with the protracted and frightful expropriation of the masses of individuals which had established the conditions of capitalism and brought into existence the proletariat, the expropriation of the few capitalists by the politically awakened class-conscious proletariat would be both quick and painless.

'The transformation of scattered private property, arising from individual labour, into capitalist private property is, naturally, a process incomparably more protracted, violent, and difficult, than the transformation of capitalistic private property, already practically resting on socialized production, into socialized property. In the former case, we had the expropriation of the mass of the people by a few usurpers; in the latter, we have the expropriation of a few usurpers by the mass of the people.' (*Capital*, Vol. I, Ch. XXXII.)

In the established socialist societies, the evils of capitalism can be remedied and its benefits fully appropriated: productive capacity will be directly expanded and applied to the reduction of socially necessary labour-time; common interest will be re-established and the sources and occasions of conflict reduced and eliminated; freedom will be realized in the sense of exploitation banished, purpose made practicable, destiny understood and fulfilled; the disrupted family will be reinstated, and reinforced by the economic independence of its members; hand and brain, enjoyment and work, production and consumption, town and country, action and responsibility, will be reunited. What is best and permanent in human life will be restored, and at a higher level of integration with multiplied powers and a richer content. It was a grand vision; and none has been so near the truth.

V

To separate the revolutionary strategy and tactics from dialectical historical materialism and the analysis of capitalism is more than an emasculation of marxism; it is its dismemberment. The world is to be understood in order to change it; and it is to be changed, not in order to bring it nearer to human wishes, aspirations, and ideals, which are subjective and conditioned, determined by the changing facts; the way in which it is to be changed is given in the disclosed development of history, which has taken shape unforeseen and unintended, but which nevertheless is an advance, or preliminary to advance, because dialectical process ensures a progressive development. This view does not necessarily imply a teleology. Self-development, self-correction, and completion may be a persistent characteristic of things in continuous interaction in the ceaseless movement of nature: and that is the meaning of dialectical materialism—as it is also the essential meaning of platonic and of hegelian dialectic in the realm of concepts. History involves men's wills which are supposedly free, but they are blind in respect of the further, unintended consequences of choice, pursuit, and action, and they are blind in respect of the deeper causes by which they are determined. On both these aspects of their position they may get enlightenment. What happens is predetermined and predictable, not because it is purposed by man or god, but because the nature of the interacting entities and their conditions are determinate and relatively stable and may be known. Men with a knowledge of historical precedents, a grasp of dialectical process, and an analysis of the current factors at work, may learn to foresee what will happen. At worst, it will happen blindly and raggedly, with more or less violence, confusion, dislocation, and suffering; at best, consciously, smoothly, quickly, with little pain, and with aesthetic finish and completeness. The difference is the part which falls to human intelligence and will; limited in scope, infinite in importance. The particular content and detailed modification which may be the work of the intelligent will within the limited scope assigned by historical determinism is of the essence of history and humanity. So that communism, without contradiction, may well be both inevitable and a consummate act of will, the most massive and spectacular in history.

The marxist does not say: I know what I want and how I am going to get it. He says: I know what is going to happen and that it will be good; therefore I know what to do. The first attitude is made rational by recourse to ethics and science; the second, it is claimed, is wholly scientific. I will recapitulate the argument, as the marxist might put it. We have discovered and proved that the ultimate historical causes are economic factors, which change and cause changes in all the other factors. Detailed study of these changes in their historical circumstances gives a general pattern for understanding and predicting the main form of critical transition in large-scale changes (economic class conflict). We have shown that the present system of capitalist economic production is stultified by the incentive which maintains it (the appropriation of surplus value), for it can only profit by cheating labour, and if it cheats labour it cannot profit. This contradiction is hidden by the complexity of factors, although there are symptoms which show that our diagnosis is right; but in the end, if the system continues, a few can profit at the expense of the many, by creating and maintaining conditions of scarcity. Their power to do this is the power of the state. But ultimate power lies with the many, and when these become conscious of the situation, as they must, the outcome is certain. The social change that then takes place must bring about the end of class conflict because the proletariat have no separate economic interest of their own to fortify and enforce against others, no privileged relation to the means of production. This radical change of conditions must result in an unprecedented change in the nature of man, since the nature of man is ultimately determined by economic conditions. In general, the problem set by the contradictions of capitalism will be solved, because it is in the nature of problems to be solved (that is the dialectical meaning of history); the general lines of the solution can be discerned, and therefore intelligent action can be taken to facilitate and expedite the solution. Put bluntly and concretely: the dictatorship of the proletariat is certain, predetermined by the logic of the situation; what follows afterwards (the content of the new society) is an inference from that, not an ideal object of will.

Is this argument scientific in form? Is it true? In history there can be no question of a repeated recurrence of a simple sequence of events (the basic presupposition of science). Marxists generalize from one or two (mainly one) large-scale transformations of society, and apply the generalization to a prediction of a similar transformation to come in a situation which in many or most characteristics is extremely dissimilar. For example, the rising bourgeois class which displaced the feudal ruling class had a technical competence for developing the new economic order which has no parallel in the proletariat. The marxist theory of the state (the state exists for violence, as the instrument of the dominant economic interest), and the marxist theory of the necessary limits of capitalist production for profit (the inherent contradiction) and the necessary form of its development determined by those limits, are theories which usefully describe general tendencies which may be more or less perfectly realized in particular cases, but they are not fixed properties or attributes of stable entities, and to use them independently for predictions of necessity in situations in which the factors involved are complex and subtle is to assume that they are. (This is a return to the aristotelian metaphysics and logic of which dialectical materialism is a repudiation.) It may be demonstrably true that the economic factors ultimately assert themselves as the efficient causes, but it has not yet been shown that economic causes directly determine human nature and behaviour, and therefore it is irresponsible speculation to maintain that the dictatorship of the proletariat by abolishing the economic class conflict will appreciably alter human nature and behaviour unless it remains in power a very long time (a whole 'historical epoch' according to Lenin and Stalin), during which (by all the precedents) it will follow its own irresistible tendencies. Finally, the general assumption that dialectical process in history is progressive (in so far as it is not merely an empirical reading of history) seems to be either the assumption that mankind really learns and systematically applies the lessons of historical experience from one generation to another, or the assumption that human consciousness is merely an epiphenomenon and that the material inheritance develops independently by its own immanent laws; otherwise, the idea seems to be either an ideal, demanding that the objective historical process be accompanied by thought and action, that its consecutive phases be truly comprehended and truly lived, or the rather grim consolation that the truth in the end will be learned because nothing else will prove any good, 'the instability of evil is the moral order of the world' (Whitehead), or in the words of Croce, an early neo-hegelian liberal critic of marxism, 'the loss of a truth is often paid for by the human race with tremendous calamities and the truth brought back by unspeakable suffering'.

It is easy in this way to make inroads into the orderly structure of marxist thought and to scatter its scientific pretensions; and this has often been done. However, it remains impressive by its penetration and usefulness; and it is more scientific than easy criticism recognizes. For example, the great differences between the bourgeois revolution and the proletarian revolution (not stressed by Marx but clearly recognized and elaborated by Stalin) are not significant if the operative factor in both cases is economic class interest. It is of course not possible in this complex field to be as precise as in the exact sciences. Unfortunately marxism does claim to be scientifically exact in this sense, with the result that marxism contradicts itself and turns into its opposite: dialectical method becomes doctrinaire ideology, materialism becomes idealism, determinism becomes voluntarism, communism becomes fascism. How does this come about?

The strategy and tactics, fully formed by the theory, were given weight and authority by the persistent criticism and opposition offered by Marx and Engels to three prevalent forms of socialist theory and practice. (1) Utopian socialism, appealing to society as a whole and offering a new model of things in strong contrast to what existed: this, of course, had no political future and after the establishment of an independent historical working-class movement was frivolous or perverse, and a dangerous weakness. (2) Ideological socialisms, led by persons or parties who planned to use the political power of the working class for the achievement of some dreamed-of form of society, some ideal: these also were sectarian and religious in character and ministered to personal ambitions and distracted and distorted the political consciousness of the proletariat. (3) So-called opportunists or gradualists who worked empirically to improve the condition of the working class by entering into bargains and getting concessions, building up the class power of the workers for achievements within the framework of the bourgeois democratic state: these, for the sake of immediate, illusory, and enervating gains, betrayed the whole future, since they dissipated their power and left the capitalist system intact, and the state in the hands of the capitalists. With strict disseverance of these deviations, Marx and Engels followed their historic line: (1) since the mere existence of the capitalist system and the bourgeois state entails necessarily exploitation, oppression, and the restriction of production, nothing less than the destruction of the wage-labour system and of the bureaucratic military machine by the dictatorship of the proletariat can possibly bring about the jump into the new orbit which economic development has now made the destiny of mankind; (2) the existence, the character, and the situation of the proletariat ensure its recognition of its historic mission; it has no interests of its own to enforce and no ideals to realize; it has only to take over, administer, and keep in its hands the economic machine developed by capitalism; what will be achieved in the new society can in general be inferred from the character of proletarian rule, that is, from the character of proletarian class interest; the proletariat does not aim at and carry through the revolution for the sake of justice or liberty or equality, all that can be said is that these and all other attributes of man and of society are advanced a further stage by proletarian rule. (When attacking communists for making the end justify the means, it is well to notice that their peculiarity is that they don't. The means are historically given, and the end is thereby determined; no ideal end is willed. How perverse? But how like the English conception of democracy.)

Now these doctrines have to be scientifically exact to carry the whole weight of human destiny which they are asked to bear. Unfortunately, in the nature of the case, no such doctrines can be universally exact. At best, they can approximate to the situation in some places at some times. And this they do. But unless they are held to be scientifically exact it is not possible to drill and discipline a communist party as an instrument of power. All manner of deviations are possible, because they are not without truth and justification. Marx and Engels, for all their strenuous controversial labours, did not convince the workers' movements, not even the most 'scientific' of them all, of which they were most proud, on which they laboured most assiduously, the great German social democratic party. How infinitely one might wish that they had been successful there! History is dark with accidents. It was Lenin who adopted, adapted, used, reinforced, and gave new authority and prestige to marxism as an historic instrument of thought and action. It was Stalin who gave us a subtle vulgarization of dialectical historical materialism, in his essay of 1938 on that subject.

VI

It is a principle of dialectics that action transforms both the object and the agent. Action so considerable as the building up of a militant workers' movement is bound to involve mutual transformation of sectional interests in a society. That is a new situation, materially different, complicated by new factors, calling for fresh exploration.

To refuse to recognize change, and impose on the situation an ideological stereotype, is to forsake dialectical materialism for idealism. The situation may be rich in new possibilities demanding dialectical study. To prefer the primacy of will to the primacy of dialectical process is to make marxism nothing else than 'an embodied will to power and government', which was Mussolini's definition of fascism. Thus marxism, which is not a social programme but a philosophy of history, when it insists on making an exact science of dialectical social study contradicts itself and turns into its opposite: it becomes destructive. One might ask, does it turn into its opposite because it is returning to what it was to begin with; is its philosophy of history a rationalization of a given revolutionary will? Its affinity with pragmatism might confirm the suspicion. That, however, is a biographical inquiry. One may fairly suppose that marxism like most philosophical tissues is woven of the warp and woof of genuine intellectual inquiry and strong volitions. Anyhow, it gave historical solidity, seriousness, and responsibility to revolution in an age of light-hearted insurrectionism.

The fundamental contradiction between dialectics and stereotyped ideology which, through its insistence on 'science', turns marxism into its negation turns historical responsibility into irresponsibility. The present role of communist parties is not necessarily everywhere mischievous, irresponsible, and destructive. But, especially in highly developed and complex social situations, its intransigence, its refusal to be changed by action, its ideological hardness, its determination at all costs to remain whole and absolute, forces every political question to the ultimate issue of, Who shall kill whom? eliminates all possibilities save the bare disjunction, Either/Or; sets everything upon the utmost exertion of inflexible will for the disposal of absolute power: and this is rank destruction, utterly and wickedly irresponsible. Our civilization is too complex and subtle to gain anything but irreparable damage from such treatment, and there is every excuse for those who take communism not merely as the enemy but as unmitigated barbarism, indistinguishable from fascism, in its turn attracting the 'armed bohemian' and the 'armed intellectual', manifesting itself most clearly in the bitterness of its hostility to successful social democracy, which gives the lie to its 'science', exposes its denial of dialectics in practice, and turns its tempered instrument of power to brittle hollowness.

Examination of the theoretical structure of marxism shows the flaw in its science, which substitutes a form of idealism for its justifiable materialism, and issues in the negation of its essence. This can be deduced from the theory and is painfully plain in the practice. But marxism means too much to too many to be left with a formal analysis of the theory, and exposure or denunciation of the practice. It attracts not only some of the worst but also some of the best. The absolute ideology joined to the political power of a class-conscious proletariat, in the hands of fanatical leaders with ability and drive, is a force unexampled in history, and when it is moving in the direction in which our sympathies lie, there is hardly anything to be said that does not swell the temptation to jump on the band-wagon. Theoretically, marxism is not a social programme, it is a reading of history; the social programme is not prescribed and is not an object of will, it is deducible from the dictatorship of the proletariat on a full reading of the meaning of that dictatorship, and is left to history; just as theoretically the social programme is left to history in a formal democracy. I think it is important to understand marxism theoretically in this way, or one gets no insight into its inwardness, its authentic self. The theory of the dictatorship of the proletariat is the epitome of marxism and contains it all, backwards and forwards. Nevertheless, the social programme is there, and is all-important to marxism as to unsophisticated judgement. What will be achieved in the society initiated by the dictatorship of the proletariat is not arbitrary, it is historical; the advent and nature of the dictatorship is assurance of that. Because it is not arbitrary, it can be precisely deduced; it is historically determined. In sum, it is simply expressed as the application of the economic machine to the production of plenty for the satisfaction of human wants, fully and freely, and the development of personality. This rational self-conscious fulfilment of human destiny is historically possible by the removal of obstructions for which the dictatorship of the proletariat is indispensable. This reasoning raises again the whole question I have been discussing, to which there is no final abstract answer: the appeal must be from dogma to facts, from idealism to materialism. The dictatorship of the proletariat in practice does not solve definitively the political problem and the economic problem; it transposes them to a different set of conditions, some advantageous, some disadvantageous to a solution. In any case, there is no final solution, once for all. Where the dictatorship of the proletariat has been historically achieved, what is accomplished is of the greatest interest and importance, not as a standard but for comparison. The conception of the end in terms of the means whether by marxists or by liberal democrats is the essence of both theories. In both cases it has an historical justification and cannot be forthwith abandoned, but it is becoming possible to conceive the future more profitably in direct terms of the content of the social programme, and even to establish objective universal standards. This involves a new way of social thinking, in which marxism survives in the only way in which a philosophy can survive, by the enduring and progressive part of its activity and the destruction of the *system* which is necessarily transitory and *reactionary*—as Engels says. Like everything else it is mortal and transitory and limited. It has to shriek and surrender its sacred egoism, its absolute otherness and universal claim, and like other influences pass into ever-living history. It has produced honey, but it is not for the hive.

In sum, then, the key concepts of marxism (capitalism, the state, the revolution and dictatorship of the proletariat) are the products of historical thinking, but they are not used by marxists as dialectical conceptions of historical existents in development; they are not even used as empirical scientific concepts: they are used absolutely as logical concepts of substances and their necessary attributes; historical characteristics and tendencies of these phenomena are treated as the propria of substances, belonging to them by definition without any need to look again. This of course is not dialectical materialism, but reactionary metaphysics. But it is useless to pretend that it might be corrigible intellectual error when manifestly it is implacable will. Marxism in this way shows that it is not true and it is not honest; it is doubly false: intellectually and ethically, objectively and subjectively. It is not marxism that is condemned, the union of militancy and dialectics; on the contrary, it is marxism that condemns the marxists: they are judged by their own doctrine, as lacking the courage and integrity to follow it through, or as using it merely to cover their naked will to power. Marxism does not turn into its own opposite by a necessary development, a dialectical process, nor by a venial or vital inconsistency on the part of marxists, but by their total though unavowed abandonment of reason and principle. If it is otherwise, the proof will be in a return to the principles of dialectical historical materialism. Meanwhile, marxists, in the main, stand for no interests but their own, and their claim to represent the historical human cause must be decisively rejected as impudent, mischievous, and destructive.

A great headstrong cocktail with a jaw of iron, with no manners and no vice, with tremendous jumping-quarters and plenty of stamina: such a beast would not be very pleasant to ride, but a good horseman would be well carried and might soon leave the field behind; and if after a time in the excitement of the chase he found he was riding a tiger, well, that could not really happen of course, that could only be a nightmare. But how like real life!

Chapter 7

THE DICTATORSHIP OF THE PROLETARIAT

I

THE first interest of Marx is capitalism, not socialism. The phrases of the *Communist Manifesto* ring with admiration in depicting the brutal materialism and irresistible energy of the bourgeoisie in action, thrusting themselves into history, sweeping aside the effete persons of place and privilege in church and state, expropriating peasant and artisan, putting all their drive into the business of organizing their own interests, compelling the world into the path of progress. For in this phase of social development this is the historical class playing the progressive role, master of the new sciences, the new techniques, the new machines, the new men; and at this stage socialism or communism is as futile, as reactionary, as attached to idealism, as the dream of restoration which consoles the dispossessed. But, as Engels says, the eyes of the dialectical philosopher see on everything and in everything the stamp of inevitable decline, and look for the newcomer which will rise and thrust it aside: the present power is always engaged in establishing the power that will destroy it; 'not only has the bourgeoisie forged the weapons that bring death to itself; it has also called into existence the men who are to wield those weapons—the modern working class—the proletarians'. In time, Lenin will concentrate in himself the audacious self-confidence of the early bourgeoisie and drive their class from power, establishing in their historical role the dictatorship of the proletariat.

This dramatic spectacle of capitalism in expansion was merely a graphic summary of events which in detail had a different aspect. In France, for example, throughout the nineteenth century it is the anarchy of capitalism rather than its efficiency that demands attention: the feverish speculation, the tariff campaigns of rival interests, the struggle for spoils, the exploitation of the powers of the state for private fortune-making. These conditions are reflected in French economic theory, which is rich in socialist utopias, by contrast with the classical British theory of an automatically self-regulating 'natural' economy. Saint-Simon proposes to organize capitalism: the new order of production requires an appropriate social order, a technocracy. Fourier dreams of regenerating society by model collective farms. Proudhon wants small-scale co-operatives and the elimination of all forms of income without work. These systems are strong in their protest and rejection, their analysis of the economic waste and moral evils of capitalism. They do not capture the interest of those who are profiting by the existing anarchy, and they cannot long appeal to those who are victims of it. These (workers who feel themselves cheated of all gains in successive revolutions) gradually come to accept the view, propounded pre-eminently by Blanqui, 'the head and the heart of the proletarian party in France', as Marx described him, that it is private property in the means of production that is the source of anarchy in production and of arbitrary power over the workers, and that it is by using the power of the state that the owners maintain their privileged position and exclude others; with the result that there is an irreconcilable antagonism between the two classes, which can only be resolved for the workers by the conquest of political power and the institution of a revolutionary dictatorship on the model of the jacobin dictatorship of Robespierre, which Babeuf had hoped to revive in order to 'withdraw the people for ever from the natural enemies of equality and give them the unity of will required for the adoption of republican institutions'. Blanqui's thought has travelled from this earlier ideal of republican institutions to the question of economic power, and for him the object of the dictatorship is the collective appropriation of the means of production by the workers, and the crushing of every attempt by the counter-revolution to regain possession. This was communism as it took shape in France, disengaged from the confused aspirations of the great revolution, sharply opposed to utopian socialism, given impetus and operational clarity by Blanqui, for half a century head and heart of the proletarian party, and born and bred to conspiracy, agitation, and insurrection. Nevertheless, French communism is not 'scientific socialism'; it is an improvisation on a theme of the revolution. In a phrase of Blanqui's it is 'the marrow of the revolution', for experience of successive revolutions had taught him to regard the class interests of all sections of the bourgeoisie as a betrayal of the revolution, and the socialist utopias as new religions no less reactionary than the old; only the proletarian class was a dependable instrument of revolution and social regeneration.

II

The practical conclusion of the revolutionary agitator Blanqui, his operational conception of communism as the dictatorship of the proletariat, could hardly have gained universality without the theoretical elaboration of Marx, whose economic and historical analysis issued in the same conclusion. Marx tried to show that capitalism, having created the proletariat by expropriation, appropriated in profits the use-value of its unpaid labour. This was not merely injustice, wage-slavery, exploitation; the worst consequence was that within the limits of the home market the system entailed the contradiction that it could only persist by selling to people who had not the money with which to buy: hence, booms and slumps, monopolies, wars, and crises of unemployment threatening chronic stagnation. The capitalist economic expansion would inevitably lead to a world-wide struggle for an increasing share of diminishing trade returns, accelerating the contraction. (And in the 1930's this happened.) Private property in the means of production constituted not merely privileges in consumption but also arbitrary power in the disposal of resources. Only the proletariat had no interest in private property in the means of production and could reconstitute the general interest in full and planned production by abolishing this form of private property. But the instruments of government were in the hands of those who enjoyed and would defend privileged relations to the means of production. Therefore, revolutionary action establishing a dictatorship of the proletariat was the only means by which the full productive capacity of the economic machine developed by capitalism could be realized. This conclusion was theoretically inevitable, since privileged relations to the means of production constitute interests at variance with the common interest, and since these privileged interests are solely interests in profit-making, that is to say, interests sometimes satisfied in expansion, sometimes in contraction, without regard to unsatisfied human needs. A society constituted of consolidated privileged interests has no common interest, and a common interest can only be created by the class which has no privileged relation to the means of production, that is, the proletariat expropriated by capitalism. The intolerable waste, anarchy, oppression, and misery inseparable from the capitalist system cannot be cured by economic reforms because these evils flow from production for profit, in which everybody is interested except the proletariat. The task of the dictatorship of the proletariat is to put everybody on a footing of equality in relation to the means of production, thus creating a common interest in full production, and then to plan the allocation of resources and the programme of work. At first Marx thought that capitalist economy would ripen into monopolies in the hands of a few and that a change of hands would be all that was required, that the proletariat representing the immense majority could take over and run the state and the economic machine. Reflection upon the course of capitalist development and the course of class conflict, especially in France and especially as seen in the experience of the Commune, convinced him that it would be necessary to reconstitute the armed forces and the administration. Blanqui's political programme, summarized by himself in two words '*dictature parisienne*', meant simply the disarming of the bourgeoisie and the arming of the workers. The Commune, first sketch of the proletarian dictatorship, proved to Marx and Engels that 'the working class cannot simply lay hold of the ready-made state machinery and wield it for its own purposes' (Preface to *The Communist Manifesto*, 1872). Thus the dictatorship of the proletariat has to 'smash the bureaucratic-military state machinery', and its regime will last 'an entire historical epoch'.

'Scientific socialism' is this analysis of the necessary consequences of production for profit based on privileged relations to the means of production. All other forms of socialism are utopian (unless the mere mockery of opportunist labour leaders) because they have no roots in effective class interest and because they seek to gather grapes off thorns. The rational allocation and full employment of resources inexorably require the abolition of private property in the means of production, which inexorably requires the dictatorship of the proletariat. It is not open to anyone to prefer the inconveniences of the present if he dislikes the means more than he desires the end. There are no alternatives. Communism is only secondarily an object of will, it is primarily the necessary sequel to capitalism, the continuation of capitalism at a higher level. It becomes an historical necessity when the proletariat becomes conscious of the necessary failure of capitalism, of the indispensable conditions of full production, of their own class interest and class power. It is made inevitable by the convergence of economic and psychological laws, and for that reason the consent or dissent of individuals cannot alter the issue, as variation in the behaviour of individual units does not affect statistical regularities.

This operational definition of communism as the condition of society created by the dictatorship of the proletariat distinguishes 'scientific socialism' from every other form. In practice it presupposes advanced capitalism and a class-conscious organized proletariat; in theory it presupposes the whole content of marxist thought. There is no marxism apart from it. On this view, socialists who are social democrats are no more able to play the historical role of the proletariat in realizing the productive capacity of a machine economy than are the bourgeoisie themselves whose part is played out and whose tools they are: their action merely confuses the issue and delays the *dénouement*. Stalin remarks of the task of the dictatorship of the proletariat: 'To think that such a revolution can be carried out peacefully, within the framework of bourgeois democracy, which is adapted to the rule of the bourgeoisie, means that one has either gone out of one's mind and lost normal human understanding, or has grossly and openly repudiated the proletarian revolution.' Marxism is not concerned with socialism as a theory or ideal of society, but solely with the dictatorship of the proletariat as the inevitable next step in the economic organization of society. What the dictatorship would do could be left to take care of itself because it could be trusted to deal with the economic conditions which made it necessary; for the rest, the economic order was the source of all things in any society.

Thus Marx says of the working class, with reference to the Commune:

'They have no ready-made utopias to introduce *par decret du peuple*. . . . They have no ideals to realize, but to set free the elements of the new society with which the old collapsing bourgeois society itself is pregnant.'

He sums up the content of the programme thus: 'The great social measure of the Commune was its own working existence.' As to the dictatorship itself, he says:

'Its true secret was this. It was essentially a working-class government, the product of the struggle of the producing against the appropriating class, the political form at last discovered under which to work out the economical emancipation of labour.' (*The Civil War in France.*)

Lenin underlines 'at last discovered' in order to contrast Marx's historical approach with the inventions of the utopians.

'And when the mass revolutionary movement of the proletariat burst forth, Marx, in spite of the failure of that movement, in spite of its short life and its patent weakness, began to study the political forms that it had *disclosed*. The Commune is the form "at last discovered" by the proletarian revolution, under which to work out the economic emancipation of labour.' (*The State and Revolution.*)

Theoretically, the Commune is the observed verification of the marxist hypothesis; historically, it is the establishment of a second and greater precedent, to be repeated, as Lenin noted, in Russia in 1905 and 1917. Similarly, Engels in a letter to Bebel commenting on Marx's *Critique of the Gotha Programme* rejects the idea of socialist society as the realm of 'liberty, equality, fraternity', and all the ideas of the socialist schools, 'for they only produce confusion in people's heads, and more precise modes of presentation have been found'. This more precise mode, instead of presenting socialism as turning principally on distribution and treating distribution as independent of the mode of production (which according to Marx is vulgar socialism and liberalism derived from bourgeois economists), is 'scientific socialism, which does not attach great importance to distribution and which explains the social system by the organization of the *relations of production* and which considers that a given system of organization of relations of production already includes a definite system of distribution . . . this idea runs like a thread through the whole of Marx's teaching'[1] (Lenin).

Lenin elsewhere sums up the approach of Marx to communism in this way:

'The whole theory of Marx is an application of the theory of development—in its most consistent, complete, well-considered and

[1] Lenin in another place says that the idea of the dictatorship of the proletariat runs like a red thread through all the teachings and all the works of Marx and Engels. Indeed, this is true, and on the two 'threads' twined together hangs the whole weight of marxist thought.

fruitful form—to modern capitalism. . . . Marx treats the question of communism in the same way as a naturalist would treat the question of the development of, say, a new biological species, if he knew that such and such was its origin, and such and such the direction in which it changed.' (*The State and Revolution.*)

The same operational approach is seen even more strikingly in Blanqui just because of his deficiency in theory: he has a blind apocalyptic belief in 'creative' revolution, and left blank even the first steps in the construction of socialism.

'The social question can only come into serious discussion and into practice after the most energetic and irrevocable solution of the political question, and by that means. . . . Ideas of social reconstruction will never have any reality until a cataclysm striking dead the old decrepit society will set free the imprisoned elements whose spontaneous and rapid germination must organize the new world. All the powers of thought, all the stretching of intelligence will not know how to anticipate this creative phenomenon which will only appear at a given moment. One can prepare the cradle but not bring to light the awaited being. Until the moment of death and re-birth, the doctrines which are to be the foundation of the future society remain vague aspirations, remote and nebulous views. It is like a silhouette formless and floating on the horizon of which no human effort can fix and grasp the outline. There also comes a time when discussion is exhausted and does not know how to move a single step towards the future. In vain it tires itself to lift a barrier which thought cannot cross, a barrier which only the revolution will be able to break. It is the mystery of future existence whose veil, impenetrable to the living, falls of itself before death. The old society once demolished, one will find the new under the rubble, the last blow of the pick will bring it to light, triumphant.

'No doubt the seminal ideas of the new society must precede and prepare the movement; but this work seems to me already a long time accomplished, the old world is sufficiently dissected, the scalpel will not dig out of it one more fact. It is now for the storms to renew the atmosphere.'

This romantic conspirator, improvisator of revolution, for ever going off at half-cock, incapable of political action, is really a carica-ture of the marxist proletarian leader, in spite of his formidable influence as a legendary hero which made him 'the head and the heart of the proletarian party'. Nevertheless he reveals the basic pattern of marxist thought: the proletariat because it is the only element which has no privileged relation to the means of production is the only element in modern society which can operate the economic machine successfully and reconstitute society on a basis of common interest in full production, and, therefore, what the proletariat in power will do can be left to take care of itself. This form of thinking is not invalid and has many comparable examples: in science, a proposition is proved by the way in which it is arrived at; the kingdom of God is the inscrutable outcome, within and without, of Christian discipleship, not a programme of social reform and personal righteousness; a decision or law or state of society may be taken as fair or as free because it is the outcome of democratic procedures, regardless of what it may be. These conceptions are products of historical thinking, established and held in position and nourished by a root system of assumptions, which may crumble to dust when exposed to the light. But the real question is whether they continue to flourish in the soil of experience.

On marxist assumptions, a dictatorship of the proletariat will have the fullest historical and philosophical sanction, a legitimacy far exceeding the conventional legitimacy of established governments. Moreover once it emerges on the historical plane and is established, marxism enters a new phase, and the dictatorship of the proletariat becomes an oecumenical authority more unchallengeable by marxists than the authority of the papacy by Christians, because the dictatorship is not the vice-regent of the authority, but the absolute authority constituted by history as prophesied by Marx and taking up and superseding the marxist phase, continuing, as Stalin says, the line of Marx and Engels. Thus the party line as determined by the leaders of a proletariat dictatorship engaged single-handed during thirty years in the socialist reconstruction of society over one-sixth of the world has unquestionable validity for marxists. Both in prestige and in authority it is incomparable. The point is well put by the Hungarian, Georges Lukacs, one of the oldest and intellectually one of the most distinguished of European marxists, in the course of a long controversy with the French existentialist socialist Maurice Merleau-Ponty.

'. . . at a time like ours, when socialism has behind it thirty years of actual history, a profession of abstract faith devoted to the final end of socialism does not mean a thing. The choice before which our social reality places the sincere thinker, the situation in which he finds himself, is the following: he must take his position in regard to socialism *such as it is*, as it has been born and is developing in the Soviet Union. He must take his position in regard to the entirely new ways which lead towards socialism and which have opened with the collapse of fascism. To say: I am for socialism, but not for soviet socialism; I am solely for a socialism which conforms to my idea of it—to say that, . . . would be comparable to the attitude of a mother who should say: the flame of maternal love consumes me, I am maternal love embodied, but I refuse to love my child, because his ears run.'

This must be the (thoroughly marxist) answer of the marxist to-day to the would-be 'classical' marxist *pur sang*.

III

Stalin defines leninism as 'the theory and tactics of the proletarian revolution in general, the theory and tactics of the dictatorship of the proletariat in particular'. Lenin is the great international ideological leader of the proletariat, he says, because the fundamental thing in leninism is the dictatorship of the proletariat.

'One of two things:
'*Either* the peasant problem is the fundamental thing in leninism, and in that case leninism is not suitable, not essential for developed capitalist countries, for those which are not peasant countries. *Or* the fundamental thing in leninism is the dictatorship of the proletariat, and in that case lenism is the international doctrine of the proletarians of all lands, suitable and essential for all countries without exception, including the developed capitalist countries. Here one must choose.'

However, there is really no choice, because the second alternative is merely a version of the first, and Stalin is turning the truth inside out. The fundamental thing in leninism, which was the fundamental thing in marxism, was decisively rejected as unsuitable by all the advanced workers' parties and leaders associated in the Second International; if it was received in Russia that was greatly due to the ideas and strategy and amazing personal force of Lenin himself, and because it came to peasant lands and to peasant lands alone as a gospel of salvation by industrial development. The intense militancy of leninism comes from his appropriation of the fundamental thing in marxism, with the result (1) that he has to engage in a 'ruthless struggle against the opportunism' of the leaders of democratic socialism in the advanced capitalist countries who rejected this fundamental thing, 'the fight against which was and remains an essential preliminary condition for a successful fight against capitalism' (Stalin); and with the result (2) that he has to fight for the ascendancy of a small proletarian party in a large peasant country. The actual ascendancy of the proletariat under Lenin in the revolution necessarily initiated the drive for industrial development which still continues. The desperate plight and appalling losses of the Russian people opposed to the German armament with sticks in their hands gave historical impetus to the efforts of the Bolsheviks to force the pace of industrial equipment. Similarly, in the neglected peasant lands which are the present satellites of the Soviet Union there was no prospect of better things without the industrial development which only the gospel of communism promised to bring them.

Thus the dictatorship of the proletariat, in the only form in which it exists or is likely to exist, is rather different in nature and in function from the dictatorship which Marx predicted by the logic of history. Instead of being the work of a numerous organized proletariat in an advanced capitalist country, bringing the established economic machine into full production, it is the strategic mastery of a small party of ideologists actually creating the machine economy and having to exploit the workers to do it. The facts as they have developed on all the national fronts require a fundamental revision of all the basic marxist conceptions: the theory of the state, the theory of surplus value, the theory of historical materialism. But there seems to be no reason to doubt that Marx would have been happy about the dictatorship in Russia and her satellites. Marxism, in a phrase, is unexampled preoccupation with economic production, which is the supreme characteristic of the Soviet Union. It is not so much interest in production for its own sake (although it easily becomes that) as the supposition that economic production is the condition and means of everything else: easy production of plenty abolishes 'bourgeois right', and the social discipline necessary to produce easy plenty is a permanent transformation of human nature. Thus the communist society to be achieved and the means of achieving it under the dictatorship of the proletariat solve at one and the same time the economic problem of full production, the political problem of the reconciliation of interests, and the moral problem of the good will; since the moral problem is identified with the political and social problem in the formula of Morelly: 'To find a situation in which man can no longer be either corrupt or wicked.'

On paper, the results produced by a dictatorship of the proletariat and by a political democracy in an advanced capitalist society might in time look near enough alike: organized plenty and security for all; educational and social opportunities and facilities for self-realization; a creative social ideal. No doubt the monolithic state can provide these conditions and produce state-determined persons to enjoy them, 'heretics in the truth' as Milton called them because they know no alternative to their orthodoxy. Only a pluralist democratic society can provide the conditions of personal self-determination and of the development of alternative views of the world and ways of life, and can respect and consider personal opinions and personal interests in all matters. Perhaps the difference in the abstract seems derisory. In practice, in terms of personality and consciousness and the finest human achievement, the difference is immeasurable. In an advanced capitalist society, organized labour is strong enough to get its own, and the productive resources are well enough developed to provide the social wealth in which all participate, and the government is bound to put an end to capitalist anarchy and take responsibility for planning the economy. In these circumstances, none but the insane, the simple and deluded idealist, and rank opportunists thirsting for power think that a dictatorship of the proletariat is necessary or desirable, or would be anything but immensely destructive and retrograde.

IV

What the dictatorship of the proletariat means in theory and practice once it is established, Stalin tells us. It is the continuation and completion of the strategy and tactics of the proletarian revolution according to marxist theory. Every person has eventually to be dispossessed of every form of ownership in the means of production, and the habits and outlook engendered by independence, privilege, and power based on private property have to be eliminated; machine production on a collective basis has to be stimulated, developed, and maximized, and socialized habits and outlook established. The dictatorship is exercised by the communist party functioning as a general staff, which is disciplined to accept and apply the party line as determined by the leaders. The 'correct' line is determined by the correct relationship of the party to the proletariat, the correct apprehension of Marx-Leninist doctrines, including the general principles of revolutionary strategy and tactics, and the correct appreciation of objective factors as confirmed by success.

The character of the dictatorship is described clearly by Stalin in *The Foundations of Leninism* and *On the Problems of Leninism* in the volume of Stalin's writings and speeches published in Great Britain in 1940 with the title *Leninism*. The following quotations from Lenin give the main outline.

'The dictatorship of the proletariat is a persistent struggle—sanguinary and bloodless, violent and peaceful, military and economic, educational and administrative—against the forces and traditions of the old society.'

But in the case of the Soviet Union the task is complicated by the backward condition of industry:

'The more backward the country which, owing to the zigzags of history, has proved to be the one to start the socialist revolution, the more difficult it is for her to pass from the old capitalist relations to socialist relations. To the tasks of destruction are added new, incredibly difficult tasks, viz., organizational tasks.'

There can be no question of the proletariat party's sharing the dictatorship with any other element in society:

'The class which took political power into its hands did so knowing that it took this power *alone*. That is a part of the concept dictatorship of the proletariat. This concept has meaning only when the single class knows that it alone is taking political power in its hands, and does not deceive itself or others with talk about "popular government, elected on the basis of universal suffrage, sanctified by the whole people".

'The supreme principle of the dictatorship is the maintenance of the alliance between the proletariat and the peasantry in order that the proletariat may retain its leading role and its political power.'

The dictatorship disposes of absolute power for the carrying out of its destructive and constructive tasks:

'The scientific concept of dictatorship means nothing more nor less than unrestricted power, absolutely unimpeded by laws or regulations and resting directly upon force.

'. . . the dictatorship of the proletariat is not only the use of force against the exploiters, and not even mainly the use of force. The economic foundation of this revolutionary force, the guarantee of its virility and its success, is in the fact that the proletariat represents and carries out a higher type of social organization of labour compared with capitalism. This is the essence. This is the source of the strength and the guarantee of the inevitable complete triumph of communism.

'Its quintessence is the organization and discipline of the advanced detachment of the working people, of their vanguard, their sole leader, the proletariat. Its object is to establish socialism, to abolish the division of society into classes, to make all members of society working people, to remove the basis for any kind of exploitation of man by man. This object cannot be achieved at one stroke. It requires a fairly long period of transition from capitalism to socialism, because the reorganization of production is a difficult matter, because radical changes in all spheres of life need time, and because the enormous force of habit of petit-bourgeois and bourgeois dealings can be overcome only by a long and stubborn struggle.'

Stalin sums up the three main aspects of the dictatorship of the proletariat:

'1. The utilization of the power of the proletariat for the suppression of the exploiters, for the defence of the country, for the consolidation of the ties with the proletarians of other lands, and for the development and the victory of the revolution in all countries.

'2. The utilization of the power of the proletariat in order to detach the toiling and exploited masses once and for all from the bourgeoisie, to consolidate the alliance of the proletariat with these masses, to enlist these masses for the work of socialist construction, and to ensure the state leadership of these masses by the proletariat.

'3. The utilization of the power of the proletariat for the organization of socialism, for the abolition of classes, for the transition to a society without classes, to a society without a state.

'The proletarian dictatorship is a combination of all three aspects. Not one of these three aspects can be advanced as the *sole* characteristic feature of the dictatorship of the proletariat. On the other hand, it is sufficient, under the conditions of capitalist encirclement, that even one of these three features be lacking for the dictatorship of the proletariat to cease being a dictatorship. Therefore, not one of these three aspects can be omitted without running the risk of distorting the concept of the dictatorship of the proletariat. Only all these three aspects taken together give us a complete and finished concept of the dictatorship of the proletariat.'

The dictatorship is exercised by the party, as Stalin explains:

'The highest expression of the leading role of the party, here, in the Soviet Union, in the land of the dictatorship of the proletariat, for example, is the fact that not a single important political or organizational question is decided by our Soviet and other mass organizations without guiding directions from the party. *In this sense* it could be said that the dictatorship of the proletariat is *in essence* the "dictatorship" of its vanguard, the "dictatorship" of its party, as the main guiding force of the proletariat.'

But the 'dictatorship' of the party over the proletariat is figurative only and means leadership and not 'power based on force'. 'Whoever attributes to the party the unnatural function of employing force against the working class violates the elementary requirements of correct mutual relationships between the vanguard and the class, between the party and the proletariat.' 'Mutual confidence' expresses the correct relations between the party and the proletariat. Stalin sums up:

'1. The prestige of the party and the iron discipline of the working class that is necessary for the dictatorship of the proletariat are built up not on fear nor on "unrestricted" rights of the party, but on the confidence of the working class in the party, on the support which the party receives from the working class.

'2. The confidence of the working class in the party is not acquired at one stroke, and not by means of force against the working class, but by the party's prolonged work among the masses, by a correct party policy, by the ability of the party to convince the masses by their own experience of the correctness of its policy, by the ability of the party to secure the support of the working class and to induce the masses of the working class to follow its lead.

'3. Without a correct party policy, reinforced by the experience of the struggle of the masses, and without the confidence of the working class, there is not and cannot be real party leadership.

'4. The party and its leadership, if the party enjoys the confidence of the class, and if this leadership is a real leadership, cannot be contrasted to the dictatorship of the proletariat, because without the leadership of the party (the "dictatorship" of the party), enjoying the confidence of the working class, a dictatorship of the proletariat to any extent durable is impossible.'

Correct relations, mutual confidence, are disturbed:

'1. If the party begins to build its prestige among the masses, not on its work and on the confidence of the masses, but on its "unrestricted" rights;

'2. If the party's policy is obviously wrong and the party is unwilling to reconsider and rectify its mistake;

'3. If the party's policy, although in general correct, is one which the masses are not yet ready to adopt, and the party is either unwilling or unable to bide its time so as to give the masses an opportunity to become convinced by their own experience that the party's policy is correct.

'The history of our party provides a number of such cases. Various groupings and factions in our party have fallen and have been dispersed because they violated one of these three conditions, and sometimes all these conditions taken together.'

Thus the dictatorship of the leaders of the party, who determine the party line, is exercised on the basis of the support, sympathy, or at least the toleration, of the majority of the workers, who are dealt with not by regulations, decrees, orders, but by demonstrations, persuasions, exhortations, rewards. Coercion in one form or another is employed against recalcitrant minorities amongst the workers, Right or Left deviationists amongst the party members and theoreticians (those who want to go too fast, 'revolutionary phrasemongers', or not fast or far enough), and against 'class enemies' who stand outside the proletarian organizations. It is employable at any time against individuals who fall under suspicion. All these features of the dictatorship are well exemplified in the struggle with the kulaks and the collective-farm movement or in the continuous effort to wind up the tempo of economic production. The party also promotes production and keeps itself in the right by looking out for and promoting people who show initiative and ability who are not in the party.

'. . . it is particularly these non-party comrades who must receive our special attention, who must be promoted to commanding positions so that they may see for themselves that the party appreciates capable and gifted workers. Some comrades think that only party members may be placed in leading positions in the mills and factories. This is the reason why they not infrequently shove aside non-party comrades who possess ability and initiative and promote party members instead, although they are less capable and show no initiative. Needless to say, there is nothing more stupid and reactionary than such a "policy", so called. It need hardly be proved that such a policy can only discredit the party and repel the non-party workers from it. Our policy is by no means to transform the party into an exclusive caste. Our policy is to create an atmosphere of "mutual confidence", of "mutual control" (*Lenin*) between party and non-party workers. One of the reasons why our party is strong among the working class is that it pursues such a policy.'

The continuous purpose of the dictatorship is production and socialization, two aspects of the same thing, since the meaning, justification, and guarantee of socialism is that it is a higher type of economic organization, that is, more efficient. Thus collective and state farms, because of model layouts, electrification, and large-scale employment of tractors and machines, greatly increase the productivity of peasant labour, and at the same time remould the stubborn individual peasants into socialist proletarians. This theoretical certainty that only a socialist organization of social relations can historically correspond to a machine economy is the ground of confidence and of world policy.

'Crises, unemployment, waste, poverty among the masses—such are the incurable diseases of capitalism. Our system does not suffer from these diseases because power is in our hands, in the hands of the working class; because we are conducting a planned economy, systematically accumulating resources and properly distributing them among the different branches of the national economy. We are free of the incurable diseases of capitalism. This is what distinguishes us from capitalism; this is what constitutes our decisive superiority over capitalism.'

When Stalin spoke these words in 1931 the capitalist anarchy in the Western world amounted to crisis and a general outlook of *sauve qui peut*, at the expense of the workers. At that time the Soviet Union was undoubtedly in a stronger position enjoying a brighter prospect. Peoples and governments in the Western democracies have learned something since then; and today observers in the Soviet Union are not so confident that a 'bourgeois' state with a mixed economy cannot overcome the worst contradictions and crises of capitalism. Even at that time Stalin said: 'We are fifty or a hundred years behind the advanced countries. We must make good this distance in ten years. Either we do it, or they crush us.' And he goes on to look forward to a success which will change the whole world and free the entire working class, who meanwhile can have no other fatherland than this first working-class state.

V

The dictatorship of the proletariat as practised in the Soviet Union and in her satellites may or may not be more efficient than the Western democracies in organizing the production and evoking the loyalty and releasing the energies of citizens. The present rivalry is working out the historical result of that practical test. On marxist assumptions, the result is not in doubt; but it is marxist assumptions that are in question. Unfortunately these assumptions involve much more than a healthy rivalry for superiority in organizational and administrative efficiency, such as the Webbs dreamed of at the time of their survey; they involve a life-and-death struggle *à outrance* from which there is no escape. On these assumptions, if there is resistance to the Soviet Union or to the communist parties, that can only be founded on the reactionary defence of profit-making interests. If democratic labour parties are associated with the resistance, that can only be because they have been misled by opportunist leaders who have 'grossly and openly repudiated the proletarian revolution', and because they have been corrupted by high wages drawn from imperialist profits. On marxist assumptions no other interpretation is possible and the only possible outcome is outright victory and domination of one side or the other; and on these assumptions the permanent victory of the capitalist elements is impossible in principle. On the other side, hopes are set on controlling the capitalist anarchy by government policy whilst working out national forms of the democratic social service state and creating a common interest, preferring evolution and compromise to revolution and dictation.

And in external relations with communism, the alternatives are: to contain Soviet expansion and penetration by the solidarity, success, and strength of social democracy, striking a world balance of power; or to force the Soviet Union into a world security system by declaration of an ultimatum.

It is tragic that the issue has been forced in this way, and it may be catastrophic. Except on marxist assumptions it is wholly unnecessary. In general, the present dictatorships of the proletariat are established in power for good or ill, and the present democracies, unless in France or Italy, are unlikely to surrender to proletarian revolution. The battle is joined, and the issue is in question most decisively in the struggle for the soul of Germany. The 'struggle for the soul of Germany' in marxist terms can only mean the class struggle in Germany supported from outside by the same opposed class interests at present dominant in world powers. However, although the actual situation in Germany is far too complicated and too fluid to simplify into a formula, 'the struggle for the soul of Germany' does mean something actual and something symbolic of the whole world issue. Marxism, although it treats the convictions and imaginations of men as ultimately the reflections of economic class interest, nevertheless appeals to conviction and imagination, and its triumphs are triumphs of conviction and imagination. Unless men are convinced that marxist assumptions are fallacious and disastrous, and unless they are themselves attached to a different vision of human life in the world more deeply rooted in experience, opposition to marxism has no head and no heart, no meaning and no strength.

It is not enough to say that dictatorship is evil in itself. The marxist argument is that there is no choice between dictatorship and democracy or freedom; there is only the choice between dictatorship of the proletariat, which is a stimulating creative leadership maximizing the productive energies and restoring the common interest of society and developing the conditions of complete stateless freedom, and the veiled dictatorship of bourgeois governments which maintain privilege, restriction, and oppression. The only answer from experience is that this certainly could be the only choice but as certainly is not necessarily the only choice. Unfortunately, here as always marxism goes one better than experience, and having done a service to mankind by refusing to cry 'Peace, peace' where there is no peace, goes on to create a dangerous problem by insisting on crying 'War, war' where there is no war; for it maintains that so long as the state exists there can only be a more or less disguised dictatorship of the bourgeoisie in favour of privileged interests or an open dictatorship of the proletariat establishing a common interest: that is the absolute nature and sole meaning of the modern state, and therefore the only question is at the right moment to force the issue between the two powers and establish the dominion of the only one with whom the future lies.

This conception is not merely nor mainly a conclusion drawn from experience of class conflict (in France, for example), nor wholly and solely a conclusion drawn from Marx's analysis of capitalism; it derives from a metaphysical theory of cosmic development in general and man's historical development in particular—as Lenin loved to declare. This marxist general theory of development, which claims to put socialism on a scientific basis, is a radical and vicious misconception of the relation of mind and matter, man and history, and ultimately, man and man. Marx was bred in hegelianism and fascinated by its dynamic grandeur and evolutionary content. At the same time he was a convinced materialist and could not but be dissatisfied with the static mechanistic materialism of the eighteenth century. In the light of its own law, to see the new idealism as the inevitable negation of this inadequate materialism and to restore materialism at a higher level including its own contradiction, thus realizing the dialectical development of historical philosophy assimilating and superseding all previous movements of thought, was a temptation not to be resisted. Unfortunately, this was to read into nature and into history characteristics proper only to mind. The terms 'contradiction', 'negation', 'dialectic', belong, properly speaking, to discourse and only metaphorically to nature or history. Marx says that they belong to discourse simply and solely because they belong to nature first; mind is a product of material development and reflects the nature of reality. Let mind be a product of material development, it has nonetheless like everything else specific characteristics: it selects and abstracts from experience, and this is precisely the reason for the dialectic development and completion of argument by contradiction (a true form of the eclecticism which marxism abhors, for one reason because it has taken this specific characteristic of the mind and planted it in things, and then superstitiously inhibited the mind in its proper functions). The abstractions of the mind correspond to aspects, phases, sequences, identities, in the order of nature, and the mind is able to seize such aspects, arrest such phases, pick upon such identities or incidents, and distort them for some intellectual or aesthetic or practical purpose; and thus you have the probing and experimental techniques of the sciences, and the development of a selected aspect of things in the arts (as when a whole world of human living is focused in an episode or phase of the drama), and the high cultivation of certain qualities in a fruit or a flower, which biologically is merely a by-product of the plant. To surrender this free activity of the mind to a fictitious logic of development in the order of nature which the mind merely reflects is a fatal folly. It is to stand theology on its head. It is the most perverse example of myth-making in history. It is the superstitious and paralysing worship of one's own powers deified in nature. It is the obsession of Narcissus.

If you think of the class struggle (which is real enough) not as the antagonism of people struggling to live in a free-for-all (in terms of social psychology, that is, as Hobbes might have thought of it), but as the reflection of a concrete contradiction between the means of production and the social relations; and if you think of this contradiction metaphysically, as a logically necessary stage in the development of man's self-consciousness and freedom; then, you are not going to analyse the problem with a view to alternative solutions, you are going to look for the resolution of the contradiction by the logic of its own development, and conform your mind to that outcome and act in a way to conform the outcome to your mind. Thought will only perfectly correspond with its object when the dictatorship of the proletariat has fully resolved the contradiction; and then the mind will reflect in self-consciousness the complete knowledge of man.

'The philosophers', Marx says, 'have only *interpreted* the world in various ways; the point however is to *change* it.' That is excellent. And he understands that the way to change it is to work with the grain. But to confuse the economy of the mind with the economy of nature by treating one as the reflection of the other is to misuse and waste the resources of both. The blunder is seen plainly in the extreme feebleness of marxist epistemology. All the philosophies of the nineteenth century developed formally out of a theory of knowledge, marxism amongst them. The problem of knowledge is a question of the nature of our knowledge; the reasonable assumption that there is an objective external world independent of and prior to the knowing mind does not answer this question. If the objective world reflected thought or thought reflected the objective world, that might be the answer to the question. It is difficult to find any meaning in either assumption, and neither has any warrant in experience. Thought develops by contradiction: a negative instance disproves the universality of the proposition and forces the mind to conceive a more general law which will include the contradictory instance. The contradiction destroys the proposition inevitably; there is no future in the thought which seeks to ignore it or explain it away. (This is the logic, aristotelian in spite of repudiation, which the marxist likes to find, and which marxism depends on finding, in nature.) This logic, in its terms, in its meaning and use, is wholly and solely a process of mind. It is unthinkable in nature. It is the way of making the schematic representation of total experience consistent and productive, as the means of further operations, intellectual, aesthetic, and practical, leading to human satisfactions. Seriously to treat knowledge as a reflection of nature (mainly a reflection of natural process, since reality is process rather than substance), would make progress in the sciences wait upon development in the phenomena studied. Marxists of course apply their theory of knowledge mainly to history; the self-consciousness of man keeps pace with social development and reflects it; at any time the theory of man and of history is determined by the stage of development and reflects it; man's full historical consciousness of himself awaits the completion of the historical process and will reflect it.

Marx's theory of man and of history, like any other, uses the conceptual and factual material available at the time, and, like any other theory, it claims to explain and predict the phenomena with which it deals. Like any other, it stands or falls by its power to explain and predict. Marxism should certainly be tried by this test; but in this field explanation and prediction are the guide to an action which cannot wait for the final proof of results, and which itself makes the results equivocal. It is therefore important to recognize that in this case explanation and prediction are *formally* the expression of natural and historical process in terms of logical process, and the prediction of what will happen in history on the assumption that the terms are related as are the terms in a logical process of thought.

This absurd metaphysics has no foundation in experience and fails to appreciate the specific processes of nature and of thought and their fertile interaction. Reducing all the interrelated processes to one process, in effect, reduces thought to a stupid, stuttering literalness, spelling back what it has read into nature; or it is like treating mathematics as merely the mental accompaniment of physical operations with quantities. Of course, that is what mathematics is at the beginning, when the child learns to count with beans. Indeed, primitivism is a striking characteristic of marxism. Philosophic primitivism is matched by economic primitivism, distrust of the artifice of thought by distrust of the artifice of money; there is the desire to return to direct and simple relations, because money and thought are veils and we are liable to find that there is nothing behind the veils: therefore it is best to deal with things direct and not at several removes. In terms of hegelian self-realization, man is conceived as estranged from himself since the days of primitive communism: the work of his own hands becomes an object which itself dominates and absorbs him (the negation which contradicts and destroys him), as the thoughts of his own mind become in religion an object which itself dominates and absorbs him. In capitalism this process of self-estrangement reaches its final phase, for man as a proletarian is himself a commodity and as a capitalist he is able to buy his terms of existence and has no reality of his own. The proletariat is brought to the historical consciousness of this self-estrangement, and the dictatorship of the proletariat by destroying capitalism (the negation of the negation) restores communism and the correspondence of thought with its real object, at a higher level (made possible by the intervening stages of objectivication), and raises man to full self-consciousness and freedom. Man is restored to himself in the consciousness of himself as a worker along with his fellow workers, joint-masters of the means of production and of a common destiny in their social use. Man is literally an economic animal, is estranged from himself in any other image, can only be himself, and, therefore, only know himself, in the literalness of communism. Thus marxism (contrary to promise) gives man a metaphysical essence in place of his historical nature, reduces to one note his chromatic range; its man is censored man, its humanism is puritanism.

There is no reason to doubt that marxism is grappling in earnest with fundamental problems, and that is the reason for taking it seriously at the intellectual level. But drastic remedies may be nearly as bad as the disease; the long-term results are not easy to foresee and may leave the health permanently impaired. There is, therefore, every reason for making quite sure that drastic remedies are called for and are absolutely necessary.

Before pursuing this point to a conclusion, I quote a passage from the recent book of an intelligent Roumanian marxist, Zevedei Barbu, in order to show that I am not fathering upon marxism the repudiated offspring of its irresponsible youth:

'The action of the proletariat is not negative; on the contrary it is constructive in the highest degree. The proletariat builds a new social structure, capable of overcoming all the contradictions which are disclosed in the practical activity of man. The most serious contradiction is that which opposes man to his own practical activity. In suppressing private property, and in instituting collective ownership, the proletariat suppresses the social classes and at the same time the state, inasmuch as it is force opposed to the natural fulfilment of man. In suppressing the social classes the proletariat suppresses itself. We then reach the consummation of the dialectical process, the season of *fruit*. In order to produce a new plant, the fruit rots, and thus appears the seed which carries within it the future plant. In the realization of a new social structure, the proletariat makes the supreme sacrifice: the sacrifice of self.' (*Le Développement de la Pensée Dialectique*.)

VI

The leading theoreticians who moulded the thought and policies of the great social democratic parties of Europe in the generation after Marx, ardent admirers and students of him as they were, as responsible and competent thinkers knew that it was necessary to purge marxism of its bastard idealism. As Bernstein put it: 'What Marx and Engels have done that is great they have done not with the help of Hegel's dialectic, but simply in spite of that dialectic.' Kautsky found more use for the dialectic than Bernstein, but strictly as a method, for formulation and analysis, as a resource of thought not as a process of nature or history. Similarly Max Adler, theoretician of the Austrian marxists, denied metaphysical contradictions in nature and history which could only be overcome by leaps, and recognized only social antagonisms to be resolved by political means. It was Lenin, fighting hard against the 'renegades', 'revisionists', and 'opportunists' of the Second International, who restored the metaphysical content to marxism. 'No one better than

Lenin', says Mr. Barbu, 'has grasped this dialectical view of matter.' It was indeed congenial to him, this endless transformation of things by the principle of contradiction, 'which makes nature a battlefield for opposing forces'. Thus he restored to marxism its fighting edge of intransigence with which to make the revolution and establish the dictatorship of the proletariat, the destined negation of the negation which restores man to himself at a higher level of attainment.

The metaphysics is put back into marxism not because it is true, for it had been cast out by the most able labour leaders in Europe as manifestly untrue, but because it is the court which pronounces the sentence on man which is executed by the dictatorship of the proletariat. It is the pretension of the dictatorship to rational authority. That is why marxists take such a vigilant interest in philosophy and take quick steps to quench any glimmer of intelligence on the question of epistemology, seemingly such an innocent and private affair of the head. They have understood well enough from the first that this small breach is enough to rive the trunk and kill the tree. Thus, before the development of marxism, Théodore Dézamy, a schoolmaster described by Marx as one of the most scientific of the French communists, had understood that 'doctrinal intransigence' was necessary to forge a communist party, that philosophy was not a secondary matter, that the proletariat must be given a line on every question, and that every sign of slipping from the theoretical line established by the proletariat would mean in practice a reformist politic tending to the liquidation of the whole movement. In other words, the proletariat had to be sealed off in mind and body, and society by their means remade in their image. The discovery of the hegelian 'contradiction' in nature and in history admirably served the purposes of such a proletarian philosophy, for if it had not met the need it would have created the mission. Then Proudhon, as the ancestor and type of all those 'sterile' thinkers who dream of tinkering with capitalism and install themselves helplessly in the contradiction instead of making up their minds to surmount it by a violent leap, can be reviled and ridiculed as an unprincipled intellectual squinter.

The sombre splendour of marxist fanaticism has its fascination: it appeals to the puritan in us. It is not an essay in the interpretation of history: it proposes to remake man for all time in the image of a metaphysical essence. There need be no doubt that it can do what it proposes to do. The dictatorship of the proletariat which carries out the metaphysical sentence during 'an entire historical epoch' has power over the inwardness of consciousness. That does not mean that the metaphysical sentence is true, pointing to the fulfilment of man in history, but only that the communist party in power can carry it out. That is why those who recognize clearly how false it is and what the resources are from which it cuts man off must oppose it with all their power as the greatest threat to the true economy of civilization.

Nevertheless, it would be blind and silly to pretend that communism, all error and evil, arises in opposition to an established good. In many parts of the world today, it is, all told, a threat to something considerably better; but its profound challenge is to the deeper level of difficult possibilities for the sake of which alone it is worth resisting. It is a challenge to those who love and want historical man not metaphysical man, humanism not puritanism.

Chapter 8

THE HUMAN ETHOS

MAN is identified with all animals by his instincts; he is distinguished by his body, by his hands. Other animals exercise at a bound in full view the perfection of their species; man's excellence is delayed, uncertain, individual, painfully acquired and pieced together, obscure even in its perfection. The human body is a model of moderation; reserved, withheld from the exotic and the erotic, it stands upright like a leaden soldier, dense, enigmatical, potential, a sign. This body with which the human spirit is formed, which transcends itself in the work of its hands and in the utterance of its mouth, is the ancestral home, and at all times separation from it is the alienation of exile, and the return to it is the restoration of selfhood, breed, tradition, the recovery of health and love. In his body man is joined to his kind and to the continent of all being, and walks out from himself to all encounters. With his body man is the author of works, the architect of a universe. By his hands and by his tongue he makes a world and he makes himself. Random movements and gestures, random cries and articulations, become the alphabet of all techniques. Success by chance is turned into success by principle. Artifice is mixed with nature, discovery with invention. Man's works extend his body into the external world and acquire the human dimension for his animal being.

In his works man makes himself an object to himself, and humanizes the world. By his works man becomes himself or becomes alienated from himself. What is he? He is what he makes himself. He is what he has been, in his way as extravagant and absurd, as exotic and erotic, as amazing amazonian flora and fauna, as bizarre as nameless subaqueous oddities, as impossible as fabulous fabrications in the museums. He is postured fakir or painted brave or coiffured sardanapalus—all that he ever has been or will be without exception. Simplicity, the simplicity of the body, is not primitive; it is natural but not obvious, prime but not prior; it is uncovered; it is uncovered by man's self-discovery in work: simplicity is culture. Doctors, teachers, administrators, technicians, such are the middle key-workers whose teams can raise the condition of a backward people or renew the face of a devastated civilization. These are the representatives of man, the common man, enemy of the pyramid builder, of the sun-king of Versailles, infantile sultans, grandees, and pontiffs, sterile as a mule, whose corrupt imagination alienates man from himself, whose power and prestige cast culture in the mould of the archaic, whose arbitrary will arrests and enslaves man in perpetuation like an animal species.

The work, wrought by hands or by word of mouth, with whatever elaboration and refinement, is always a work of art, of culture, of tradition, sustained and advanced by individual achievement. In his works man contemplates himself and by his works he changes himself; and in his works he contemplates nature, and by them he changes nature. Also, the work, however individual the achievement, is always the work of man. Not only is the work of one also the product of many more than one, it is also the concern of all: it is always man's work. Thus, in the work each man both attains himself and rejoins mankind and the natural world, from which he is separated in self-conscious personal existence. The work is the specifically human consummation. Not every work realizes man. It is not the particular character of the job that authenticates it, for the breeding of a horse, the execution of a deed, the mining of coal, the formulation of a philological sound-law, the scaling of Everest, the dressing of a bar, each in its way, can be a work. The measure of the work is in the polar exchange of life, the life that is in the worker and the life beyond his own: the work is the drawing of him out, the drawing upon him, the entry into him of the life beyond his own, and it is his drawing upon that life and entry into it. And this may be trivial or playful or casual or everyday or titanic.

The body is human not only in the work of the hands and the utterance of the mouth by which it transcends itself, but also in man's awareness of it. In the body he is separated from and joined to his fellows, separated from and joined to nature: in this awareness of his body he is aware of himself, the awareness that may be the error of Narcissus and may be the pilgrim's ascent to the total self-awareness of man that is the end of scientific and humanistic studies. The body is in itself human and personal, but to separate it from its works is to pose man's being as a problem: I transcend my body. The body apart from its works is an abstraction. The self which cannot be identified with the body is identified with it in its works by which it transcends itself. That is a fate which man wishes to refuse. The body is in itself human and personal as soon as man is able in reflection to separate himself from his works. It becomes then the point of retreat and the starting-point, the home. This awareness of the body is the beginning of human existence; this love for it is the beginning of all seriousness.

The body falls to disease, decays; it is abused, debauched; it is neglected, treated with contempt; it is pampered, idolized. Work becomes routine, drudgery, exploitation. Body and work are symbols of man's servitude and degradation. From both he craves release. Good is the occasion of evil; vital human interests are menaced by betrayal. Release is the last recourse of bitter irredeemable failure. The dangers which beset body and work set the human task, the ceaseless task of conservation, development, utilization, enjoyment. Heroism is sometimes required, for instance in resistance to exploitation, or even to raise the head from drudgery. And there is work, physical and mental toil and danger, for which only heroes are fit, Titans. And there are enterprises which seem to fail and on which everything seems to hang, until nothing is left save

to hope till Hope creates
From its own wreck the thing it contemplates.

But in nursing the sacred source of all human life in the body each has it ever alone in his own daily hands that work is a brave thing and that monotony of work does not become monotony of life.

The ethos of human life, then, is affirmation, striving, becoming, upsurge and attainment, springing from the body and manifested in the work of the hands and the utterance of the mouth. Also it is repose, at the level of established order; then it is quietude and a virgilian sweetness. The tongue itself speaks both languages, the body has the habit of activity and of repose, can stretch and relax, and can acquire competence and grace in the one and dignity and collection in the other.

There is room on the earth for all temperaments and for all types:

there are forbidden places, inaccessible peaks and abysses, and there are the domestic provinces; there are cities and villages diverse and innumerable; there are seasons and climates, there is the past and the future; there is much much else, far far more than any human being can entertain or enter into. Life is excess.

PART TWO

PART TWO

Chapter 9

THE CHRISTIAN TRADITION

I

IN one of his essays, Baron von Hügel recalls a conversation with a charming young lutheran theological student as they stood together on the Malvern Hills looking down on the priory church. The Baron is gently regretful that the Dissolution of the Monasteries should have been at all deserved, and finds in the young lutheran no sympathy with such feelings, since for him religion has nothing to do with anything but mind and doctrine, it is nothing else but acknowledgement of sin and faith in the redemptive work of Christ. '. . . my one mind abstracted from other minds, and driven in upon its own state with regard to one single issue: my friend found this entrancingly simple, spiritual, northern, modern; and I found it inassimilably thin, abstract, doctrinaire, inhuman, driving me into endless self-occupation and scruples instead of unto God, our liberty and home.' He adds: 'After all, I had already found up on Alpine heights, some thirty years before, that pure glacier water cannot be retained by the human body—at least, not by my own.' (*Essays and Addresses*, II, pp. 97–9.)

The difference between protestant and catholic exemplified in this incident is of course historical and traditional before it is personal and temperamental. These two voices in their two languages spoke for Christianity even before the Reformation, and they echo two voices which spoke in simpler terms for Israel before Christianity existed: the voice of the prophet and the voice of the priest, of the desert and of the city.

Hegel characteristically seized on Abraham as the prototype of Israel, a man who separated himself from his kin and tore himself free from all the dear intimate ties which bound him to his fellows and to nature and, implicitly, to God. He separated himself from life, became a stranger and a wanderer on the face of the earth, and this disruption of the one spontaneous life brought into existence a consciousness of the self as autonomous, of the world as objective, and of God as 'wholly other', infinite and inaccessible. Abraham formally healed this broken unity by choosing for himself and his people the destiny of obedience to God for the objective goods of the world. From this utter dependence on a unique, jealous, and holy God, derive both Jewish literalism and priestly servitude and the prophetic interpretations weaning the people of corn and wine and empire. The prophetic interpretations reach a consummation in Jesus who reveals the unique God, the infinite 'wholly other', as a loving Father who requires only love of his children. This restores the immediacy of love and the unity of the finite and the infinite, but takes it out of the world, out of history; religion becomes a relation between the soul and God, the Christian loses interest in the state and the objective goods of this world. This for Hegel is at best an anticipation of the final historical reconciliation of the finite and the infinite, in both of which the human spirit participates and be-tween which it is torn in the tension of reflection and in the long historical separation which embodies the phase of reflection. It is this reflective separation and its doctrinal healing, individually appro-priated and realized, which is reproduced and represented in the young lutheran friend of Baron von Hügel. Over against this line of development initiated by a drastic separation, Hegel conceived the classical city community with its undivided participation in the finite and the infinite, rationalized and idealized in Plato's Republic. Nevertheless, the personal autonomy, man's individual conscious-ness of himself in his universality beyond his social relations in time and place, is lacking in the city state and in the Republic. It is Christianity which makes historically indefeasible the claim to per-sonal autonomy, liberty of conscience over against church and state, and this work of Christianity is reinforced in such historical move-ments as protestantism and liberalism and in rationalist philosophies (kantian ethics). At the same time, the claim of the state, and of the church in its identification with the state, is no less indefeasible, as the principle of the unity of the universal and the particular, the infinite and the finite. It is the task of history to effect the reconcilia-tion of these two principles without doing violence to either, through the concrete development of each and in the cultural process by which the individual becomes conscious of the meaning and the claims of both. Then, with the historical elaboration of institutions and the working out of national destinies, men would become conscious of the destiny of man and enabled to achieve the union of man with man and with nature and the infinite.

In this philosophy of history, Hegel sought to establish a total human tradition in which everything found a place, in which religion was taken seriously, and in which the necessary and leading role of Christianity was recognized. From a Christian point of view this was inadmissible, since it included Christianity in the whole and did not subordinate the whole to Christianity. For Hegel, the history of the world is the judgement of the world. For the Christian, the world is under judgement and only individual souls may be saved: it is not the business of Christianity to be serviceable to civilization, for it has the authority to call on civilization to be serviceable to the Christian mission. Kierkegaard emphatically rejected Hegel's version and vision of Christianity and history. In his own vision, Christianity maintained itself only by resistance to assimilation, by persistently unravelling its own tradition, by insistence on its separation from culture, by continuing without alternative to isolate each individual life and to compel a personal choice in the face of its challenge and its claim. True, this alone, in the modern world as in history, saved the individual from nonentity, from merger in the mass; but Christianity had the power to do this only in so far as it was and remained a living faith, a supreme and exhaustive personal decision, a consummation which placed and kept the whole content of history under the seal of the Incarnation. In the perspective of Kierkegaard's vision of Christianity, the predominant role accorded to it by Hegel had no more importance than the obscurest footnote; evaluated objectively from outside and not accepted from within as the standard of all measurement, historical Christianity was a trail of embers. From these divergent points of view, humanist and Christian cannot begin to discuss historical Christianity; they speak different languages about different things. Christianity is in the world to make Christians, and no other effects upon the world are relevant.

This is the judgement of Arnold Toynbee, for instance. The most erudite and the most imaginative and speculative of historians, he willingly entertains all possibilities. Christianity will not necessarily prevail. Souls may be saved outside the Christian faith, but there is no human interest other than the salvation of the soul, and for this purpose the Christian revelation and the Christian church furnish incomparably the best historical means. The earth is a province of the Kingdom of God, to be lost or won. The establishment of the Kingdom entails a society of free, equal, and brotherly persons, but this is a by-product of Christian salvation and cannot be attained by a direct aim. Professor Butterfield also speaks of these ideals as mundane by-products of Christianity in the context of a very advanced state of society; adopted as secular ideals, they are severed from their Christian roots and perish, destroyed by the means used to attain them. The Kingdom of God, however, although it may be established on earth as a Christian dispensation, can never be established here fully and finally as a realized ideal, because the conditions of earthly life can never be fully assimilated to the Christian ideal. In one of his speculative flights, Professor Toynbee thinks that the Christian church, which has proved so tough an institution, may outlast the nation states and the other higher religions and come to inherit the earth. In that event, it will still have to rely on a secular power, as in the middle ages, or exert a like discipline in its own name since unredeemed human nature is not likely to alter, and the work of redemption in the salvation of any one soul is more like a natural process than a miracle. The great advantage in such an event would be the multiplied means and opportunities for the work of individual redemption to go on. Professor Toynbee in this context quotes St. Augustine as having said the last word on this matter:

'It is written of Cain that he founded a commonwealth; but Abel —true to the type of the pilgrim and sojourner that he was—did not do the like. For the Commonwealth of the Saints is not of this world, though it does give birth to citizens here in whose persons it performs its pilgrimage until the time of its kingdom shall come—the time when it will gather them all together.' (*De Civitate Dei*, Book xv, Ch. I.)

Yet no one speaks more firmly than St. Augustine of the hierarchical sacramental institution of the church as the one ordained administration of the divine dispensation. In him the ambiguity of the Christian mission is already evident, and he is the father of both catholicism and protestantism. Professor Butterfield speaks of the medieval ascendancy and temporal privilege of the church as the product of very special circumstances not likely to be repeated, and as wholly unsuitable to an advanced state of society. It is only one among many possible forms of interplay between religion and human systems. 'Modern man is wrong if he looks back upon it with resentment, but the modern Christian is presumptuous if he demands anything like its restoration as though it were a thing that believers had a right to claim from the world. Perhaps it is not repeatable except after a catastrophe that should have overwhelmed modern civilization altogether.' (*Christianity in European History*, p. 19.) It is such a catastrophe Professor Toynbee thinks the church might be fit to survive.

Medieval Christendom, 'one among many possible forms of interplay between religion and human systems', is indeed a very special case. Nothing in history is more fascinating and instructive than the long and intricate story of the forming of Europe by the Christian church. The early Christian churches, independent communities with their humble members and their missionary gospel and eschatology in an alien and hostile world, were not much interested nor much involved in secular society. After the adoption of the faith by the emperor, so long as the empire survived in the West, the leaders of the churches were forced to take on new responsibilities and to take advantage of new opportunities and became a clerical caste. It was the one Christian church that was in the making, but it was a church within an empire, built up by its means, relying on its conveniences, assimilating its culture, sheltered by its structure, accepting it, supporting it, criticizing it, aloof from it, idealizing it. By the time Christianity was adopted by Constantine the civil administration of the empire had been separated from military functions. The church had no direct part in the administration but became increasingly associated with it in the development of ecclesiastical administration and in the difficulties brought about by the barbarian invasions and social disorder. By the sixth century, the military organization of the empire in the West was in the hands of the barbarian leaders and the civil administration in the hands of the bishops. The church had no specifically Christian system of society; it was the Roman system the bishops adapted to new needs and new problems. The Bishop of Rome turned from the emperor at Constantinople to the barbarian kings as allies in the work of christianizing the new nations; and Latin Christianity, with its practical concern for unity and order, excluded the sophisticated Greek church with its passion for dialectical subtlety, and concentrated on the administrative and missionary problems of the new

Europe. There was no longer one church within one empire; each of the new barbarian kingdoms lay within the church. This ascendancy of the church within the new society, with direct responsibility for administration as well as for preaching the gospel, so that in some sense society lay within the church and not the church within society, was a source of corruption as well as advantage, and issued in the protestant Reformation.

In spite of the idealization of Christendom in the high middle ages, and the irrevocable claims of the Roman Catholic Church to this day, it was only 'one among many possible forms of interplay between religion and human systems'. Christianity carried on the Roman tradition, the church even romanized its own organization, until a new secular civilization emerged at the end of the seventeenth century, and looked back with recognition to the Graeco-Roman world. This does not necessarily make of Christianity 'the egg, grub, and chrysalis between butterfly and butterfly', another of the possible forms of interplay between religion and human systems. Even if the Christian system of the middle ages does not last and is destroyed by a new secular civilization, the Christian mission survives, and is indeed set free, Christianity as the highest of the higher religions, and enables Toynbee to make his thesis that the higher religions are ends not means, the supreme ends of history, superior to the civilizations whose encounters they survive; so that our contemporary Western civilization is 'an almost meaningless repetition of something that the Greeks and Romans did before us and did supremely well'; and if it perishes, 'Christianity may be expected not only to endure but to grow in wisdom and stature as the result of a fresh experience of secular catastrophe'. On this view, civilizations are to be judged by their service to the Christian mission, and they may serve it best by coming to grief and teaching men through suffering the spiritual truth. 'Does a shift of human interest and energy from trying to create the values aimed at in the civilizations to trying to create the values aimed at in the higher religions mean that the values for which the civilizations stand are bound to suffer? . . . Is it true that the fabric of civilization is undermined if the salvation of the individual soul is taken as the supreme aim of life?' Professor Toynbee asks these questions because he is well aware of the humanist's criticism of his view. His answer is triumphant. When Christians make it their highest purpose to make themselves and others Christians, to save souls, they are embarked upon a social task;

they seek fellowship with God and to make themselves like God, and they seek to bring others, and all, into that fellowship and likeness: they are thus creating the good society. The establishment of the best possible human society in this world, if that is the aim of civilization, is not the Christian aim, but it is an almost certain by-product of the Christian aim, and to aim at it directly is to miss it altogether. Professor Butterfield says the same thing: the seculariza-tion of Christian ideals dooms them; a Christian civilization is not necessarily a society in which the church is dominant, for it can be nothing other than a civilization created by Christians. There is no historically achieved and no ready-made Christian civilization, but the gospel in any social context may be the source of a Christian civilization producing distinctively Christian things. 'Above all, throughout our history it has been of the first importance that our church has not merely launched or inspired great human enterprises . . . but, by being here, the church stands as a perpetual centre from which the whole process can be for ever starting over again. Those who preach the gospel . . . are guarding the very fountain, dealing with the problems of civilization at its very source, and keeping open the spring from which new things will still arise. . . . The continually renascent power of our religion seems to consist in this unlimited opportunity to return to the original spring, the original simplicities of the faith.' In this view, history is perpetually renewed in the preaching of the gospel, as in Croce's view history is perpetually renewed in the demand for liberty.[1]

The idea that history is perpetually renewed in the preaching of the gospel is a protestant idea. But that is too crude a statement of it for contemporary sophistication. We must turn from eminent Christian historians to a theologian, a Christian philosopher, to Professor Paul Tillich. He has attempted to analyse the protestant tradition and to reaffirm the protestant principle.

The problem can be stated objectively, as the problem of the rela-tion of religion to culture, how to preach the gospel, or it can be stated subjectively, as the problem of my relation to the infinite, how to gain grace. This problem does not exist for the Catholic

[1] 'There is no philosophy of history in the sense of a predetermined plan or of a hegelian dialectic, but there is an ever-developing, ever-renewed pattern grouped about the central, eternal truth of liberty as a moral ideal and a moral need, never to be finally forgotten or suppressed, never satisfied with less than its real personal force and liberating quality.' (*History of Europe in the Nineteenth Century*.)

Church which alone has an unbroken and massive tradition and authority, which has wrought for itself a religious culture out of assimilated elements of its Graeco-Roman inheritance, and which claims a unique office and power of mediation between God and man. The Catholic Church remains virtually unchangeable and universal at the price of being archaic; its historical achievement was in the early and high middle ages, when it was forming itself and its people in living touch with the culture of the time, establishing personality and community in their interdependence with one another and with the universal divine life. 'Although personality and community were guaranteed in this period, they were not really developed.' The claim to autonomy which broke up the medieval synthesis and has been the mainspring of the modern movements was necessary. Nevertheless, Christendom remains in some sense a model of historical achievement in the relations of religion and culture, and the present Catholic Church with its fossilized religious culture remains fascinating to nostalgic longings for a lost simpler and happier youth, as well as attractive to those who feel the responsibilities and anxieties of autonomy, and the weary weight of all this unintelligible world.

The protestant break with catholic Christianity was not the claim of the individual to autonomy, to be his own authority and his own priest; it was, rather, a rediscovery of the invincible uncertainty of the whole matter: he found the bottom of the human situation to be his helpless ignorance and impotence in relation to the infinite, his inadequacy as measured by his sense of his need of the infinite and his sense of its demands of him, and, at the same time, he knew his own inescapable responsibility for facing this situation and taking it upon himself without evasion and for making himself open to and dependent upon the infinite, unconditionally. This was the ground of the protestant protest against the catholic claim to guarantee divine grace and personal salvation, to channel and limit by prescriptive right the divine operations, and to separate and label the holy. This was the meaning of the high debate about justification by faith which rent Europe and turned the course of history, was passionately discussed by every mouth, and today is unintelligible even to the intelligent, 'a breaking-down of tradition that has few parallels'.

This break in the protestant tradition, so that its capital doctrine has become unintelligible to modern man, exemplifies and emphasizes the interdependence and independence of religion and culture.

The doctrine has to go, has gone; but its religious meaning was never more valid and vital, relevant to the needs of contemporary man. But it is the protestant mission to free religion from all the irrelevant transitory elements of religious cultural tradition: thomistic philosophy, but also the protestant ideal of personality (manifest in von Hügel's young lutheran friend); Greek theological concepts and the feudal pattern of the Roman hierarchy, but also even the cultural traditions embodied in the Biblical language and world view. It is the protestant mission to free itself from the prison of its own orthodoxy and to purify the gospel from the traditional accretions gathered in its relations with former cultures and times, so that its permanent truth and perpetual relevance are recovered and made good in new relations with contemporary culture.

It is not to my present purpose to follow Professor Tillich in his development of the protestant mission in the modern world. It is enough to say that he relies little on the religious cultural tradition and much on sensitive adherence to the permanent human situation, dependence on the infinite without circumscription, and insight into the strength and the weakness of contemporary secular movements. Merely to preach the gospel is to fail in the contemporary mission, it is to deliver a report about grace which the secular world will not receive. On the other hand, within the secular movements that are shaping the modern world, religious thinking and acting can bring into conscious expression their hidden meaning and ultimate aim, that is, bring them into relation with grace and awaken men to their need of it. He sums up this relation of religion and culture in two sentences. 'Culture is not subjected to religion, nor is religion dissolved in culture.' 'Religion is the substance of culture and culture the form of religion.' His verdict is this. 'Either the protestant churches will be reduced to insignificance between catholicism and secularism, or they will prevail against both of them, in the power of the protestant principle and of the reality to which it witnesses. Either protestantism will become a sect, isolated from the main trend of history, or it will become the starting-point of a new embodiment of the spirit of Christianity in which a demonic sacramentalism and an empty secularism are overcome.' (*The Protestant Era*, p. 221.)

The sense of dependence upon the natural order and upon culture for the efficacy of revelation and of grace has been of course much stronger in the catholic tradition. The constant theme of Thomas Aquinas is that 'nature is the preface to grace'.

'Nature is to blessedness as first to second. Blessedness is grounded on nature. The groundwork is safeguarded in the achievement, and therefore nature is preserved in blessedness, likewise the activity of nature in the act of bliss.' (*Summa Theologica*, 1a, lxii, 7.)

'The divine rights of grace do not abolish the human rights of natural reason.' (*Summa Theologica*, 2a–2ae, x, 10.)

'Grace does not destroy nature but completes it. Hence the natural reason subserves faith as the natural desire of will is the undercurrent of charity.' (*Summa Theologica*, 1a, i, 8.)

It is this pervasive doctrine which the heart of thomism pumps through the whole system, that 'faith presupposes natural knowledge, as grace presupposes nature, and perfection the capacity for it'. Von Hügel continually stresses it, both in appreciative references to St. Thomas and in his own statements. '. . . there is no such thing as an exclusively spiritual awakening to, or apprehension of, spiritual realities. This, to my mind, is already decisive against all purely spiritual, entirely mystical, quite non-historical, quite non-successive religion.' The work of Gabriel Marcel is informed and impelled by the conviction that there can be no recovery of a Christian life irradiated by grace and sustained by hope unless there is first a restoration of the vital bond, the happy nuptial tie, which unites man to his natural existence on earth. It is in following through natural experiences rooted in the body, the affections, creative interests, the reflective operations of the intelligence, that our responsiveness to the world and participation in it unfolds the divine implications in our natural existence, required to complete it, a divine aid which should be invoked with a confidence engendered in the natural order, not with a despair bred by rejection of the natural order.

'Everything leads us to think that the giving way of religious beliefs which has been going on for five centuries in large sections of the civilized world has brought as its consequence a weakening of the natural foundations on which those beliefs were built. If this be so it means that what we need to reawaken within and around us is this piety, not Christian but pre-Christian, or more exactly peri-Christian. Each one of us probably knows Christians who are over super-naturalized and who have lost the sense, we will not say of nature but of the nascent grace which stirs at the heart of nature. I am strongly inclined to think that, apart from Revelation, this piety is the only true *vinculum* which can bind men together, and that all abstract universalism which claims to do without it, however up-right its intention, really serves only to prepare the way for a nihilism whose devastating action we can discern on all sides.' (*Homo Viator*, pp. 161-2.)

M. Maritain, above suspicion in his respect for and loyalty to his church, founds his vision of a new Christendom on acceptance of and respect for the autonomous culture developed since the break-up of the old Christendom, which can never be restored on the old terms. In the new Christendom, the temporal order is not merely a means to the supernatural ends of the spiritual order; as Christian, it is concerned to facilitate and further the mission of the spiritual order, but in its own way and with respect for liberty of conscience. The temporal field is the plane of action of Christians not of Christians *as such*, instruments or agents of the church.

Dr. H. D. A. Major, a scientist before he was a theologian, speak-ing for Christian modernists, says that the future of Christianity (and of mankind) is bound up with the attempt to win both traditionalist Christians and scientific humanists to acceptance of the gospel of the Kingdom of God as the essence of the Christian religion, so that Christianity may prevail in the West and thereby in the world. By the Kingdom of God he means 'the humanization of man in society' (Arnold) through the power of the immanent and transcen-dent God revealed in Christ. The gospel is the leaven which leavens the whole lump, and works in the world secretly but with visible results.

Finally, and in sum, a quotation from the mission field. '... tension is inescapable in a church which is in the paradoxical position of living in two worlds at once. It must make terms with this un-redeemed world in which it lives; yet it must never be satisfied with those terms.'

II

The clue through all the complications of the Christian tradition is the essential character of the Christian mission, which is to adapt natural human existence to the requirements of a divine order and a supernatural end, whether it is done joyfully without tears by adoption of the sons of men as children of God enjoined to love one another and be like their heavenly Father, or by a painful pilgrim's progress through conviction of sin, repentance, and sanctification by obtaining the atonement provided by the blood of the Lamb; whether justification be by faith or works or obedience to the church. The preliminary question is whether there is any difference in the message, the pure gospel, or only in the ways in which it is presented and brought home to the conscience in different times and different places. The long list of historical heresies, the bitter and endless theological disputes, bloody and endless religious wars, the multiplication of sects, these characteristic features of the history of Christianity seem to make a mockery of the one universal indisputable gospel. The many and great differences may be stressed, and the universal substance disappears; or the total events may be thrown into a long perspective with a bold accent on the universal substance: the two pictures are in violent contrast. It is pointless to ask which is the true picture. Theologians, especially Greek intellects, restlessly press their questions and drag everybody into labyrinthine subtleties. Administrators, especially Latin minds, require faithfulness to a defined truth and loyalty to an established order. Both are justified, and, temperament apart, both preoccupations are inevitable in the historical circumstances. The Greek Church was fully established in a theocratic state; the Latin Church had to deal with new barbarian nations brought into the fold by mass conversions. A parallel difference remains between the nature and needs of ordinary Christians in an established Christian community and the nature and needs, intellectual and moral, of those 'twice-born' souls who lay hold of the Christian teaching to enable them to heal the trauma of their broken condition, those who have fallen into the abyss of the human situation. This is only one sort of difference, underlying the wide range of cultural differences, amongst the many which tend to obscure the simplicity and unity of the original gospel—if simplicity and unity there be.

There are plenty of questions to make difficulties. Does the church derive its commission from the New Testament documents, or are these documents the expression of the faith of the church, the witness to, not the source of, the experience on which the faith is founded? What type of order in the world realizes the divine order and has divine sanction? There have been many types of social order in Christian history, each claiming special validity. All the many questions which may be raised make room for disagreement and difference. The unity and simplicity of the gospel seem to disappear when it is looked for beyond the bewildering variety of interpretations and applications. There was point in old Hobbes's sardonic remark: 'it is with the mysteries of our religion, as with wholesome pills for the sick; which swallowed whole, have the virtue to cure; but chewed, are for the most part cast up again without effect'. But although there is no possible statement of the Christian gospel which will not sooner or later disclose ambiguities, raise questions, start arguments, and promote differences, that does not discredit it, that only means that in this respect at least it is not unique amongst doctrines on earth: in entering into human discourse it shares the mortal weaknesses of that mode of existence. There may be a common gospel at work in the varied phenomena of Christian history, nevertheless. At least, Christian history is made by the perpetually renewed effort to rediscover the gospel and apply it more effectively.

Assume, then, a common original gospel as the source of the main streams of the Christian tradition, without asking what it is, and look at the ways in which it is applied, its relations with culture and how it works with and on culture.

The early centuries of the Christian era are dominated by the Roman Church, and its achievement to this day remains for Christians both a model and a provocation. It is tempting for the outsider to say with the Roman Catholic that in origin and history the Roman Church is the Christian tradition, the rest is aberration, heresy, and schism. This will not do, however, for many reasons. The coming of age of the Western societies, the demand for autonomy, can be labelled as sin, but protestantism is also the historical development of certain Christian principles obscured by the imperium of the Roman Church. For the very ascendancy of the church in the new Europe, the unparalleled opportunity of the church to make a Christian civilization, identified Christianity with its own creation; the power of assimilation which the church developed, its adoption and adaptation of what was alien to itself, its omnipresence in every field of interest and activity, giving the rules and regulations and providing the interpretations, this power was not wholly and solely informed by Christian purpose and furnished with Christian means, for in making the Christian tradition the church was carrying on the tradition of Rome. Especially, it was on unity of faith and order that the leaders of the church insisted, a unity cast in the mould of the Roman imperium and stamped with the universality and majesty of Roman law. Natural law which was the ideal pattern of positive law was in the Roman tradition. Catholic theology was less philosophic thinking than papal legislation, in the earlier formative stage. Christian moral teaching was at first not a critique of society nor an ideal of civilization but an appeal to the piety and sobriety and charity of men in all walks and relations of life, and later an idealization of the *status quo* in terms of the rights and duties attaching to station in society. The church which had educated, regulated, and moralized the new nations developed a vested interest in an order of society stabilized under a law and a regime deemed worthy to last until kingdom come. On Christian premises the rebellious heart of man might not gain any great good for itself by breaking out of the bonds of ecclesiastical discipline and pursuing its own courses at its own peril. But also on Christian premises such a church was itself in danger; apart altogether from notable corruptions and fallings away and shortcomings, the saving Christian truth was too much identified with the declared means of salvation and the total embodiment of the church in society; the claims of the church laid it wide open to the retort of the gospel: that 'the wind bloweth where it listeth', that grace might be found with the despised and rejected. The Christian message that there was no strength but in weakness, no hope on this side of despair, that no divine commission could relieve one of the perpetual need to make oneself as nothing to be raised up by grace, that justification is by faith alone, this message could be used against the church even more unanswerably than against the world. Whenever this message is heard again it entails withdrawal from established relations with the world and new initiatives for the sake of the gospel. As Professor Tillich insists, protestantism is as opposed to its own orthodoxy as to Rome; it is the perpetually necessary detachment of the gospel from the mission, of faith from works. Rome, the majestically successful mission, has to be dissolved for the sake of the mission.

But the church that is too mindful of the gospel in its own case may perish before its work is done. Professor Tillich thinks that the protestant churches may perish because they are not mindful enough of the true conditions and the profound meaning of their mission. Professor Toynbee has a different view. In a passage in which he examines the catholic form of the church, in which he sees 'two fundamental institutions, the Sacrifice of the Mass and the Hierarchy, which are indissolubly welded together by the fact that the priest, by definition, is the person with the power to perform the rite', he traces the Mass to rudimentary fertility rites and the hierarchy to the imperial civil service, and he goes on to say this:

'The church in its traditional form thus stands forth armed with the spear of the Mass, the shield of the Hierarchy, and the helmet of the papacy; and perhaps the subconscious purpose—or the divine intention, if you prefer that language—of this heavy panoply of institutions in which the church has clad herself is the very practical one of outlasting the toughest of the secular institutions of this world, including all the civilizations. If we survey all the institutions of which we have knowledge in the present and in the past, I think that the institutions created, or adopted and adapted, by Christianity are the toughest and the most enduring of any that we know and are therefore the most likely to last—and outlast all the rest. The history of protestantism would seem to indicate that the protestant act of casting off this armour four hundred years ago was premature; but that would not necessarily mean that this step would always be a mistake; and, however that may be, the institutional element in the traditional catholic form of the Church Militant on Earth, even if it proves to be an invaluable and indispensable means of survival, is all the same a mundane feature which makes the Church Militant's life different from that of the Kingdom of Heaven. . . .' (*Civilization on Trial*, pp. 242–3.)

There is a difference between these two Christians, but it is a subtle one. The difference in their judgement of the expediency of retaining or abandoning catholic institutions is not important in this connection. The important, and subtle, difference is in their conceptions of the relation between Christianity and culture. For Professor Toynbee, civilization is a means to Christianity and at the same time civilization is a by-product of Christianity. The more the soul is freed of civilization and becomes entirely preoccupied with its relationship to God and its life in the divine fellowship and is active in bringing it about on earth, the more Christian it is and the further advanced on its pilgrimage of salvation. This is exactly Professor Tillich's view. The difference is that Professor Toynbee thinks of Christian salvation as the destiny of each individual soul, and thinks of the social heritage as able to provide, mainly through Christian institutions, increasingly available means of grace to aid each soul in its pilgrimage; whereas Professor Tillich, and (I take it) Professor Butterfield, think of the autonomous development of secular culture as providing the conditions of a higher realization of Christian personality and Christian community. Thus, although they are at one with him in looking only for Christian ends and Christian values, they would not be so likely to follow him in the appalling folly of supposing that secular catastrophe could produce spiritual gain. But this difference, real and important though it is, should not mislead the humanist into thinking that other Christians, unlike Toynbee, do value civilization and secular culture for the sake of human existence and not merely for the sake of Christian salvation, as the means of grace. They are crude and subtle versions of the same doctrine, that is all.

Toynbee quotes from Gibbon and Frazer the characteristic humanist view that Christianity has been the destroyer of civilization, sapping the civic virtues on which it is founded, and devotes an essay to its refutation, stating the contrary thesis, that civilizations have collapsed from their own inherent defects and that Christian devotion to the making of Christians and the salvation of the soul is the salt which preserves civilization, is the only motivation capable of creating and sustaining a brotherly community that will endure, and that to aim at this directly is to destroy it inevitably by the means employed to attain it. He states, also to refute it, the alternative humanist thesis that Christianity has proved serviceable to civilization in a time of social breakdown by fortifying the will to live and by carrying on the tradition of civilization.

Both these humanist theses crudely stated are easily shown to be blind and wilful misrepresentations. Adequately stated, both are, and will remain, final and unanswerable judgements of the Christian tradition from the humanist point of view.

III

Whether the Christian faith is justified or not, and whether the heaviest items are showed as paid out to Christianity or as paid in by Christianity, there have been substantial Christian contributions to civilization. It was as Romans rather than as Christians that the Latin bishops carried on the Roman tradition of law and administration and educated the barbarian nations of the new Europe, but the establishment of Christendom was a distinctive contribution of the church. On the other hand, it was as Christians rather than as social reformers that most of the protestant sectaries, especially in England, carried on their agitations, but in so doing they contributed to liberalism and democracy and even to science; and the infusion of Christian sentiment, principle, and belief into liberal programmes helped to establish a solidarity of social tradition in England since the end of the seventeenth century which has been in strong contrast with the split national traditions on the Continent, where Christianity has seemed to be identified with reactionary causes. There are substantial Christian credits in humanitarian service in the mission fields and at home, through hospitals, schools, and colleges, and in the denunciation and mitigation of cruelties and oppressions. There is the specifically religious culture (in music and architecture, for example) which was bequeathed to humanity by the Christianity of Christendom. All this, and the like, although it is specifically Christian, the humanist may value as human.

On his part, too, the Christian may value specifically humanist contributions as needful to Christianity. 'Christian humanism', says M. Maritain, '. . . is able to accept all, since it knows that God has no opposite, and that all is borne on irresistibly by the tide of his providence. It does not reject what springs from heresies and schisms in its human heritage, the works of the heart or of the reason gone astray. . . . It knows that these historical forces energized by error have served the work of God despite themselves, and that in their own despite throughout the whole modern period they have felt the surge not only of illusory, but also of Christian energies in this temporal life. In the scheme of Christian humanism there is a place, not for the errors of Luther or Voltaire, but for Luther and Voltaire to the extent to which, in despite of themselves, they contributed to human history a certain increase and growth (which belong to Christ, as does all the good we know). . . . But in the scheme of Marx's humanism there is no place for St. Augustine or St. Theresa of Avila.'

Any mature scheme of humanism must find room for the Christian contribution, just as a percipient Christian will not fail to see the humanist contribution to the Christian tradition. Of course this common ground is no basis for reconciliation; they contribute to each other 'in despite of themselves'. A humanist must look at the Christian tradition in this way, from his own point of view. But unless he also tries to see it through Christian eyes he is not able to evaluate the Christian tradition even from his own point of view, because he is looking only at the residual embers in the path of the *élan vital* instead of trying to discern its probable course. The relics of Christendom, even actual cathedrals and liturgies, are materials for the antiquary and the connoisseur. The Christianity that is and will be active in history, purged of its archaic products and by-products, has to be discerned with other eyes.

From a Christian point of view, the Christian tradition is a clarification of the gospel and the Christian mission. Christianity is at first equivocal, doubtful, in its relations with the human order in the world; with the creation of Christendom, it becomes univocal; emancipated by the development of modern autonomous culture, it is ready to become multivocal (Maritain says *analogical*, following Aquinas), related in more ways than one and not all of them traditional and expected. A Christianity learning from its past and purging itself of archaism and freeing itself from a perishing and perishable order may not wish any longer to insist with protestantism on man's consciousness of separation from God, nor with catholicism on man's union with God in and through the church, but may think itself able to unite modern man in all the dimensions of his being with God in and through the autonomous culture which has alienated him from God. This seems to be the Christian project both of the catholic Maritain and of the protestant Tillich. Differences remain, and both these Christians are far from dispensing with the church of their adherence, and both are unshakably founded on their faith in the truth of the Incarnation, but each of these two thinkers from his own standpoint has a Christian project which is inseparably Christian and humanist and free from the weakness of earlier Christian modernism, and both seem to converge on the same historical goal.

Whatever fortune may attend the systems of thought of these two Christians, there are influences which do favour a bold Christian bid of this kind. Christianity need no longer be on the defensive against science nor in opposition to social reform, nor excessively dependent on distinctively Christian institutions and traditions. The severe losses which Christianity has suffered in the Europe which it brought into existence have served to release the essential universality of the Christian gospel by setting it free from too close an association with certain social classes and with ecclesiastical peculiarities. This universality has been helped also, as Professor Latourette has shown, by the expansion of Christianity in the mission fields during the past hundred and fifty years when no other historical religion was vital enough to gain converts abroad, and by the returning contribution from these mission fields to the oecumenical movement.

It would be rash, then, to conclude that Christianity is an exploded fallacy which can no longer be active to any purpose in history. The resounding blows and severe losses are obvious; the strength is secret. It is the strength of an historical religion, not the strength of an impregnable doctrine. In the evolution of a natural or cultural religion, there is a tendency towards agnosticism, and finally the infinite is properly recognized as unconditioned and inconceivable, definable only by negatives. Christianity announces with Paul, 'Whom you ignorantly worship, him I declare unto you'. The declaration is a declaration of historical acts and of divinely appointed persons and institutions. Even so, the divine cannot be imprisoned in any historical manifestations, past or present. There is a Christian, prophetic, protestant form of agnosticism, which turns away from all extant manifestations to the unknown and unknowable God, but which depends on those manifestations as the ground of trust in and the justification of waiting on that God for new initiatives bearing new witness to his inexhaustible concern for human souls and issues. A God that has ceased to be active in history, that is only an unknowable infinite or only the god of an established cult, is not the Christian God. The *élan vital* of the Christian mission depends on the continued self-revelation of the living God of Christian faith. The Christian tradition founds and supports this faith with its witness, endangers it by its claims and its temporal success, rescues it by reflection upon the trials and tribulations which shatter that success.

Suppose that Christianity should throw off archaism and prepare itself for a new historical project that would be both Christian and humanist, is not the gospel itself archaic? Is Christianity not the defeatism of a primitive and helpless civilization? Such a gospel for the hopeless is always good news to the race of men, amongst whom disillusionment is endemic in their hours of fatigue, failure, frustration, and reflection. The reasons which made it succeed in the Roman world may serve another turn. Mortals are not in a hurry to put themselves beyond reach of the temptation to accept the offer of a chance to hope against hope. Nothing can be archaic that remains always relevant. Moreover, from the point of view of a strenuous missionary humanism the Christian gospel may be more acceptable than the enervating influence of a parasitical humanism, which feels the vanity of life and enjoys with tender melancholy (or with any other emotion) the spectacle of the triumph of time. The literary spell of a Santayana may put an enchantment on the world, but it is a world in which the imagination is divorced from the will and does not breed a future. Such a humanism, not less than Christianity, saps the civic virtues and destroys civilization. Whereas, Christian humanism does offer a homoeopathic treatment of natural despair, telling men that they never can establish truth and justice on earth in order to show them how they may, condemning humanism in order to save it. As Jaspers says: 'We have no more confidence in humanism. But we love it and we wish to do everything to preserve it.'

The humanist, perhaps, ought to be only grateful for a renascent Christianity so solicitous for humanism, so anxious not merely to save souls out of the world but also to redeem the total human order in the world.

However grateful humanists may be for specific Christian contributions to civilization, now or at any time, they cannot tolerate the idea of a regenerate and liberal Christendom in which they would be tolerated, any more than Christians can tolerate the idea of a humanist civilization in which they are a tolerated minority. In either event, the toleration would no doubt be genuine and would no doubt be accepted, but for either party to accept the necessity of either event whilst the alternative is still possible is no doubt intolerable to each. In other words, the issue is still open and is felt to be vital. Why cannot humanists accept a civilization that is a by-product of Christianity (Toynbee) or a work of Christian inspiration (Maritain) or a form of which Christianity is the substance (Tillich)? One reason might be that they are even more justified in believing that there is no chance of getting it than Christians are in believing that humanists will never succeed in establishing a rational civilization. And if the effort is doomed the misguided attempt lessens the chances of better-founded enterprises. But assuming the improbable, that Christian humanists are able to give us a Christian civilization that enjoys a human measure of the quality of their dreams, humanists would be bound, with whatever mixed feelings, to resent and resist it. Why? Not only because they could not be persuaded of the truth of the beliefs on which it was founded, but also because Christian humanism is not humanism and Christian civilization produced by Christian humanism is not civilization: it is not civilization with an extra motive and meaning, but civilization with the motive and meaning taken away.

The roots of Christianity run deep into the soil of disillusionment and despair, the historical experience of the utter collapse of hope, the experience of Israel and of Job that righteousness is no security, that for all one may be and do one may come to have left only God or nothing. This sense of unqualified dependence upon God, and with it the sense that there is nothing but God, reduces the difference between Christian humanism and an extreme Christian asceticism to nothing at all compared with the difference between humanism and any kind of Christianity. The two voices which speak for Christianity, and spoke for Israel before, say only the same thing. When Christianity values nature and culture, it is solely for their Christian uses; they enjoy only a local and functional autonomy. The gospel is the sun, let science produce what beams it can. All the enchantment and potentiality there are in nature and in human culture are conditional, an incipiency which promises and requires a supernatural and superhuman completion, and if that fail, the fore-taste of blessedness turns to ashes in the mouth of the Christian. For the humanist, on the contrary, all is staked on the sufficiency of nature and human culture; there is no thought or hope of any possi-bility of independence of them; and if and when they fail, all fails. The unqualified dependence of the Christian upon God, and with it the sense that there is nothing but God, is for the humanist an un-qualified dependence upon nature and human culture taken together, and with that goes a sense, on the one hand, of responsibility and devotion, on the other, of final good in the enjoyments and achieve-ments and pursuits which nature and culture offer to human capaci-ties: the dear city, the beloved community, the career, the companion, the theatre and the workshop of nature, the web of thought and action, the great past and the hopeful future, everything taken together in its intricate interdependence, its preciousness and its pre-cariousness, its immediacy and its continuity. The Christian cannot embrace this prospect with all its risks, responsibilities, opportunities, and savours; he is wholly staked upon dread and refusal and the remedy for despair in a primitive culture. He makes his choice, and he destroys the meaning of civilization by giving it another meaning which it will not bear.

It is the self-sufficient concreteness of the whole complex of his-torical human existence, the total economy of a civilization, that appeals to a humanist. Devotion to this, even devotion to a science or to an art, is not idolatry for him; he finds actual human interests, his own and another's, are not indifferent, merely the means to good personal relationships; social harmony is an incremental value, a by-product of civilization, and civilization can never be a by-product of Christian love, nor Christian love a substitute for civilization; individual enjoyments, achievements, pursuits, are not merely occasions for something else, sublimer things more deeply interfused, although they may and must have their own abundant and expanding personal meanings, their own forms of transcendence. Allied to this concreteness of humanism rooted in actual interests, is the satisfaction of humanists not merely with the possibilities of human existence but also with human experience. Humanists are not ashamed to say that they do not look for more in principle than what humanity has already proved itself capable of attaining and enjoying: there is far more than enough in that for any life; and nobody is cheated, although many may come to grief through no fault of their own. Against this, Christianity is an abstraction and a sham, because its interpretation takes all the self-sufficiency out of things; and Christian humanism is the greatest abstraction and sham of all, because it does so all the more surely by pretending that it is preserving the reality of things and distilling their essence. These are hard sayings, but a candid humanism can hardly speak otherwise. The verdict of Gibbon and of Frazer has in the end to be upheld and reinforced, that Christianity, not least in its warmer modern developments, tends to destroy civilization by cultivating an unalterable distaste for temporal things, even when it gives them its blessing. Fortunately, the practical effects of a diluted lay Christianity are less deleterious.

If, finally, a humanist constructed in the manner of Hegel a synopsis of the total human tradition, what place in his scheme would he assign to Christianity? Perhaps it would not differ essentially from Hegel's function, for Christianity challenges man's confidence in his own self-sufficiency and his belief in the self-sufficiency of things; it puts him and his life in question with himself by facing him with an alternative, it reminds him of the permanent religious problem; and it will continue to do this not less efficaciously in the more refined versions and visions of modern Christian humanism.

Chapter 10

CHRISTIAN ETHICS

I

THE true Christian, according to invincible popular opinion, is one who loves his neighbour as himself, who is ready also to turn the other cheek and love his enemy, who is meek and peaceable, long-suffering and kind, and whose religion is doing good and living for others. To be a Christian, said Montaigne long ago, is to be more than ordinarily just, charitable, kind. To be a Christian, says the theologian, is to be joined to God in grace through Christ. The gospel was first preached, and only then was it a question how those who had heard the gospel and responded to it should fitly conduct themselves whilst in the world. Nothing shakes the ordinary opinion that the Christian is proved by his temper and behaviour, and by nothing else; Christian behaviour is exemplary and recommends itself to all; Christian beliefs are not easy to understand, and perhaps not easy to swallow, but what matters is the conduct and that is the only thing men will ever be judged for. Theologians are aware that this solid ground is the thinnest ice, that the Golden Rule and neighbour love and the compassionate heart and the peaceful temper are not peculiar to Christianity, and cannot be claimed as its distinctive contribution to human good, that the gospel sounds a far higher note and the injunction to turn the other cheek would hardly be reasonable save as the venture of faith in response to its call. When all is said, however, the ordinary person remains of the same opinion still, and one reason is that theologians in the past by their insistence on correctness of belief as necessary to salvation have revolted the conscience of ordinary people, who have judged differently. They are sure that if they try to live as Christians in the ethical sense they can aim no higher, and nothing more can be required of them; they are sure that the correct beliefs required by the theologians are no more pleasing and acceptable to God than the blood of bulls required by the priests; and they have Biblical warrant for their feelings, sacred scriptural encouragement in treating lightly all the doctors.

It has not escaped observation of course that the ethical teaching of Jesus is extremely revolutionary, in a moral sense. He turns upside down accepted notions of justice and good conduct and of well-being. The last hired labourers in the vineyard who work only one hour get the same pay as those who have borne the heat and burden of the day. The prodigal is preferred before the dutiful son. The last are put first and the first last, the despised and outcast, sunk in sin and dishonour, are raised above the most eminent and honourable in the land. Mary is praised, not Martha. A loose woman who lavishes costly ointment upon him is justified before all those who dutifully toil at good works. The money-changers following their customary business are violently outraged. Every child in a Christian country grows up to think of the Pharisees as monsters of self-righteous callousness, but, looked at through the eyes of an orthodox Jew, the conduct of Jesus towards them is simply fanatical and outrageous. No doubt they were as humanly imperfect as other men in similar positions, but one could find under Christian dispensation much better examples of hypocrisy and righteous pedantry. The passion for law and strict observance which characterized the Jews was an expression of their religious humility, their zealous desire to keep the covenant. One may respond ardently to Jesus' exaltation of the generous, imaginative, personal impulses and qualities, and rejoice in their triumph over system and rule. That is always in place. Also it is always destructive. What can one ever put in place of settled rules, established usage? Never the spontaneous impulses of the heart. You can as soon remove mountains with a pair of hands. Protest, vigorous and dramatic, against the inhumanity, the pedantry, the blindness of the law and the system and of those bred in it and subdued to it is always in place if it brings to the system only new efficacy, not fatal discredit. Jesus came not to destroy but to fulfil. In what sense, in bringing new efficacy to the law or in some more radical sense? Clearly, in a more radical sense; the gospel may be the fulfilment of the law, but in a sense which is its abrogation. And this is the theme of the first Christian theology.

The one outcome of Jewish historical experience, cherished

amongst the humble-hearted elect few of the remnant of the remnant, was the conviction that God was all, and all in all. Older ideas, that God was their saviour from the hands of their enemies, that God was the giver of corn and wine, were superseded in this ultimate chastened discovery that God was himself the good and perfect gift. The personal relationship, developed out of simple-hearted dependence on his grace, was all-sufficient. Those who enjoyed this secret travelled the same road with others under the toilsome dispensation of the Torah, but travelled so light, ran forward with such power of eagerness and imagination and anticipation that when they were met halfway there was no more sense in lumbering on with the old caravan. The new dispensation of the gospel presented God as the loving Father waiting and longing for the return of the prodigal; and the kingdom of heaven, the new Israel, was a family chosen by their own humble eager-heartedness to be sons and joint heirs with Christ.

Now the economy of the divine family is not the same as the economy of the just society, and it is the economy of the divine family, not of the just society, with which the New Testament is concerned, the City of God, not the City of Man. Love, not justice, is the supreme virtue here because it is a membership in one body, in which there is no more *meum* and *tuum*, but union. The context of St. Paul's encomium on love is a discussion of the respective status and dignity of the various functions and gifts in the church. There is such a hierarchy, says St. Paul, but it is not important, there is a more excellent way, since all the functions and gifts are equally wanted for the common life of the one body in which they all are in Christ. Regard for their own part is vain, since it is through this union only that they are anything at all. It is the common life in which they share that is their only good, and love is the proof that they are in and of this body, and not seeking the things of their own. Since union here is the life, there is no meaning in the justice of to each his own.

Formally, the philosophic notion of justice may not be very different from the New Testament notion of love. In Plato's elaborate definition of justice, which the *Republic* is, justice supervenes as the resultant harmony when each citizen plays his appropriate and allotted part in the social union; justice is the proof that they are in and of the Republic. There is one question that is not asked, that cannot be raised, on Christian or on platonic assumptions: is any person or class of persons in fulfilling what is demanded of him not fulfilling himself? This question does not mean anything when the whole good and the sole good is union with God and when what is asked is God's will and when God is loving Father-creator who knows the most intimate secrets of nature and nurture. It is not a serious question either if the rulers are so wise and disinterested that they alone know and are capable of knowing the good for man. But if there is no question of union with God by God's grace and if there are no perfectly wise and perfectly disinterested persons in high office, then the question of justice cannot exclude the inquiry, am I being exploited? are there any who are able to do injustice and not to suffer it? And if I allow myself to be exploited or allow others to do injustice and not to suffer it, or if I merely bear witness against this when action is possible and promising, I am not doing what I can do to promote the genuine social union in which all interests are reconciled. All the laws, traditions, procedures, and institutions which help to bring this about and demand my loyalty and active service are forms of justice, and love is incapable of taking their place. In the social union, I am one among many; I have my own set of interests to take care of, my own personal theme to work out; these are not more important than those of others, and not less. I want to be able to enjoy my own achievements and theirs too, and to promote that kind of society and that kind of intercourse. In union with God, I have no set of interests of my own to take care of, no personal theme to pursue. If in the social union I abandon my own interests and personal theme and think only of others and work for theirs, I endanger them and myself. For I lose my orientation; I cease to be one among many, I am either allowing myself to be exploited, which is evil, or I am casting myself for the role of God, which is presumptuous and silly. Even the catholic saint Thomas Aquinas, like the liberal philosopher John Locke, allows that in the state of nature any unprovoked attack on me or on my property justifies me in destroying my attacker as a noxious animal, for man if he ceases to be reasonable ceases to enjoy the dignity and rights of personality, and may be disposed of and treated as a utility. Social union presupposes the law which gives security and, as Hobbes says (with better psychology and more charitable judgement), makes morality reasonable. Love without it goes down, not in a fruitful martyrdom but in nameless oblivion, and because of folly or pretension.

II

Is love or justice the ultimate social ideal? Christian love, which derives from and is bound up with the conception of union with God, confuses the issue, for it can only be translated into history on the assumption that it is the truth of human life, and even then there is a division of opinion on what it enjoins on men in history. Karl Barth during the last war held that if men in a Christian country who had been offered the means of grace refused to be governed by love they must be governed by violence, since the world was not handed over to the devil and men must be governed by the best effective means available. The good must on occasion meet evil on its own terms, or suffer eclipse. This may be orthodox Christian teaching, but in practice it means preferring justice to love when it is justice that is threatened. It makes love a higher not an absolute value, a possibility founded on the achievement of at least rough justice.

Many reformers who were not Christians have dreamed of the social utopia as a spontaneous union of sentiment. 'I am convinced', wrote Diderot, 'that there can be no true happiness for the human race except in a social state in which there is neither king nor magistrate, nor priest nor laws, nor *meum* nor *tuum*, nor property in goods or land, nor vices nor virtues.' He admitted that this heaven was 'devilishly ideal'. But it is common form in prophecy. Marxist sobriety cannot do without the withering away of the state and the disappearance of the bourgeois virtue of justice, which is a name for organized scarcity and unfair division. Tolstoy thought that government must mean enforced injustice, since by definition justice was a state of affairs which gave satisfaction to all, who would for that very reason most jealously resist the setting up of any government. Such utopian anarchists have some support from the elaborate analyses of a modern scientific sociologist, Pitirim Sorokin. He sees the modern world as given over to unlimited, unrestrained, insatiable appetites, and he thinks that unless and until we rediscover religious ideals and ethical values, and thereby restore the family pattern of social relationship to a dominant position, mankind is doomed to enslavement inward and outward. 'In spite of the infinite variety of the patterns of social relationships of man to man, or of group to group,' he writes, 'they all fall into three main classes: familistic relationships, permeated by mutual love, devotion, and sacrifice; free contractual agreements of the parties for their mutual advantage, devoid either of love or of hatred, but profitable to both; and compulsory relationships imposed by one party upon the others, contrary to their wishes and interests. The familistic relations are most frequently found among the members of a devoted family or among real friends. In such contracts the individual ego is merged in the sense of "we". Joys and sorrows are shared in common. The individuals need one another, seek one another, love one another, and gladly sacrifice themselves for one another—in brief, they represent a single solidary body. This is the supreme and noblest type of social relationship, a real *consortium omnis vitae, divini et humani juris communicatio*. In such a unity a special contract, with its prescription "no more and no less", becomes superfluous. Unlimited, all-embracing, all-forgiving, and all-bestowing mutual devotion renders unnecessary any contract, with its limitations and reservations.'

With all due respect and gratitude for creditable if incredible idealism, the response must be to insist that neither family union nor union with God is a suitable pattern for social union. The distinction is important, the confusion dangerous. There is no imperfection to be regretted in admitting that social union cannot be an enlarged form of family union, that justice here is superior to love because more appropriate. The reason is not merely that society is on too big a scale and therefore requires machinery which stands in the way of the spontaneity of immediate face-to-face relationships, a mechanical difficulty. The reason is that social relationships are differently structured and have a different content and are between human adults, an essential difference. In these relationships there is nobody to play the part of God and nobody to play the part of Father, and therefore both the roles of these persons and the responses to them are inappropriate. Nor is individual personal attraction in question, which goes to the making of families and friendships. In the fluid situation of the family, the parents, rightly, feel themselves responsible for creating just policies and harmonious society. In the great society no one has such moral empire, and to play the part of high-minded parent is presumptuously inappropriate; what is called for is to do effectively what is rightly expected of one, and to require the same of others, and beyond that to advance one's own legitimate interests and to seek to make them more rational, and in this way to help, as one among many, to create just policies and harmonious society. This is justice founded on utility, not love founded on personal attachment or on unconditional surrender to a divine order.

There is nothing to be gained, by Christians or by humanists, from confusing the family or the church with society at large; they are different in kind, and what is appropriate to the one will never be appropriate to the other. The divine union in which the church believes can never be realized in this world: that is another aspect of the same conclusion. The result must be, and has been, a duality in Christian ethics, according to whether it is concerned with the divine union or with how Christians shall conduct themselves in this world and with their part in the social union. The ethics of love on a universal scale requires the divine union, and it is in that sense, and only in that sense, that ethics requires a Christian sanction. Outside the church, there is no universal ethics but that of justice founded on utility. The highest success in this mode could still fairly be called the brotherhood of man.

Chapter 11

THE RETURN TO CHRISTIAN DOGMA

I

PROTESTANT Christian apologists have changed their ground. Not many of them now present the evidence for Christian beliefs and seek to defend them in detail against the scepticism induced by the development of science. The severe losses and many withdrawals on this front have made the positions untenable, and those who continue to hold on, the liberals and modernists, are only able to do so by fraternizing with the enemy, and are virtually lost to the Christian cause. It is possible for Christians to abandon these positions and to try other tactics: it is possible for them to say that the arguments of rationalists against the credibility of this or that belief or the probability of this or that happening are irrelevant, that the physics or metaphysics of the Incarnation or the Resurrection, on the assumptions of their faith, are not matters on which they have any reason to be able to give satisfactory answers, that they hold their convictions on other grounds and will not therefore attempt to defend them on this ground. Thus avoiding engagement on ground of the rationalist's choosing, they boldly take their stand on the Christian faith and deploy the content of the Biblical conception of human nature and destiny to convince the reason and convict the conscience of modern man, so that he is prepared to believe that the Christian gospel is the only answer to his condition. Setting aside the question of its truth, they set out to show that the Christian faith is highly relevant today, so relevant that history is presumptive evidence of its truth.

Many recent works of protestant theologians might be cited in evidence of this tendency. Outstanding are the two volumes of

Reinhold Niebuhr's Gifford Lectures, *The Nature and Destiny of Man*. This restatement of the content and relevance of the Christian faith may be taken as normative for the protestant view. Its treatment of the pretensions of the church makes it definitely protestant. It is normative because Niebuhr skilfully uses the main variant developments in theology and in secular thought to recover the distinctively Biblical conception of human nature and destiny, and shows its perpetual relevance by using it as a clue to historical interpretation and to the achievement of a modern synthesis. Thus his work is neither eclectic nor branded with the name of a school, but stands forth as a powerful hypothesis claiming to do justice to all the facts. For this reason, and because Niebuhr tries to take nature and history seriously, his restatement of Christian faith is worth the reconsideration of humanists.

Niebuhr fully accepts the Renaissance discovery that history is filled with endless possibilities of good and evil open to man, a discovery which sets the themes and tasks of history and gives it prospects and seriousness. He notes the characteristic humanist assumption that they are possibilities of good and that they can be realized. He is concerned to show that they are also possibilities of evil, and that the good cannot be fully nor finally realized. All achievements are new occasions of evil because man's nature and condition make it inevitable that he shall will good and do evil. The good and evil in him are not separable principles, as the Greeks thought: body and spirit, or reason and appetite. Evil is essentially spiritual, but both reason and the vital impulses are ambivalent, sometimes creative, sometimes destructive; and their creative phases involve destruction. The good and evil flow from man's nature and condition. He is a finite self, but he transcends himself and reflects upon his own deed and judges it. Such judgements may inform his will but cannot control his acts. Not because vital urges (his body) are too strong or run too deep for rational restraint, but because of the predicament of his situation. As a finite self he is necessarily anxious for his own survival and security, and his rational nature makes him anxious, resourceful, and persistent far beyond the survival impulse of animals. His anxiety prompts him to seek advantage and to secure the future, both in dealing with nature and with his fellows; and in the nature of the case, anxiety is unlimited and security never assured: the further he goes in trying to make himself secure, the further he has to go, because he gives himself more to lose and both tempts and threatens, and perhaps injures, others in the same case as himself. If this logic of anxious self-frustration inherent in the human situation is not always clearly discernible in the life of the individual, it is plain enough in the policies of the collective organizations with which he is insured against his anxieties. The lust for power, the exploitation of nature and of men, give general evidence of this condition. They are endemic amongst human beings in this world; there will be no lack of prescriptions, but there can be no cure, even if mankind perfected their institutions and universalized goodwill. History cannot solve its own problem. And the evil that men inevitably do, individually and collectively, is almost inextricably mixed and confused with moral pretensions and rationalizations, so that it does not seem to be what it is. Thus man's will is determined, in spite of himself (by his situation), to do evil, and his responsibility and sin are less in his individual acts than in his condition. His sin is original sin. It is the sin of trying in his condition, out of his own resources, to complete his life and achieve his good. This course inevitably bogs him more deeply and desperately in evil. The only cure for his anxiety, which expresses his true situation and which prompts him to do evil, is trust in God. That gives him the only genuine security he can achieve, exempts him from the inescapable pressure of the human situation, remakes him on a new model; he is released and enabled in principle to do good; sin is overcome in him in principle, although not in fact: he is justified by faith.

This is the Biblical conception of man's nature and condition, recovered and reaffirmed at the protestant Reformation. The protestant concentration on the Pauline version of the human predicament (Romans vii, 15–24) and the Christian deliverance from it by faith slighted the possibilities of secular progress on which the Renaissance concentrated. Niebuhr is concerned to correct the emphasis of both by recovering the Biblical warrant and interpretation for the Renaissance view.

One of the tasks which confronts us in reassessing the human situation today is to reject what is false and to accept what is true in the Renaissance world view. Human history is indeed filled with *endless possibilities*; and the Renaissance saw this more clearly than either classicism, catholicism, or the Reformation. But it did not recognize that history is filled with endless possibilities *of good and evil*. It believed that the cumulations of knowledge and the extensions of reason, the progressive conquest of nature and (in its later developments) the technical extension of social cohesion, all of which inhere in the 'progress' of history, were guarantees of the gradual conquest of chaos and evil by the forces of reason and order. It did not recognize that every new human potency may be an instrument of chaos as well as of order; and that history, therefore, has no solution of its own problem.

'This tragic aspect of history, towards which the Renaissance was partly oblivious, was precisely the aspect of history which the Reformation most fully comprehended. This comprehension is contained in the Reformation polemic against all doctrines of sanctification, whether catholic, secular, or sectarian-Christian, in which it detects a too-simple confidence in historical possibilities. Its doctrine of "justification by faith" contains implications for an adequate interpretation of history which have never been fully appropriated and exploited, probably because most protestant theologies which are interested in the historical problem have drawn their inspiration from the Renaissance, rather than from the Reformation.

'It must be noted, however, that the understanding of the Reformation for the ultimate problem of historic existence was not (and probably could not be) elaborated without tendencies toward moral and cultural defeatism. Its consciousness of the ultimate frustration which faces every human enterprise inclined it towards indifference when dealing with all the proximate problems. When confronting these problems every moral situation, whether individual or collective, actually discloses, when fully analysed, unending possibilities of higher fulfilment. There is no limit to either sanctification in individual life, or social perfection in collective life, or to the discovery of truth in cultural life; except, of course, the one limit, that there will be some corruption, as well as deficiency, of virtue and truth on the new level of achievement.

'This moral pessimism and cultural indifferentism of the Reformation was one cause of its defeat by the forces of the Renaissance. It must be recognized that the spiritual life of modernity has been primarily determined by this defeat. The other was that the phenomenal development of all the sciences and social techniques, of the conquest of nature and the general extension of human capacities in the modern period, was bound to emphasize what was true, and to hide what was false, in the Renaissance estimate of life. . . . It is particularly important to understand why and how those aspects of the truth about human nature and destiny, in which the Renaissance and the Reformation contradict one another, represent valuable insights into human nature and history, which are partially blunted and obscured in the medieval synthesis in which both were contained. The question is whether they can be so conceived and defined that they will not contradict or tend to defeat each other. If this were possible a philosophy of human nature and destiny could emerge which would reach farther into the heights and depths of life than the medieval synthesis; and would yet be immune to the alternate moods of pessimism and optimism, of cynicism and of sentimentality, to which modern culture is now so prone.' (Vol. II, p. 160.)

History is a divine imperative, serious, purposive, and progressive, as the Jewish prophets believed. (Niebuhr insists that progress is a Biblical conception.) But the meaning of Christianity is that no consummation is to be looked for within history, and only those who live out of the world can live in it to any purpose. Christians, accepting the witness of Christ, obediently trusting to God for their existence, can give themselves to the achievement and establishment in the world of truth and justice, never ceasing to disavow 'every effort and pretension to complete life, whether in collective or individual terms, every desire to stand beyond the contradictions of history, or to eliminate the final corruptions of history'. The achievements of Christians in history on these lines are real and progressive, and bring the world nearer to the perfection which can never be finally attained within history because of the nature of man. Those who reject the Christian faith may also participate in this process; but because they have not the inner security of trust in the divine love, they are under the determination of the human predicament and cannot do the good they will; and because they pretend to be able to interpret and complete life out of human resources, they are doomed to perpetual disillusionment and an ultimate futility. Disinterested Christian love, which is the leaven of the world and creates new possibilities of human achievement within history, cannot be sustained unrequited except on the assumptions of the Christian faith, which thus enables men to act in a way that transcends historical conditions and historical judgements and is only justified beyond history. Christians may, and are morally bound to, take sides in history according to their judgement of the better or worse cause, although they do so without pretensions and illusions;

but the divine love, as the Jewish prophets learned to see, cannot champion any human cause, even that of the faithful, can only appear in history as the sufferer on the Cross; beyond history, as the judge. Thus both divine and Christian love produce results in history but have their full scope and consummation beyond history. Human nature is limited by but may transcend history because human destiny does transcend history.

Of course this is an old story and it is not open to Niebuhr to introduce into it anything new which demands attention. Long enough ago Pascal elaborated a cry of reflective despair at the human predicament, since re-echoed by Kierkegaard and still reverberating; their backward leap into the Christian faith to escape the abyss of nihilism at their feet is more than ever possible today. That is why Niebuhr's restatement of the faith, highly competent and mature, familiar with, and not indifferent to, the achievements of secular culture as well as the ramification of theology, merits reconsideration from a humanist point of view. He and other Christian thinkers are today saying to humanists in effect: Think again now, at this moment of history, in the context of modern experience, and ask yourselves whether the inescapable recognition of the impossibility of ultimate human achievement in the pursuit of truth or of justice does not break the spring of humanism and leave the field of history to the Christians: is there not more relevance and validity than you had dreamed of in the Christian doctrines of original sin, justification by faith, incarnation, atonement, resurrection, and judgement? And if relevant and philosophically apt, may they not be credible and verifiable?

'There are periods of hope in history in which the Christian faith would seem to be irrelevant, because history itself seems to offer both the judgement and the redemption which the Christian faith finds in the God who has been revealed in Christ. There are other periods of disillusionment when the vanity of such hopes is fully revealed. We have lived through such centuries of hope and we are now in such a period of disillusionment. The centuries of historical hope have wellnigh destroyed the Christian faith as a potent force in modern culture and civilization. We do not maintain that the period of disillusionment in which we now find ourselves will necessarily restore the Christian faith. It has merely re-established its relevance. There is always the alternative of despair, the "sorrow of the world", to the creative despair which induces a new faith. (Vol. II, p. 212.)

II

The humanist does not, indeed cannot, hide his wounds. Wells and Russell have expressed their despair. The Christian is in a superior position and can say, I told you so. Niebuhr is very nice about it and points out the good reason there seemed to be for secular optimism. But the point of his argument which is intended to hurt is in the restatement of the doctrine of original sin; it is a doctrine which humanists have always found peculiarly fantastic and irritating, but perhaps in their present mood they will have the patience to see what it means and to what conclusion it leads. Niebuhr's account of human nature and of the human condition, for all the points of difference, is strikingly like that of Hobbes, the earliest naturalistic English thinker. Their conclusions of course are different. Hobbes finds the security which makes justice possible (and rational) in the Great Society, Niebuhr in the Kingdom of God beyond the world. The reason why Niebuhr finds in the Great Society, or any other human improvement, no solution of the problem is because it merely reproduces in a new form or a new context the ineradicable evil. The moral of all history is, 'new presbyter is but old priest writ large'. Similarly, every new philosophy which claims to be true is doomed to be superseded like the others. How, then, on humanist assumptions can there be anything but scepticism and cynicism, except blind illusion?

The answer which humanists usually give will not do: that in bad times the black side of human nature is painfully conspicuous and colours the view; that the bright side concealed by the times will again have its day; that nature 'red in tooth and claw' is also the scene of mutual aid; that egoism is balanced by altruism in the human make-up. It was in principle this answer, skilfully elaborated with subtlety and insight, which the Christian Bishop Butler gave to the naturalistic Hobbes. But the argument does not touch the position to which it is opposed: that human beings willy-nilly, good and bad, act under the constraint of their human situation; that the human predicament compels all to assert themselves, in the first place in order to live, in the second place in order to live well; that this situation can be aggravated but cannot be abrogated. The conclusion which Hobbes drew is that morality is only rational and possible if political power can give assurance that it will be enforced on all: in that case, a common interest is created and the initial situation is virtually abrogated. Niebuhr agrees that institutions can make the situation more favourable to the possibility of human goodness, but insists that it can only be virtually abrogated by trust in God.

Undoubtedly humanist psychology and ethics in the past have oversimplified the problem, have assumed too lightly a natural harmony of selfish and benevolent principles in the structure of human nature, of a natural coincidence of private interest and public interest in the social order. Any reading of human nature is inadequate which confines attention to an inventory of innate propensities and abilities, or to the physiological and psychological structure and functions of personality, or to the situations in which human nature manifests behaviour. All such matters are inseparably related in the total human complex, and are in constant interaction and reciprocally influence and change each other. It may be possible and fruitful to isolate for theoretic analysis constant elements in human nature, but these are known only in behaviour which is profoundly modified both by the situations created by social institutions and by concepts, ideals, aims, purposes, occasions, and tasks furnished by patterns of culture: and these are indefinitely modifiable by policies. That is to say, the actual content of human interests is variable and modifiable, and also there is no obvious limit to the possibilities of social method by which interests may be reconciled, harmonized, or identified. Indeed, it is true to say that there is no determinate human nature and no determinate human situation; these are misleading abstractions, distracting attention from the real concrete cultural and social phenomena in history. Human nature and the human situation do not together determine history, nor does history determine human nature and the human situation. It is not so simple as that: the determination is reciprocal, or dialectical. There emerges a possibility of self-conscious human freedom, through understanding control of the process. This freedom is a clear aim, conscious selection from alternative possibilities, not mere self-identification with a natural historical process recognized as inevitable. Such freedom is both collective and personal, and an understanding of the precise relation of interdependence of the two is of crucial importance for the characteristic disputes and problems of our time. A grand strategy of human advance on many fronts is conceivable and would be likely to produce remarkable results. The situation is far more complex (the interrelated factors more variable and reacting together more intimately and powerfully) than has been generally recognized, and the possibilities and the difficulties far greater. The humanist who is aware of this can be neither defeatist nor sanguine; he is both disillusioned and immensely stimulated. His philosophy of human nature and destiny does 'reach . . . into the heights and depths of life', and is 'immune to the alternate moods of pessimism and optimism, of cynicism and sentimentality, to which modern culture is now so prone'.

Therefore, humanists who have put away fatuous beliefs in a golden age of the past and in utopias of the present or the future (and many have not), who do not see much that is black or white in the human spectacle, who agree with Joubert, 'Il ne peut y avoir de bon temps à venir que celui qui resemblera aux bons temps passés', and, 'Demander la nature humaine infaillible, incorruptible, c'est demander du vent qui n'ait point de mobilité', whose humanism is seasoned and mature, that is, will reject Niebuhr's reformulation of the doctrine of original sin as itself too simple for the facts, as nothing but the other side of the medal which has been put away with childish things. There is no fatality in the structure of human nature in its relation to the human situation which puts a blight on human hopes, unless those hopes are so foolish as to look for 'la nature humaine infaillible, incorruptible'.

It is with this last point that we can begin to develop the decisive difference between Christians and humanists, cutting out all mere debating points. Both Christians and humanists (unless they are simple-minded or fanatical, as some are) recognize that human nature neither is nor can be made in time (even with the endless possibilities of improvement before it) infallible and incorruptible. Christians cannot bear the prospect, and the Christian faith is their answer. Humanists (some, at least) accept the conditions of human living as they find them and found their hopes, conceptions, and ideals on what seems to be possible. The ultimate failure to eliminate evil and error does not worry them at all, because: (1) the difference between better and worse is so enormous as to give them all the incentive and occupation they need; (2) the achievements are real and have a finality and individual quality which informs judgements and ideals, rather than is subject to them; ideals have no secure superiority, owe much to the actual, and are frequently surpassed by the actual; (3) the final elimination of evil and error simply does not mean anything, it is a wind that does not blow.

I will apply this analysis of the issue to Niebuhr's treatment of the historical enterprise, characterized by him as the cultural quest for truth and the social quest for justice and love. He accepts Karl Mannheim's sociology of knowledge in *Ideology and Utopia*. Mannheim accepts the substance of the marxist critique of culture: summarily, the view that culture is necessarily concerned with the elaboration, development, and defence of a set of interests rooted in the politico-economic structure of society. But Mannheim will not allow that marxism is an exception, and he applies the critique to its pretensions to universality: this also is an 'ideology'. The argument runs thus: whatever your interests, they are your interests as a political person; but the fact that you have this or that set of interests implies also that you must do this or that to realize them, and that you must know the specific position you occupy in the whole social process; this is the deeper logic and dynamic of human thinking, but since this structural relationship between the conditioning point of view and particular judgements can be taught, the point of view can be transcended by recognition of its limitation, no universality or absolute status is assumed or demanded for it, and therefore particular judgements can be qualified from points of view representing other interests accepted as equally entitled to historical existence and destiny. Thus Mannheim indicates an historical (as distinct from abstract or metaphysical) universality and freedom for human thinking, to be achieved by an adequate sociology of knowledge, which does not impair the dynamics of thought and progress: the ship is taken skilfully through the narrow and dangerous waters between scepticism and fanaticism.

It is characteristic of Niebuhr that he chooses to accept Mannheim's account of human thinking as 'embodied', having a given locus and dynamic, a position in society and a set of interests to be maintained and developed. He explicitly criticizes and rejects Greek rationalism and philosophical idealism, and these elements in Christian thought, which assume in human nature a pure reason which by disciplines may free itself of finite conditions and gain cognition of absolute truth. He is even more scathing in his criticism and rejection of Dewey's empiricist's faith in co-operative inquiry as a means of establishing a universal human order, because he thinks that Dewey too simply assumes the unconditioned universality of 'scientific method' and has no adequate 'sociology of knowledge'. But it is equally characteristic of him that he chooses to reject Mannheim's conclusion, his indication of the historical conditions of universality and freedom in human thinking. He taxes Mannheim with seeking (in vain) to escape the logic of his own analysis. If the analysis delivers the reader from fanaticism, it is only because it leads to scepticism and breaks the historical spring of the cultural enterprise. Only the Christian pilot can take the ship out. Men as finite selves are bound to take partial views, and as transcending their condition they are bound either to claim universal truth for their partial views or to recognize their partiality and give up the quest for truth. This, of course, is descriptively true of what frequently happens, but that is not at all to say that it is a dilemma in which human life is shut up. Mannheim's way out to historical freedom and universality is in principle open and true to experience. His sociology of knowledge is not a complete account of human thinking and the status of knowledge, a complete epistemology, but the argument so far as it goes is permanently valid. Since Niebuhr has chosen to accept it, the humanist can be quite ready to agree to this account of the matter. But he insists on the essential conclusion: that historically conditioned human thinking, by recognition of all its conditions and presuppositions, by taking full account of alternatives, above all by being relied on, used, and lived by, can transcend historical conditions without losing the dynamic inherent in those conditions which make achievement and progress; that human thinking on these conditions is a self-correcting and self-completing process.

Niebuhr is not interested in this conclusion not merely because it is not the Christian conclusion but fundamentally because although he rejects Greek rationalism and philosophical idealism and accepts a descriptive sociological account of human knowledge, he retains the ideal notion of truth as disembodied, pure, universal, eternal. He is not really seeing through the pretensions of both sides and reconciling the truth in them through the mediation of the relevant Biblical conceptions. He comes from the idealist camp, in spite of his disclaimers, and is found in the other camp solely for the sake of the idealist cause. What he sees is the incapacity of men to achieve on the historical plane the truth they seek; but it is the idealist conception of truth he has in mind, and he does not stop to criticize it, nor to consider the humanist conception of truth. He does not face the possibility that this truth which is not achieved in history is an unmeaning abstraction. Of course philosophical idealism is important; and there are normative universal abstract truths which are outside history, so to speak, because they do not wait on further experience although they are the fruit of experience and are only relevant to human life. But such truths are attainable, are indeed commonplace, although perpetually forgotten or ignored. Any other sense of absolute truth and secure possession of it seems to imply not merely conditions of life which do not happen to obtain, but conditions of life purely rational, immaterial, and eternal, that is to say, purely universal. If it is assumed that such conditions of life, although not obtainable in history, are conceivable and ideal, in the sense of interesting and desirable, humanists are at least entitled to object that this belongs to the metaphysical realm of pure possibility and is not required for the interpretation of history or participation in it. I would go further and say not only that such conditions have no bearing on human life and are strictly inconceivable and meaningless, but also that in so far as meaning is found in them they indicate conditions of life which do not stand above but fall below the historical conditions of human life; just as 'un vent qui n'ait point de mobilité' does not really excel the real thing, neither does 'une nature humaine infaillible, incorruptible'. This is not a piece of bravado, a defiant extravagance; it is a profound meditation, and he who does not understand it does not catch the full seriousness of humanism. It is the imagined ideal that is shallow. In the history of thought as in the history of the individual soul, true perceptions and typical errors constantly recur, but in both there is growth and may be progress; and the end of that process in the life of the individual and in the history of the race is never absolute truth joined to infallible mind, but reliable knowledge fruitfully applied to the creation of experience. In this concrete context of actual living, knowledge may be relevant and sufficient, and cannot be more than this in heaven or earth. The humanist who understands these things does not fall into scepticism nor make absurd claims for his knowledge, nor need recourse to Christian doctrines to reconcile nonsensical notions of truth with historical possibilities. (At the same time, he need not grudge others the comfort of being sustained in arduous labours by the feeling that they are saying the last word: nor neglect to profit by their real achievements because these are not exactly what they are claimed to be.)

Niebuhr's account of the historical attempt to establish justice and love follows the same lines and is open to the same criticism. He sees the political struggles within nations and between nations, overt and concealed; he appreciates the construction of stable policies and wider structures of political cohesion; he recognizes that there can be no final historical achievement in which oppression is eliminated and conflict resolved. This ultimate frustration, he concludes, can only breed despair in those who will recognize it, without the Christian faith in a consummation of history beyond history, in other than human hands. Within history, the realization of mutual love is possible, although it is difficult because the manifestation of love risks the failure to elicit response and may merely make a victim; but sacrificial love which looks for no response and gets none is on historical conditions both impossible and irrational: it can only be sustained by divine intervention and example and on extra-historical conditions. To be fair, one must consider exactly what he says.

'Sacrificial love transcends history . . . it cannot justify itself in history. From the standpoint of history mutual love is the highest good. Only in mutual love, in which the concern of one person for the interests of another prompts and elicits a reciprocal affection, are the social demands of historical existence satisfied. All claims within the general field of interests must be proportionately satisfied and related to each other harmoniously. The sacrifice of the self for others is therefore a violation of natural standards of morals, as limited by historical existence.

'Furthermore the sacrifice of self-interest is psychologically impossible when life is conceived only in terms of nature-history. If the self identifies life with physical existence the basic ethical paradox of the gospel ethic, Whosoever loseth his life shall find it, can have no meaning. This paradox can have meaning only if the dimension of life is known to transcend historical existence. . . . Sacrificial love thus represents a tangent towards "eternity" in the field of historical ethics. It is nevertheless the support of all historical ethics; for the self cannot achieve relations of mutual and reciprocal affection with others if its actions are dominated by the fear that they may not be reciprocated. Mutuality is not a possible achievement if it is made the intention and goal of any action. Sacrificial love is thus paradoxically related to mutual love; and this relation is an ethical counterpart of the general relation of super-history to history. . . . The final majesty, the ultimate freedom, and the perfect disinterestedness of the divine love can have a counterpart in history only in a life which ends tragically, because it refuses to participate in the claims and counter-claims of historical existence. It portrays a love "which seeketh not its own" . . . even the most perfectly balanced system of justice in history is a balance of competing wills and interests, and must therefore worst anyone who does not participate in the balance. . . . It is impossible to symbolize the divine goodness in history in any other way than by complete powerlessness, or rather by a consistent refusal to use power in the rivalries of history.' (Vol. II, p. 71.)

Here Niebuhr confuses justice and love and perversely exalts sacrificial love over mutual love. The passage is characteristic in that it shows how quick he is to seize the essential point in humanist thought and how he lets it go again, how discerning he is and how the preconceptions of orthodox Christian thought blur the meaning of what he sees. Thus he rightly sees that in the humanist view self-sacrifice is an evil, a violation of morals; and more faintly he seems to see why, because it indicates the failure to realize a richer complex of good: yet he makes of historical heroic human remedies applied to redeem such failures a transcendent principle, irrational, sublime, and superior to successful normal historical realizations of love—which is to defeat the whole intent of historical sacrificial love and make nonsense of it. Sacrificial love cannot be an historical norm (true insight); therefore it is a super-historical norm (*non sequitur*, but orthodox Christian teaching). 'There is . . . no pure ethical norm in history; nor any hope of history gradually purifying itself so that it will achieve this norm. The "essential", the normative man, is thus a "God-man" whose sacrificial love seeks conformity with, and finds justification in, the divine and eternal agape, the ultimate and final harmony of life with life.' (Vol. II, p. 84.) Self-sacrifice is often called for in human life, and occurs on a considerable scale (even in conditions which make it 'psychologically impossible'); it is far more exacting than the sacrifice sustained by reciprocated love, and may be more admirable; but it is only admirable when it is strictly 'historical', when it is a turning aside from strong interests and pursuits to help another, or a refraining from a particular pursuit for the sake of another; when it is professional self-sacrifice, so to speak, self-sacrifice as a vocation and on principle, when you set out to have no interests, pursuits, and life of your own because you believe that human beings have a divine calling to live that way, then such 'super-historical' self-sacrifice is apt to be most mischievous, and Christian teaching has often engendered it with ruinous consequences. Of course there may be a considered life-long setting aside of personal interests and pursuits in a specific course chosen because of the state of the world, but this is historical sacrificial love nourished by historical hopes and sustained by historical effects; it is exceptional and has no meaning except by reference to a life of positive worth-while interests and to the achievement of a state of the world in which it would be unnecessary and wrong. The content of love is historical, namely, real interests, real pursuits, real achievements, real goods. Mutual love is explicitly concerned with this content, and so is sacrificial love within history. But make sacrificial love a principle and a norm superseding or outdoing mutual love and you empty it of all historical content. As with absolute truth, that is not to put it in heaven but in limbo, incapable of any content or meaning. Of course interests and pursuits, the historical content of human lives and personalities, are ambiguous; they may be producers or consumers, so to speak, they may be making claims or creating goods: inevitably they are doing both to some extent, and with infinitely various shades of difference, and it is in this theatre that the subtle interplay of altruism and egoism takes place; to abstract and hypostasize one principle, or a particular manifestation of one principle, and create a new world out of it is sheer fantasy, and hopeless falsification. In any case, the divine love manifested in Christ (for the sake of argument) is not sacrificial; it is accomplishing the divine will and fulfilling the divine interest. It is the supreme example, in which the difference between egoism and altruism vanishes: God is good and it is his interest to will the true interest of man; but the true interest of man is God's conception and God's interest; it is only saved from odious comparison with painfully familiar cases of alterocentric egoism in family relationships by being put above suspicion and outside human judgement. Nevertheless, the difficulty is real enough to have occasioned tensions in theological thought and to have left its mark on orthodox doctrine. The point is that the divine example is a special and difficult case which is neither like sacrificial love in history nor a justification of sacrificial love as an absolute ideal. It is mere Christian bias to say 'the divine love can have a counterpart in history only in the life which ends tragically, because it refuses to participate in the claims and

counterclaims of historical existence'. The tragic end is merely accidental and irrelevant and the refusal to participate in the claims and
counterclaims of historical existence (sacrificial love) is merely one
mode of creative living, not the specifically divine. Devotion to the
care of the broken and helpless, the weak and oppressed, is one half
of goodness, and the other half which makes sense of it is participation in the creative and regulative tasks of historical existence, cultural and social. If one must speak of the divine, let it be found not
less manifest in the promethean culture heroes than in the sacrificial
figures. Deification of the one type by Christians leads to the exaltation of the other type by humanists, to the extravagances of Nietzsche,
for example, who, it is important to notice, reacts violently against
Christianity just because he is a profound and subtle mind, not because he is not. Fortunately, the mass of mankind are incapable of
taking Christianity seriously, and treat it as equivalent to compassion
(of which they approve) and get on with the day's work. But the
joining of these two aspects of human living is too important to be
left entirely to casual common sense. Indeed, Niebuhr from the
Christian side is making a sustained and critical attempt to effect just
this synthesis, but in spite of himself he fails to take seriously enough
the tasks and content of historical existence, and subordinates them
(in spite of his remarkable insight) to the sacrificial historical element
translated and transfigured in the Christian manner.

Apart from his Christian preconceptions, or bound up with them,
is his horror of the element of egoism, self-assertion, aggressiveness,
inseparable from cultural and political enterprises in historical
existence. That is the essence of his doctrine of original sin, his insistence on its perpetual relevance, and his warning to this secular age
of the folly of the humanist hope. That is why the divine is precluded
from participation in the specifically human historical tasks, and
identified in history with renunciation of the world and sacrificial
love. That is why the divine consummation of history is outside history. Freudian psychologists have insisted on the powerful influence
in our lives of repressed aggressiveness; some are wrecked by the
struggle, many or most of us have feelings of anxiety and guilt
which give rise to the longing for a state of pure love. The Christian
scheme of salvation obviously applies to this condition and has
therapeutic value, but whether it is the best therapeutic treatment and
has sound results is quite another question. Marxist or other utopianism which believes in an historical consummation either existing

somewhere or coming some time also gives ideal relief to this condition and is a source of justification. The conception of a super-historical state of pure sacrificial love is an abstract notion without meaning; the conception of an historical state of pure mutual love has some meaning. Neither conception is mature. The achieved stabilities and harmonies of human interest are in the nature of things not permanent, and whilst they last have perpetually to be re-enacted and repossessed; and the vitality and renewal which make them final and good are inseparable from aggressiveness, change, and death. You cannot be pious about the fairest flowers of human living, and be impious about the conditions in which they are rooted. Death and aggressiveness are sacred as well as love, or for the sake of love. It is fatal not to take them seriously, or to seek to disguise or abolish them: they are essential to freedom and creative vitality, in heaven as elsewhere. History does not wait for a consummation to which all things move and for the sake of which they exist and in which they are justified: the finalities of history (and of nature) are always present; although the possibilities are always more. There is indeed a love 'which seeketh not its own', but that love does not make all forms of seeking one's own reprehensible; there is no other foothold in history, no other witness to the reality of living and of the good; no other means of creating the content of existence. Let one seek one's own, in the sense of having real interests and building up real achievements, with due regard to the interests of others and with use and enjoyment of their achievements. This normal pattern of modern secular living is delusively simple, but it is none the less not infrequently realized, and sustained by success. The hopes of humanists, too often extravagant and absurd, are exciting enough for moderate and mature minds even when bound to the feasible.

Niebuhr's synthesis, then, falls apart, because it is impossible to unite Christian and humanist views: they are developed alternatives, contradictions which never can be reconciled if both are taken seriously. The very earnestness and acumen of his attempt to take history and nature seriously show the impossibility, for he cannot succeed in taking them as seriously as the humanist does, and he fails to measure the strength and resources which the humanist gains from his position. He does not even succeed in establishing a distinctively Christian position which must be respected even by those who cannot share it, for he falls into just those Christian positions which from a quasi-humanist standpoint he undermines. He rejects Greek and modern philosophical idealism and that tradition in Christian theology, yet he retains uncritically an idealist notion of truth; he rejects Christian and other mysticism, yet in effect he shatters all the categories and meanings of human historical existence and looks for another life on unthinkable super-historical conditions of undifferentiable oneness: his notions of truth and love, unless they are simple and sentimental, are universal, and only justifiable and explicable in terms of idealism and mysticism. The sentimental view of life, leading to cynicism, with which he taxes humanists, is the very view with which he is left when the support of his untenable position is withdrawn. The paradoxes in which he escapes recognition of these contradictions do not really effect a modern synthesis or show the modern relevance of orthodox Christian doctrines. Of course these doctrines are relevant in the sense that they deal with the human situation and with human experience, but when they are examined it is not their credentials which are dubious, the power to perform what they promise, but what they promise does not mean anything to any profound human purpose. It is impossible to be agnostic about the Christian faith: its claims and evidences demand to be accepted or rejected; and some humanists at any rate who reject them after prolonged and serious consideration do so not with the sadness and reluctance of one who would be glad to accept them but is not able to find the evidence good enough, but with the definitive decision of one who finds that they have no real meaning. This ultimate rejection is once for all and does not wait on further evidence. It is not of course obvious that a doctrine has no meaning; it has or has not meaning in relation to certain presuppositions and ultimates of thought. I have tried to indicate how the Christian scheme is not consistent with human experience, is a distortion of it and does not help to solve its problems. There are protestant Christian apologists (like W. S. Urquhart in *Humanism and Christianity*) who assume or pretend that the rejection by humanists of Christian doctrine is out-of-date rationalism, the unnecessary caution of timidly sceptical and old-fashioned minds, and that humanists only need a little encouragement from Christians, and a little reassurance against the extremism of Barth, to make them glad to be able to 'dispense with the limitations which it [humanism] has unnecessarily and illogically imposed on itself' and embrace a position in which 'the truth of humanism is conserved, its errors removed, and its failures overcome'. This view is an utter, although excusable, failure to understand what humanism means, and to recognize that Christianity is rejected not solely on grounds of evidence but mainly because its content is false. It is important that this misconception should be removed, for it is a waste of effort to proceed further on such assumptions. The practical problems of human living are indeed formidable, the great possibilities exceedingly difficult, and the dangers appalling: but the naturalism of modern secular thought has resources and is better able to cope with the situation than thought which, although historically venerable, is hopelessly inadequate, and may be dangerously misleading.

Beyond the scope of argument, at the bottom of the difference between Christians and humanists is a mass of feeling about the world. There are indeed some who are humanists because their sense of evidence will not let them be Christians, and there are humanists who, knowing that human beings are physically incapable of any other life or any other conditions of life, have so learned to know and to love life in the world that they are spiritually incapable of wanting or liking the salvation of the gospel: in their skin is grained a mosaic of chequered experience, created and suffered, of concrete existence, and to their mind the mighty abstract existence of glorified Christian saints in the continual presence of God, like a dream, hangs to historical existence like drifts of fog under the drag of the land, like Virgil's wan and wistful *umbrae silentes*. Humanists of this sort compare with Christians as those who love and are long-versed in music or painting with those who just like a tune or a picture. The comparison is unfair: probably Christians and humanists of the deeper sort are nearer to each other than they are to the ruck of others of their own persuasion; and probably the ruck of Christians and humanists are only formally divided from one another, and spiritually separated from the subtle spirits in their own camp. But the comparison leads to the not unfair suggestion that from the humanist standpoint the Christian faith looks more respectable as starting-point than as goal of the pilgrim's progress; it seems at first sight to be a vital and valid ideal, but with long-developed reflective experience, following a naturalistic grain, it loses both impulse and stamp and looks like a thin and unrelated idea, an emanation. Then the accumulated solidity of experience has a settled equilibrium in which it must persist; it cannot be turned on to another axis; it cannot be reinterpreted: it can only be destroyed.

Chapter 12

HOW CHRISTIAN IS ENGLAND?

THE religious ideas which are popularly held may be studied either with curiosity about what people believe or in order to assess the influence and social value of organized religion. This paper will examine the contribution which such studies make to the latter purpose, with special reference to *Puzzled People*.[1] Nobody would suppose that popular opinions even in a mass democracy ever told the whole story. Just how much of it they do tell is the question for investigation.

In the eighteenth century when Christianity was under fire from the deists and Bishop Butler marshalled in its defence the argument of his *Analogy* (1736), it is a balance of things doubtful dipping in favour of Revelation which he presents. But there are no popular doubts; the defenders of Christian orthodoxy appeal to popular passions, and all parties in the church repose complacently upon 'the never-to-be-shaken constancy of the multitude'.[2] Later, when methodism and the evangelical party gain their great influence, and prudential moralism is superseded by the drama of sin and salvation, it is again the multitude who respond, encouraged from above by those who fear the social ideas of the French Revolution. For Wesley's revival is not a return to the turbulence, the collisions, the ferment of ideas of the seventeenth century: its romanticism offered no adventures in this world, and thus it proved an instrument of social discipline of great importance in our history, as Elie Halévy

---

[1] *Puzzled People*. Report prepared for the Ethical Union by *Mass Observation*. Gollancz, 1947.

[2] 'Tendencies of Religious Thought in England, 1688-1750.' By Mark Pattison. In *Essays and Reviews*.

has shown. In France, on the other hand, in the later stages of the Revolution, when the new republic was dominated by the outside threat to its existence, the Christian religion was abolished overnight without a murmur of protest from anybody. The peasants were indifferent, the workers liked the fun of masquerade and mockery, the ex-nobles and middle classes were imbued with the natural religion of Voltaire or of Rousseau.[1] Probably France was more rapidly and completely de-christianized than Russia under the Soviet policy of militant atheism. If the multitude can give passionate support to the defence of Christian orthodoxy, accept the Christian theme of sin and salvation as the whole content of their lives, and accept the total abolition of the Christian religion with complete indifference, what is the explanation of these differences?

In the first place, there is a difference between established ecclesiastical institutions and persons, and Christianity as a simple faith and teaching taken hold of by the people for themselves and practised and propagated by evangelical sects. There is this difference popularly made between Christianity and the church; and there is the older and more widespread difference popularly made between the church and the clergy, of which William Langland's *The Vision of William Concerning Piers the Plowman* is the most eloquent and sustained example in early England. Mark Pattison, writing of the period of controversy with the deists mentioned earlier, says: 'Though the general feeling of the country was sufficiently decided to oblige all who wished to write against Christianity, to do so under a mask, this was not the case with attacks upon the clergy. Since the days of the Lollards there had never been a time when the established ministers of religion were held in so much contempt as in the Hanoverian period, or when satire upon churchmen was so congenial to general feeling. This too was the more extraordinary, as there was no feeling against the Church Establishment, nor was nonconformity as a theory ever less in favour. The contempt was for the persons, manners, and character of the ecclesiastics.' In our time when anti-clericalism tends to be freethinking and secularist, perhaps the analogy with earlier popular distinctions should be looked for in the minds of the Russian masses.

In the second place, Christianity and the church cannot be eclipsed and replaced until events and independent movements provide the

[1] *Christianity and the French Revolution.* By A. Aulard. *L'Eglise Catholique et la Révolution Française.* Vol. I. By André Latreille.

occasions and the alternatives. There was probably as much popular scepticism, wayward thinking, and gross superstition in the middle ages as at any time; but the omnipresence of the church, its pageantry and festivals, and its administrative functions, rooted it in the day-to-day lives of the people: even their revolts and their independent thinking derived from Christian teaching and threatened the church in its own name and for its own sake. The Wesleyan revival dramatized the life of the humblest and redeemed him from the bitterness of living, and put the people in possession of the Christian faith as the pearl of great price. Today the situation is very different: secular progress has taken administrative functions out of the hands of the church; pageantry and festivals have been replaced by sporting events and the cinema; the working class has its own movement and the sound hope of social betterment by united action, and easy access to science and non-Christian schools of thought and bodies of doctrine. The reason why the Christian religion could be abolished without protest in France in the later phase of the Revolution was mainly that attachment to the principles of the Revolution was stimulated to religious fervour by the danger from enemies within and without: patriotism inspiring philosophy and philosophy inspiring patriotism became the ardent religion of Frenchmen; and the rural masses indifferent to the church had no reason for resistance or resentment.

One may sum up by saying that Christianity holds the people directly in three ways: (1) when they depend directly upon its services and doctrines for their thought, their daily needs, their emotional and imaginative life; (2) when its appeal does stimulate, engage, and focus their energies upon some personal or social goal; (3) when Christian ministers are personally adequate and achieve results and win respect. In the circumstances of today Christianity is reduced to heavy dependence upon the third of these ways. A difference is still popularly made between Christianity and the church, but seldom between the clergy and the church; because there are still vague and respectful feelings about Christianity as an ethical ideal, but hardly a vestigial concept of the church, its doctrine, and mission. Taking the effects of social progress upon the church and taking the evidence of *Puzzled People*, there is some justification for concluding that so far as the mass of people are concerned, Christianity has been reduced to a matter of private philosophy in which they are little interested and not competent. A minister of religion who is energetic, realistic, and has popular gifts may still crowd his church and draw people from a distance; he may handle themes of contemporary and permanent human interest and exert an effective influence on his hearers; or another man with sense and initiative and kindliness may win universal goodwill by his parish work. The point is that there is very little hostility or prejudice against Christianity and still less reasoned criticism of its doctrines; it is rather that organized religion impinges on ordinary personal life at so few points in the contemporary world and it requires intelligent and vigorous personal action to make it do so at all, and even then it is action on general grounds of human interest which is effective rather than on the specific ground of Christian doctrine. Mr. J. W. Robertson Scott in his recently republished *England's Green and Pleasant Land* makes the influence of the church in the rural parishes under his observation the principal theme of his study, and has to deplore the personal inadequacy of the clergy who in most instances conspicuously fail to provide anything like leadership in worth-while living.

This part of the subject, the popular hold of Christianity in England today, may be concluded by saying that popular interest in Christianity and the church has been diluted many times by competing interests, opportunities, and institutions. It is a weak but still identifiable fluid, recognizable in general goodwill to Christianity and to ministers of religion who prove themselves in personal qualities and services. The old popular distinction between the church and the clergy has given place to the current popular distinction between Christianity and all its institutional and dogmatic forms. That, or something like it, is the popular background to faith and order, life and work, in the Christian church in this country today.

One may regard this popular condition as the failure of the churches and as dangerous to the people and to the state. This is the view taken by the writer of the report of *Mass Observation*. He is looking at the situation summarized above in its detail, broken down into individual cases; he is concerned about the pitifully bewildered or ignorant answers to the questions put. However, a survey of popular religious opinion is not sufficient evidence of the religious condition of society. There are other factors to be taken into account: educated opinion; the number and influence of believers and active adherents; the opinion of national leaders. Popular religious opinion is only one variable in the formula. There have been no studies in this country to evaluate these other variables; but there are certain assumptions and indications which it is worth while to bring under review for the sake of giving provisional meaning to the survey of popular opinion.

(1) Educated religious opinion is not a more or less casual personal opinion on religious questions: beyond the personal judgement of acceptance or rejection of particular doctrines and claims, is the view of their historical development and meaning and the recognition of religion as an objective problem and a permanent social need. It involves a more or less firm and informed thought-out line of one's own, and not merely respect for the religious convictions of others but also frank and lively interest in their views and the reasons for which they hold them. Such a person, whether he holds any form of the Christian faith or not, recognizes the variety of Christian belief and something of what has gone to the making of that variety. Believers and non-believers take an intelligent and tolerant interest in each other's views, and in so far as this easiness is characteristic of educated people and prevails generally, there is in process a continuous mutual modification not so much of opinions as of claims; there is created a mental and moral climate favourable to variety and resistant to exclusiveness, to fanaticism and infallibility, to ambitious aims and bids for supremacy. When this is the prevailing temper of educated people who hold all the key positions in a society, that society is as safe as it can be from domination by a party; it is as immune as it can be made from the disease of orthodoxy. When persons and parties of opposed views and principles are not raising the issue of who shall suppress whom, and are therefore not in fear of each other, they discover virtues and uses in each other, as well as stimulus and challenge, and become mutually constructive. In such a situation, for example, the Christian church becomes hospitable to much that is not specifically Christian, and by its social acceptance, which is not acceptance of its doctrines, assimilates vitality and modernity that does more for its survival and influence than a mere reform of doctrine, statement, and usage. Thus one should not jump to conclusions when Bishop Barry says that humanism is the religion of half the intelligent persons in the modern world, or Dr. Sperry of America that the men who are doing much if not most of the serious work of the modern world in the professions and at the universities are one generation removed from the church and the Christian faith,[1] or Sir Henry Slesser that educated people in this country hold the views of Bertrand Russell and a modernized

[1] *Religion in America.* By Willard L. Sperry. Cambridge University Press.

stoicism has supplanted religion with them. The pessimism of the Christian observer is not new: one may recall that Butler in the *Advertisement* to his *Analogy* says, not without irony one may suppose, that it is come to be taken for granted as if it were an agreed point among all people of discernment that Christianity is not so much a subject of inquiry but that it is at length discovered to be fictitious. That was more than two hundred years ago, and since then scholarship and science have discovered all the evidence that can ever be used against the Christian case. All the same, there are still many educated persons and subtle thinkers who find themselves able and bound to accept the Christian faith. Indeed, some of those who have been emancipated by scientific education have second thoughts, and with these the churches may have nothing to gain by trying to be liberal and up to date. Dr. Sperry remarks that many of those who have been trained in the biological and social sciences have no use for the liberal churches on account of their optimism about human nature. On both sides, the wise and the knowledge-able have no reason to be cocksure and superior, have every reason to be tolerant and respectful, with a lively interest in each other's minds. Therefore it is reasonable to conclude that educated opinion has not turned definitely against Christianity and is not much likely to in the foreseeable future; and further, that in so far as it has, the humanists even if they were organized (as they are not) would still have a respect and use for the church such as one political party in this country has for another: that in effect the church in this country (comprehensively considered in Coleridge's sense as the whole nation on its ideal side) is not identified with the state, still less with one party, and is not likely to be, but is a twin sphere of like structure. This is a conclusion which most of us on reflection would accept and most of us more often than not forget.

(2) The figure for church attachment and attendance in this country at this time is generally taken to be about ten per cent. of the population. The corresponding figure for America is more than fifty per cent., and for Holland, for example, more than eighty per cent. Assuming that such figures are reliable and strictly comparable, we cannot certainly say what they mean. It may mean that there is a cultural lag, and that the higher figures have a downward trend; and there is evidence for this view. On the other hand, there is enough difference in the situations to account for the difference in figures and leave very little evidence for the thesis that the decline

and fall of the Christian churches has set in, beginning with Britain. The social habit of churchgoing in Britain has lapsed, and that is all that can be positively said. Members of the communist party in the Soviet Union are a small minority of the people. The ten per cent. attached to the churches in Britain include ardent Christians of the highest quality, rare anywhere, who although they are scattered and isolated, and by no means highly organized and disciplined and in power, may leaven the whole lump and have no small influence on the conscience and leadership of the nation. It is they who with a people unconsciously responsive to Christian principles can make a Christian society.[1]

(3) One is bound to consider separately educated and popular opinion, and also to evaluate separately the influence of the small number of deeply Christian persons: but why count separately the opinion of national leaders? The simple answer is that in this matter each does not count for one and no one for more than one. National leaders in the great interests in a democratic country could not flout Christian sentiment if it were actively strong and represented, but if it were weak and unorganized it would not count for much with them unless they were imbued with it themselves. It would appear that in Britain today many of the leaders in politics, in the trade unions, in the civil service, in the professions, and in education are either professed Christians or else Christian in sentiment. The mixture of Christians and non-Christians in the leadership of the nation reproduces at that level the situation characteristic of educated opinion, and ensures respect both for Christian principles and for different views. At the same time, those national leaders who are professed and practising Christians help to bring about an interpenetration of the churches and the great organized interests, interpreting the one to the other, making each more real to the other. For the Christian cause, each is a host in himself, not because he makes converts but because he is a representative public man. Further, sometimes through leading men and sometimes not, there is the use which other interests make of Christian agencies, and the use which Christian interests make of other agencies; and there may be alliances of other interests with the churches or with the Christian cause, marriages of convenience or of love.

The evaluation of the formula for Christian influence in a society is therefore likely to be much higher than the figure merely repre-

[1] *The Idea of a Christian Society.* By T. S. Eliot. Faber and Faber.

senting popular opinion. The figure for popular opinion does not measure the failure of the churches. Of course no accurate computation could be made, and the factors which have to be represented in the product are likely to be more subtle, more powerful, more unpredictable than could be indicated by any weight one would be justified in giving them on abstract considerations such as those which have been reviewed in this paper. The factors themselves have no absolute meaning: it is in their intricate interaction that what they may mean has to be studied. Thus the vague Christian sentiment of the masses may become too diffuse to conduct the current of active Christian appeal on a public issue or a specific occasion. Or Christian leaders and their friends may become suspected of ambitions which non-Christians will not tolerate, and at once goodwill dries up and the situation is transformed. Or the provocation may come from a non-Christian totalitarian party. Moreover, we see nearly every day democratic sentiment, common kindliness, the sense of fair play, and the like, coming to the call of Christian principles or Christian action. The specifically Christian is as difficult to isolate in social influence as a virus or a vitamin; indeed it is much more difficult to isolate. One may say with equal exaggeration and equal truth that the pure life of grace of fundamental Christianity is the only operative Christian principle, and that Christianity is only operative at all when it is so heavily diluted with the life of the natural world that it is hard to detect its trace in any sample.

The main argument of this paper has been that popular religious ideas, always interesting and important, are never in themselves a measure of the influence of religion in a society; they have meant quite different things at different times and never mean anything outside of their relations to other factors in a total situation. It is only by studying fully the total situation in its living complexity that the sociologist or the religious statesman can hope to understand what is going on, and, following his interests and purposes, judge where danger is most real or action most promising. Religion in a modern society is a field of study more difficult than politics and one for which there are fewer techniques and instruments for making assessments. The tortoise of sober judgement is making a slow start, but may still some time overtake the confident conclusions which meanwhile jump into sight and attract the public interest.

Chapter 13

HUMANISM AND CHRISTIANITY

LOGICALLY, there are three mutually exclusive and exhaustive possibilities in the relations between the Christian gospel and civilization: (1) the refusal to compromise the gospel with any tincture or taint of secular interest; (2) the opposite ideal, to christianize civilization completely, to turn all secular interests to Christian account and imprint on every cultural activity a Christian motive and end; (3) the various possibilities of compromise. Historically, all three alternatives have been tried repeatedly. It may be said, supporting the contention also from the history of buddhism, that the utmost which can be done on the first and second alternatives, the extremes, has been demonstrated, and that experience and the pressure of events will confine the future to exploration of the last alternative. There will still be echoes of the others in the major forms of Christianity as well as in eccentric sects, and a surprising turn of events may install one or the other as the dominant alternative again. Normally, however, one can expect future developments to be an elaboration of the theme of compromise. Such forms of compromise will not necessarily lean in the direction of either extreme, quietism or theocracy. In so far as Christians have learned the lessons of history, and hold their faith in that light, they will not want to reconquer the ground lost to autonomous secular culture, for that development is also the development of Christianity itself, and has created the cultural context in which to elaborate its most mature and refined meanings. If, as Richard Niebuhr says in a recent book, 'the problem of Christ and culture can and must come to an end only in a realm beyond all study in the free decision of individual believers and responsible communities', that free decision is not free to ignore historical experience and to treat the logical alternatives as equally live options. Historical experience can never be quite conclusive, but the free decision should be one that can give a reasonable account of itself in the light of that experience. If the Christian chooses again an alternative that has proved illusory or unviable, he must count heavily on a present difference which may reasonably be expected to make a difference. With this reservation, one may fairly say that the most enlightened and effective Christian policy in the future may be expected to follow the alternative of compromise in a way that will recognize the autonomy of secular culture and make full use of it, whilst preserving and restating the full content and authority of the gospel. The policy of Christians, of course, cannot be unaffected by the form which humanism takes and the policy humanists follow. The compromise with culture is, in part, a compromise with humanism. How far it is so, and how far it is entirely an independent evaluation of culture, is the question of main interest to ask of Christians.

Humanism, being itself a conscious self-critical cultural tradition, has not the same theoretical alternatives as Christianity; it is substantially, although perhaps not finally, identified with culture. Its relations with Christianity depend very much on the claims and policies which Christians stress. Historically, in regard to Christianity there is ground for humanist gratitude and for humanist resentment, both profound: gratitude for inestimable services to Western civilization; resentment of the authoritarian repression and obscurantism, as well as of the sectarian fanaticism, which have bedevilled human development in the modern phase, and made the struggle for enlightenment and emancipation bloody and bitter. This ambivalent attitude of humanists to Christianity in the historical perspective is quite familiar; it is too often painfully paralleled in the relations of colonies to their mother country and of sons and daughters to their parents. Christians dominated the discredited past. They will have to play a new creative role if they are to earn lost prestige. The humanist revolution of the last century and a half will go on; its success is in question, and Christians are at least in the position of being able to help to make it disastrous. On the other hand, if Christians abandon once for all authoritarian claims and pretensions and sincerely embrace science and democracy and the liberal welfare-civilization which they imply, the great difference in ultimate beliefs, in motivations and hopes, need not divide the common effort. They can regard humanists as weaker brethren, needlessly self-blinded and superstitiously refusing to use their legs, yet struggling forward in the right direction. They can respect with gratitude the secular development which has enlightened and emancipated Christianity in spite of itself. How much each does owe to the other is a matter for profound and subtle study and for mutual gratitude, which helps to awaken the sense of a common human tradition.

The Christian sense that humanism is all right as far as it goes, that it does not go far enough, that it ought to become 'true humanism', theocentric humanism, is of course matched by the humanist conviction that humanism is both sufficient and more universal and certain than 'true humanism'. And this reproduces in a modern context the eighteenth-century argument between deists and Christians, who shared as common ground morality fertilized by the truths of natural religion, but who differed about the truth and necessity of revelation. In the sequel, the position of the deists proved more vulnerable both intellectually and practically; the new critical philosophy hit it harder and the new disturbance of the foundations of social order was more successfully resisted by the witness and teaching of the evangelicals. History will repeat itself, think many Christians today: Christian theology is better able to stand up to philosophical scrutiny than a rudderless empiricism, and Christianity is the only doctrine that can rationally defend the liberal interpretation and use of science and democracy against the challenge of communism. In so far as this is really the argument, and Christians are not in any way undermining science and democracy, humanists are ready to collaborate with them both in practical policies and programmes and in genuine controversy about foundations and aims, premises and conclusions. Christians who think it is important that people shall be able and willing to think for themselves, to make up their minds and take their decisions and commit themselves, and communicate their experience and respect and interest themselves in the experience of others, more important than that they shall be induced to make Christian decisions and to propagate Christian teaching, and who therefore propose and work for social and educational policies and programmes which promote this kind of spiritual autonomy and intercourse, such Christians, who recognize that the highest values are weakest and are founded on the establishment of stronger and lower values, which therefore have a necessary priority, that Christianity even for the Christian depends on civilization, such Christians are expressing in their Christian policy the humanity and toleration, the liberal values, the enlightenment and emancipation, which humanists uphold. Both are upholding in the structure of their policy the same civilized ideal, not as a common end of action but as a common basis of all that is reasonable and worth while.[1]

The tree is known by its fruit. The profession of this policy is meaningless if in fact Christians do not acknowledge and respect the humanist alternative, if the Christian position is entrenched in the B.B.C., in the schools, and, more figuratively, in most British institutions, on the ground that this is a Christian country, in sentiment if not in theology nor in law. Humanists should not exaggerate this monopoly, nor misrepresent it. Mr. Butler, as minister of education, claimed that the statutory provision for religious instruction and worship in state schools in the 1944 Act was desired by the overwhelming majority of parents; and there is no evidence to show that he was wrong. The Anglican Commissioners reporting on church and state cannot be contradicted when they say: 'There is small sign that any large section of public opinion actively resents the national profession of Christianity involved in its establishment.' The B.B.C. as a public monopoly with an educational responsibility cannot merely hold the mirror to contemporary cultural disintegration, nor has it the authority and the competence to provide a new synthesis; all it can attempt to do is to give predominance to the traditional orthodoxy and to mitigate that partiality by concessions to unorthodox alternatives and by the introduction of free discussion. Finally, the humanist alternative itself can hardly be said to exist yet in an intellectually coherent and compelling form which commands wide assent; it is still for the most part negative disbelief, individual unorthodoxy, and a certain tradition.

In this situation, the strength of the humanist position is in the claim that the great majority who are acknowledged to be outside the churches are not so much lapsed Christians who may be reclaimed as virtual humanists who can be edified. The claims of both Christians and humanists in this respect are idle save as they are

---

[1] It is perhaps also worth while to recall by the way the Anglican conception of the church which Coleridge expounded in his essay *On the Constitution of the Church and State, According to the Idea of Each*. We must be men in order to be citizens, and we must be men and citizens in order to be Christians. Therefore it is the duty of the clergy to humanize and civilize men before it is their duty to win them to Christian faith and life.

realized in fact. Meanwhile, the most that humanists can reasonably ask is that the indifference to and the rejection of Christianity, and the existence of a humanist alternative, shall be openly acknowledged in our public life, and in our schools, that the real situation, whatever it may be, shall be fully accepted as a starting-point by all. Even this simple honesty would in fact take us a long way towards a unity that can never be approached by any other route. Uniformity is out of the question for a long time to come. Active Christians want to have a Christian society with room left for humanists as a tolerated minority. Active humanists would like to be in a position to return the compliment. The bulk of the people are probably indifferent to the question and are not going to be forced to decide where they stand. Public policy in these circumstances is constructive in the degree in which it is honest, and in which Christians and humanists are honest with themselves and with each other.

The crux of the problem is in the schools. The homogeneous believing community naturally wants its children to be brought up within the church, and in this case the school is inside the church, penetrated and enfolded by its ethos, and is not merely a place in which the Christian catechism is taught. This situation is destroyed by the rivalry of sects within the unity of nations as well as by the incidence of disbelief. It belongs to the past unity and uniformity of Christendom for which the church of Rome still stands, one of the logical extremes which, in spite of survivals, has proved incapable of making good its pretensions. Where resistance to the church or the acute rivalry of sects has forced the state to make the neutral school the principle of public educational policy, a school that excludes religious teaching and is founded on common citizenship and moral values, humanists are offered an entrenched battle-front, and they are ready to defend it with all their strength. Although for historical and political reasons such a solution may have been acceptable to the great majority of Christian citizens, in so far as the effect of the policy is, or seems to be, to strengthen the tendency to secularization and to empty the churches, with the abatement of serious conflict between the sects, Christians will naturally want to call the policy in question —as it is now being called in question in the United States. It probably would be true to say that the vast majority of parents (not churches) throughout the Western world, including catholic countries, want their children to have religious teaching at school, and would prefer that it is not dogmatic and not hostile to other faiths.

The statutory provision for religious teaching in English state schools almost fulfils this impossible lay requirement.

Public policy in this matter as in others is determined by political compromise, not by ideals. But what is the ideal? It is not hard to imagine a secular school, in which there is no religious teaching, in which the moral and social development of the child is promoted along with his intellectual and physical development by means of the materials, activities, and situations which make up the life of the school, and in which at the end of the secondary course he is introduced to the main alternative interpretations and evaluations of life on which he may be expected sooner or later to make up his mind and take a decision. Such a procedure, properly followed, would be likely to lead to a more sensitive and thoughtful response to the question of life, to more respect for rejected alternatives and less crude and violent rejections, than present practices do. For it would conform more faithfully both to the actual social situation and to the process by which intellectual and moral convictions and decisions are genuinely formed.

Even if Christians and humanists were agreed and happy about the foundations of public policy on the question of religion at the present time, they would remain in vital opposition and regard each other's view as essentially pernicious, Christians because humanists leave no room for transcendence, have no eternal perspective (or conceive very differently their transcendence and their eternal prospect), and leave man to the wretchedness of his state, subject to sin and death, humanists because Christians deceive men with false hopes, undermine and disparage true satisfactions, and leave the spirit impaired and debilitated save in so far as it is stayed on faith in illusions. That Christians and humanists who do remain in vital opposition and regard each other's view as disastrously mistaken can reasonably co-operate and respect and tolerate each other is possible only on one condition, namely, the recognition of fallibility. I think my chosen alternative is right and I think that the others are monstrously incredible and, in so far as they are taken seriously, extremely injurious. Nevertheless, I may be wrong; and even in so far as I am right, the existence and influence of other alternatives bear witness to the insufficiency of mine; their questioning, their challenge, their chastening is necessary to the truth and soundness, or, rather, to the vital self-awareness of my alternative. A view that does not include recognition of its insufficiencies is too narrow to be a view of the human situation. This is a hard doctrine, hard to accept, harder still to apply sensibly. (Of course it is not a doctrine that has any meaning if it is the bid for power and not the appeal to reason that is in question.) Theoretically, other views may be wrong-headed and damnable, yet in practice they may meet the needs and suit the condition of many people more effectively than the right view. Moreover, no alternative is before the world exclusively in its highest development and most refined elaboration, and each alternative in its crudity requires the confrontation of others. Such considerations are not over-subtle, such a state of affairs is not a happy one, but it is made far unhappier by the intolerance and intransigence in practice which purely theoretical considerations might seem to justify and to recommend. Coleridge's warning against fanaticism, 'He who begins by loving Christianity better than the Truth will proceed by loving his own sect or church better than Christianity, and end in loving himself better than all', may be generalized against him who puts his own alternative, his preferred reading of human life in the world, in place of the human situation itself, and without looking at the human tradition in which it is mirrored. In this deep soil is rooted the toleration that can be shaken and seasoned by the storms of controversy, the only toleration that is not shallow indifference.

PART THREE

Chapter 14

AN ANATOMY OF ATTITUDES

I

SOMETIMES it is said (facetiously or maliciously) that philosophies are nothing but elaborate rationalizations of underlying attitudes which have no rational foundation. If this were simply true, it would be possible and useful to construct, in place of the history of philosophy, a morphology of attitudes, by digging down to and exposing and classifying these underlying fundamental attitudes. Because the clue to some philosophies is rather obviously in the make-up of the philosopher (take Nietzsche for an example), it is tempting to think or to say that the truth about philosophy is the truth about the philosophers. Two cautions ought to check this short way with philosophers. One is that attitudes are not psychological ultimates or constants, independent of assumptions and judgements about the world, a stock of elements found pure or compounded in human nature and determining the individual's way of taking and tackling things. They are personal responses to judgements, implicit or explicit, about the world; and philosophy, as the explication and justification of such judgements, is not merely rationalizing nor merely expressing an underlying attitude but is elaborating its rational foundation. Let reason raze a rationalization, and the psychological roots feed immediate sprouts. But if reason finally destroys a philosophy, the attitudes rooted in it are shrivelled. Views are not simply determined by attitudes. But neither are attitudes simply determined by views, for the attitude is a personal response to the assumptions and judgements held, and other responses are possible. The second caution is that the word attitude is ambiguous in this context. The philosopher's attitude may be his response to his personal situation, favourable or unfavourable, which he generalizes and projects on to the world, or it may be his reasoned response to a reasoned reading of the human situation; the philosophy may be a symptom of an inferiority complex or it may be simply what it pretends to be. Both types of philosophy are found, with their variations and complications, amongst the great philosophical productions. The theoretical distinction is a clue and a criterion.

With these cautions in mind, it is legitimate to inquire whether there are not typical attitudes bound up with typical views of the world which are more ultimate than any of the historical doctrines. Family likenesses amongst the historical doctrines are often noticed. Are the resemblances superficial or significant? Do they help us to interpret the historical development of thought? Can we hope to formulate in philosophy a true disjunction, an exhaustive set of mutually exclusive alternatives, and would it be useful if we could? Such questions may be answered by examining some scheme of classification of the most general patterns of thought and attitude that have prevailed in the West. The scheme proposed here for this purpose distinguishes three main types: (1) stoic, protestant, and existentialist individualism; (2) epicurean, renaissance, romantic, and liberal individualism; (3) theocratic, platonic, and marxist communism. Each member of each of these groups is a special complex of judgements and attitudes, approximating more or less to a pure type. What follows is an attempt to define each type and to describe each of its leading historical examplars in terms of it.

II

(1) TRANSCENDENTAL INDIVIDUALISM. The essential characteristic of this group is a total acceptance of the human situation founded upon a total rejection. Acceptance does not follow and replace rejection, nor do they alternate; they are consciously maintained in tension, and each is used to make the other more profound and real, complete. There is no withdrawal from and no abandonment to the world; daily life is used to realize both the rejection and the acceptance, and the sole theme and whole content of living is to perfect oneself in this realization. By this extreme tension, the human situation is transcended in some way and resolved. Faith, philosophic or religious, may play a part in the resolution, an essential part, but it does not itself provide the resolution, its uncertainty increases the tension. The attitude is a struggle

to hold tenaciously and courageously to what are held to be the fundamental realities, even though they threaten to pull one apart: the evil and irrationality of the world in one's experience of it; the indefeasible demand for rationality and a moral order; the possibility of a transcendental solution; the uncertainty of it. The stubborn refusal to abandon or to allow anyone to take away any one of these abiding realities forbids a solution, but the very refusal of illusory solutions is the necessary condition of a true solution, and opens the way to a possible experience of the solution: the best the individual can do is to keep himself open to this experience. The explanation of the paradox that the world is at the same time rejected and accepted is that normal human responses to the world are inhibited and yet the demands of the world are complied with, and this attitude is bound up with orientation towards a transcendental solution—which may be literary, or sustained by moral pride, and does not necessarily involve religious faith.

Stoicism. The stoic teaching exemplifies the position historically in its simplest developed form (a rudimentary form is exemplified by the cynics). The stoic makes a total acceptance of the world without discrimination: whatever falls out, whatever comes to him, he accepts it absolutely as his good because he has no power over events and he has, if he will, full power over his own attitude. In order to be able to accept as good what he naturally dislikes, he has to school himself in detachment and indifference: his absolute acceptance is absolute rejection, and the other way round. He remains in daily life and realizes the absoluteness of rejection and acceptance as best he can in every transaction. To help him out and to make it reasonable, he postulates a divine reason which ordains all things, so that whatever is is best. But that is a matter of faith, and even if the epicureans were right and the world had come into existence by chance, he would remain constant and continue to put reason and order into things by consistently accepting with an equal temper whatever befell because consistently rejecting the appeal to his natural likes and dislikes, fears and hopes. By this attempt to transcend the human situation, he hopes to enjoy independence and immunity, autarky.

Protestantism. There are of course many protestant sects, with their own forms of Christian belief, but if protestant insistence on the right of the individual believer to throw himself without mediation before God, and his responsibility before God to seek his salvation by the light of the Bible, be taken together with the characteristic protestant return to the Old Testament, there is a discernible type of protestantism which stands very close to the universal type of this group. The conception of the world as under divine judgement, and of the individual as bound to a personal creator in obedience and for salvation, sharply distinguishes Christian from Greek thought. It derives of course from the historical experience of Israel as interpreted by the prophets. The nation was smashed, and Judah survived only as a religious congregation. Out of this situation emerged a consciousness of individual, not merely national, dependence upon God, and a readiness for total rejection of the personal will, as a measure of that dependence. The total rejection was the obverse of the total acceptance of God's will; moreover God willed both the total rejection and the total acceptance, and that was the meaning of their historical experience. Belief in the Christian revelation was a sequel to this fundamental interpretation of the human situation, into which the Scriptures of the Jews baptized all men. Rejection of the world as the theatre of man's hopes and fears, his triumphs and failures, and acceptance of it as the appointed school of probation, a probation that was to prove in daily conduct not so much virtues as faith, that is, the reality of the total rejection and the total acceptance, this is a Biblical individualism, perhaps universally Christian, but characteristically protestant. (The original closeness of stoicism to semitic ways of thought and its later assimilation by Christianity make it not surprising that protestantism should resemble it.) The world is rejected totally as not answering to human hopes and desires; at the same time it is accepted totally in faith; and the reality of both rejection and acceptance is proved in everyday life; and always the uncertainty of faith, the impossibility of deferring or delegating the decision, the personal risk and responsibility of the course taken, leaves the individual in moral isolation and therefore compels him to seek the assurance of his hope, to remain open to the experience of transcendence.

Existentialism. The movement of thought to which the name existentialism has been given developed in the context of Christian conceptions. Indeed, Kierkegaard was applying the characteristic judgements and attitudes of transcendental individualism precisely to an established Christian society. He made a total rejection and a total acceptance of Christianity itself, or, to look at the other side of the medal, of reason itself. Neither Christianity nor reason could be renounced, nor could they be reconciled. He rejects the finite world with its limited hopes and fears, ruined by infinite uncertainties and longings. The possible transcendental solution is for him identified with the historical Christian revelation, but it is not merely uncertain, it is inconceivable. The question bears down with its full weight upon the individual, standing alone without the possibility of support from another individual nor from the established authorities or traditions of society. No decision which the individual makes at personal risk lightens the weight of the burden; in his daily tasks he goes on bearing the strain of acceptance of what he has rejected, just as he goes on bearing the strain of accepting with his whole life what his reason goes on rejecting totally. The strains are felt to be necessary, inescapable realities of the human situation; the only hope is in bearing them: that can lead somewhere, nothing less can.

To turn to the catholic Gabriel Marcel is to be struck by a difference, for here is a Christian humanist insisting that the recovery of faith, which is necessary in a ruined world that cries out for salvation, begins with the recreation of the poetry of everyday existence, restoration of the happy nuptial tie which unites man to his natural life; the responsive, open spirit begins to trace an arc which faith and hope round out to the full circle. Yet Marcel, not less than the others, insists that the world is a standing invitation to despair, the transcendental solution which the human situation demands cannot in principle be ever objectively assured. It is only by courageous building on certain revealing and intensely intimate experiences that we can dare to reject totally the objective evidence and issue a call to which there can be a response, and be ready to hear a call to which we can respond. This openness and creativeness which make possible a transcendental solution are maintained by striving to use the objective forms which are the structure of everyday living (institutions, third-party relationships and judgements, possessions, etc.) as the means of achieving a personal transcendence: here again is the total acceptance which is a total rejection. Marcel began his thinking with the ideas of the idealists, but from the start worked his way towards existentialism: 'from the beginning my researches were explicitly directed towards what might be called the concrete examination of the individual and of the transcendent, as opposed to all idealism based on the impersonal or the immanent'.

Of the existentialists who are not Christians, Jaspers is nearest to Christianity. For him, too, human life in principle cannot be realized in the world, for science cannot be completed in knowledge of the whole, which reason cannot renounce, nor can human aims escape the frustration imposed by the unalterable structure of the human situation (death, conflict, etc.). Nevertheless, there is no other knowledge than science and no other life than life in this world. By total acceptance which is a total rejection, we keep ourselves open to the experience of transcendence, in which we can have a philosophic faith: but it cannot be assured by any method, nor communicated.

Heidegger's identification of all individual possibilities with the ultimate possibility of death, the nothingness of human existence, is the most drastic of all rejections. And his insistence on realizing in daily life this mortification is the most thoroughgoing total acceptance of the totally rejected life. He uses it for the same purpose, to open the individual to the possible experience of transcendence, in which lies the only hope of a solution of the human situation.

Sartre finds in the structure of human reality the contradiction which is the dynamic and the invincible frustration of human living. We exist in being not identified with anything; the distinctiveness of a personal consciousness is that it is not anything it knows, nor what it has been, nor even what it is. On the other hand, it seeks to be something self-dependent and self-founded, but if it could succeed it would extinguish its personal consciousness: it cannot be both identified with a positive existence and conscious of it. The structure of our reality involves us in other similar invincible frustrations and indefeasible efforts. All we can do is to recognize and accept the situation as the condition of our existence and try to get as near as we can in all that we do to the impossible triumph of surmounting the contradictions. On the basis of this total acceptance of the human situation, the individual totally rejects provisionally the civilization which has been built upon it (as Kierkegaard rejected Christian civilization) and totally accepts responsibility for it, responsibility for conforming to it or for remaking it; otherwise he has not constituted himself fully personal. Nothing relieves him of individual responsibility for making the world in all that he does.

The case of Nietzsche is instructive. Roughly speaking, he began with Schopenhauer's judgement of the world as irremediably evil, on which Schopenhauer based a total rejection; but Nietzsche wanted to achieve a total acceptance, and he rejected not Schopenhauer's judgement but the standard of his judgement, his rejection. Nietzsche's total acceptance was a complete identification with the world as it is (or as it was in his judgement of it), not an acceptance founded upon rejection; he rejected instead the values and standards by which the rejection of the world as he judged it could have been made. The transcendence he sought was not immediately and personally enjoyed, with the power of tension beneath him, it was merely postulated, an evolutionary human goal. One cannot and need not say that his madness was the catastrophic result of this solution, but it was a solution which tended to destroy the characteristically human qualities of human existence, as the other solutions more typical of this group tend to maintain them at all costs, personalizing the self not only by an act of acceptance of the objective world but by also rejecting it, not being identified with it.

The solution effected by transcendental individualism may be called a religious solution, whether or not it is Christian; and it may not be even theistic. It makes total and radical judgements of the world, and insists that only total and radical solutions are real. The world is transcended by means of a total rejection and acceptance of it, in a critical act of total choice re-enacted in daily realizations, and this can only be done by the individual on his own responsibility. The risk is sharply recognized as very real and incapable of being mitigated by or shared with social authorities or traditions, for the transcendent reality it is hoped to experience cannot be reduced nor objectified by human measures: it is by definition beyond the world, although it embraces the world and is indirectly accessible from within the world.

(2) HUMANISTIC INDIVIDUALISM. The members of this group do not make a global judgement on the human situation and found a universal attitude upon it which they strive to realize in every act and relationship and response of daily existence, an heroic attempt to be equal to the worst in human fate and private lot by anticipation. They are readier naïvely to take happiness and success at their face value. They are intent on achievement rather than transcendence, on careers rather than inwardness. The pleasures and opportunities, the promise and possibilities of human life in the world engage their interest and their energies. The world offers them raw material and they are confident in their powers. They seek to know the world in order to adapt it to their needs, their desires, their designs, rather than in order to adapt themselves to its inexorable requirements; they survey the obstacles in order to remove them, and do not submit to them in order to surmount them. With them, 'mankind has not learned to renounce anything, has not outgrown

the instinctive egotism and optimism of the young animal, and has not removed the centre of its being, or of its faith, from the will to the imagination'. The risks they run and the responsibilities they take in their solitary individualism are not the responsibilities and risks of a philosophic choice of life which goes against all appearances, or does not dare to, but the responsibilities and risks of trusting to their judgement and capacities in practical ventures. They do not accept life, nor do they reject it: they handle it.

Epicurus. Like the stoics, the epicureans exemplify their type with an antique simplicity. In the teaching of Epicurus there is so much moderation and adaptation of the will, so little modification and adaptation of the environment, so much the same aim as the stoics professed, to enjoy a self-sufficiency that would ensure freedom, tranquillity, that it makes a transition from the one type to the other. The essential difference is in assumptions, method, and temper. By wise choice and avoidance, and by limiting desires to those that are simple, easily satisfied, proved, and lasting, Epicurus sought to create a social environment in which success in living a natural satisfying human life is not merely possible but normal and fairly assured. He withdrew from the world as the stoics did not, but that was the condition of his making a world that was safe for the human values he chose and cherished. It was a simple and primitive model of the modern democratic social enterprise, as interpreted by John Dewey for example, a community of friends co-operating to secure the shared satisfactions of a good life. And the underlying assumption, which basically divided the teaching from that of the stoics, was that the world and human history were not ordained by divine reason, but that the one constituted a natural order which could be studied and the other a human order which could be improved and developed by reason, making inventive use of the natural order. The whole teaching is that the conditions are favourable enough and it is in our own hands to live a natural and successful human life, if we are guided by reason; and that it is better to fail in a life that is guided by reason than to succeed by chance in one that is not.

The Renaissance. Burckhardt has emphasized the emergence of the self-conscious personality at the close of the thirteenth century in Italy, and the cult of individualism and of fame. However much the historical generalization may stand in need of correction and refinement, the Renaissance accent on the individual is loud enough to be heard by everyone, and the individualism of this type is in bold contrast to the individualism of the protestant Reformation. Of course it contrasts hardly less strongly with epicurean individualism. The strings of passion are not muted, the competition of the rough world is not eschewed, the complexities are not simplified, the many-sided possibilities are not renounced, there is no playing for safety; and in place of the individual satisfactions cultivated by the epicureans, so impersonal in their simple human generality, like the drinking of water for the satisfaction of thirst, the Renaissance individual cultivated the rare satisfactions of the eminently great, the stupendously accomplished, the fully developed, the astonishing achievement. Not, 'The man who is not satisfied with little is satisfied with nothing', but, 'Men can do all things if they will', set the limits. Nevertheless, the contrasts are not greater than the essential identity, for both are using the resources disposed of to treat human life as a work of art; the style and temper are as different as classic and romantic, but the aim and the accomplishment are artistic rather than religious or intellectual. Of course the epicurean life is pre-eminently a life of reason, and the stoic may play the game of life in such a way that the style is all; but that is only to say that there are intellectual and aesthetic aspects, with many others, of all complete human enterprises; for the stoic glorifies the style of playing to show his contempt for the outcome of the game rather than because he cares so much for style, it is his triumph over the natural human concern that he cares about; and the epicurean uses his reason in order to construct a natural human life that is craftsmanlike and world-worthy, as he uses science to remove his superstitious fears not to satisfy curiosity nor attain contemplation. To stress the aesthetic aspect of humanistic individualism as its essential character does not mean that the individual values specially the formal qualities of his achievement, still less that he is spectator of the human theatre, it means that he uses the materials furnished by nature and by man to construct his life. The individual construction may be a work of reason or of passion, or of any other temper, but the humanist treats his materials for their qualities and uses, and does not impose on them indifferently, as the transcendental individualist does, the same chosen general pattern of living.

Romanticism. The romantic is even further removed than the Renaissance ideal from the epicurean model. Its indiscipline and excess, its mutability and insatiability, its reckless abandonment to experience rather than control of the self and of the materials used in a pattern of achievement inwardly enjoyed and outwardly recognized, its utter insobriety and intransigence, separate it absolutely from an ideal that is designed to succeed and can succeed. Yet it is an ideal, and it does exemplify the type, and exemplify it superbly, in the freedom and boldness of its interpretation and of its pursuit of its chosen ideal, in its choice of this world for its own sake and the completeness of its commitment to that choice, without a thought of prudential reservations and safeguards. There is a brilliant delineation of the romantic ideal in Santayana's essay on Goethe in his *Three Philosophical Poets*. 'The zest of romanticism consists in taking what you know is an independent and ancient world as if it were material for your private emotions. In the romantic hero the civilized man and the barbarian must be combined; he should be the heir to all civilization, and, nevertheless, he should take life arrogantly and egotistically, as if it were an absolute personal experiment. . . . If only his will is done, he does not ask whether, judged by its fruits, it will be worth doing.' It makes an ideal of full-blooded acceptance of the world without ideals and without illusions, and plunges into an infinite experience that refuses all conditions and all goals. 'To live, to live just as we do, that is the purpose and the crown of living. The worth of life lies in pursuit, not in attainment; therefore everything is worth pursuing, and nothing brings satisfaction—save this endless destiny itself.' The romantic ideal is the destruction and dissolution of everything established and standing, and at the same time it is the renewal of the springs of life, spontaneity, immediacy, originality, freedom, sincerity, first-hand genuineness, innocence, freshness, naïvety, infinite possibility. It is impossible to classify because it is the perpetually recurrent challenge to all ideals. 'No construction, however broadly based, will have an *absolute* authority; the indomitable freedom of life to be more, to be new, to be what it has not entered into the heart of man as yet to conceive, must always remain standing. With that freedom goes the modesty of reason that can lay claim only to partial knowledge, or to the ordering of a particular soul, or city, or civilization.'

Liberalism. The liberal ideal is a political or social ideal, a theory of the way in which society should be organized, not a personal idea, not a judgement of the world with an attitude and choice of life founded upon it: it affirms and seeks to ensure the freedom of each to seek his happiness or his salvation in his own way. Liberals may be, and typically have been, protestant Christians. Its inclusion therefore as an example of humanistic individualism requires some justification. Historically, it is a revolt and a protest against ideals of the third type, against an authoritarian social order founded upon an authoritative interpretation of the world. The personal outlook of the first type is theoretically compatible with any type of social order, because of the totality of its interdependent acceptance and rejection. Ideals of the second type make a point of non-acceptance and non-rejection, they insist on picking and choosing and making the world safe for their chosen constructions of individual satisfaction. The insistence of liberalism on the freedom of each individual to think for himself and to pursue his own happiness in his own way certainly does not and cannot exclude ideals of the first type, and indeed includes as part of its aim the intention of making the world safe for them, but the liberal ideal would hardly exist (in spite of the historical contribution to its formation by the protestant reformers) if it were not founded on belief in the value and use of personal self-development, of successful careers, and of a progressive culture. Rather than itself a particular example of humanistic individualism, it is perhaps a union of all historical and possible forms of such individualism for their common protection, to create the social conditions of their successful coexistence. But it then becomes a theory of human life, with an attitude founded upon it, an historical theory; for Croce, liberalism is a concept of reality and an ethics that conforms to this concept, that is, it is essentially a religion, 'the irreplaceable religion'.

This is a type of liberalism which is not concerned to make the world safe for individualism (after all, Hobbes and the early Bentham were just as concerned for that), but to make way for the self-revelation of the historical process through the self-determination of peoples exercising and maintaining political freedom and freedom of thought as the foundation of all self-realization. This hegelian conception of liberalism, prevalent under many forms in the nineteenth century, so different from the utilitarian conception, is liberal in its insistence on freedom, but in its essential conception of human good and the solution of the human problem it exemplifies the third type and not the second.

(3) ORGANIC THEORIES. The individualistic attitudes so far described are of course practised in a society, and are integrated into the society and satisfy its requirements. In general, attitudes of the first type conform to social requirements, whatever they may be,

in the course of practising the discipline of acceptance and rejection. The things that are Caesar's are faithfully returned to Caesar. Responsibility for the personal attitude and its realization is the one thing that is not surrendered. Attitudes of the second type require a society that will protect, or at least tolerate, them. Such a society is not necessarily liberal. Indeed, the purpose of the absolute power in Hobbes's *Leviathan* is to make the world safe for private pursuits, for individualism. Whereas most liberal thinkers have been concerned about the benefits to society to be gained by promoting the liberty, independence, and activity of its individual members. Liberalism is a theory of society. On the other hand, it arises as a charter of individualism, a repudiation of the organic theories, a claim that the individual must be allowed and enabled to construct for himself his own individually satisfying solution. On the organic theories, the individual can never construct his own good, however free and endowed with resources society makes him, because human good is a social construction to which the individual is required to contribute and in which he can participate, but which he can never appropriate. The individual does not stand alone in moral isolation to wrestle with his problem and risk his destiny on his own responsibility. He is born into an already constituted good which he is called on to sustain and to share. What is evil or irrational in the world is attributable to the failure of individuals to fill their place and play their part in the realization of the universal good, by which they bring evil not only on themselves but also to all. Therefore there is no escape from evil by the heroic measures exemplified by the first type, and there is no achievement of good by attempting to construct it for oneself in the manner exemplified by the second type. The whole glory and tragedy of human existence is played out within the bounds of the one system of universal good, social and cosmic.

Platonism. The *Republic*, Plato's ideal construction of the good, reflects and repeats the organic harmony of the cosmos and of its microcosm, the individual man, whose cardinal virtues perfect and harmonize his individual powers, as they perfect and harmonize the social functions by which the absolute good is realized, in which all participate, each in the measure of his ability. The *Republic* exemplifies the Greek quest for the perfect constitution, or a complete and final body of laws which would regulate human relations once for all, and would be as an impersonal passionless mind, from which each would learn without resentment the conduct that would lead

to his own and the general good, and which would not only harmonize individuals in their social relations but also harmonize them
within themselves and harmonize human society with the universal
order of the cosmos. This ideal pattern moulded Christian thought,
pre-eminently in Augustine and in Aquinas.

Theocracies. The phrase 'Kingdom of God' expresses the notion of
rule by God of a society ordained to some consummation, outside
of which there cannot be any good or prosperous thing. The idea of
their being a chosen people whose destiny lay in the hands of their
God existed and persisted in Israel with an unparalleled absoluteness
and development of content. Until the worst disaster befell them,
the prophet and the king played the major roles in developing the
theocratic polity. After the return of the remnant of Judah from
exile, emphasis returned to the priest, the law, and the altar. The
completion of the law, the consummation of the ritual, routinized
the rule of God, but the living idea awaited the act of God, the
apocalypse. The teaching of Jesus that the kingdom of God was
within the individual man reaffirmed ideas in the Old Testament
prophets (for example, Jeremiah xxxi, 31-4) of a kingdom directly
ruled by God, because each man, and not merely the prophet, was
filled with the spirit of God and knew and fulfilled the law.

In the medieval church, the double conception persists. On the
one hand, there is a hierarchical, sacramental system, administering
in the divine dispensation the priesthood of Christ, claiming to be
the sole means of approach to and knowledge of God and the sole
appointed means of God's grace and salvation; on the other hand,
there is the invisible church, the 'congregation of saints', enjoying
grace in simple dependence upon God. The difference is like the difference between the notion that the church is in the world not for
the sake of the world but for the sake of the elect, and the idea that
the church is in the world to rule the world in order to christianize
it and perfect it. The leading idea in the system of Thomas Aquinas,
an idea borrowed from the metaphysics of Aristotle, is expressed in
a simple sentence in one of his sermons. 'The highest perfection of a
thing is that it should be subject to that which perfects it.' As 'matter
is not perfect unless it be subjected to form', so the soul is perfected
in being subject to God, and society in being subject to the church.
For the soul is not directly subject to God; on earth, it is under angels,
prelates, and teachers and conforms to the law and is formed in the
image of God. But in heaven all 'principality' is done away with and

each directly enjoys the vision of God, as in the prophecy of Jeremiah. Similarly, in society each has his station and his duty and is instructed what he shall do for the common good; and on earth men are unequal, but in heaven there is no regard for what they have been, only for what their faithfulness has been. Thus the entire economy of God is a perfect community founded on a common good, the same for each, which is the chief end of all action and for the sake of which the law rules and regulates each individual life. The vision of Jeremiah, the 'congregatio sanctorum', and the like, are foretastes of the consummation of the labours of the church. On this view, disobedience is not only the first sin, it is also the last, and typical, sin. Persecution is justified. There is no private good. Enjoyment of the final good is not totally postponed, since there is anticipation of it in the blessing of grace which supervenes on obedience to the law in faith.

Communism. Under a divine dispensation, the common good is not a social construction, since it is the gift of God to each individual soul, but the whole social order and divine economy is ordained to the end of bringing each to the state of being able to enjoy the given good; the historical society is a conditioning process in which all are called to participate as the condition of their possessing the good laid up for them. Political and social ideals which derive from Hegel bear a strong family likeness to this conception of the divine order. Hegel thought of human good as a social creation in the platonic sense, with the individual integrated into the social order which produced it. At the same time, he saw that the actual historical society was not planned and ruled by rational legislation providing for the social construction and maintenance of human good in the manner of Plato and Aristotle, or of Bentham. The happy realization of community in the Greek city-state was temporary and partial, and was challenged by the theocratic idea, which separated the nation from secular history and the individual soul from secular society. He therefore saw an historical process, to which he applied the platonic notion of dialectical development. On the macroscopic scale, historical development was the archetype of self-realization; the life of the individual might be futile and abortive, that of the nation could not be, and therefore the stoic faith in the real world as rational, as what ought to be, was justified, and the individual got his reality and his worth through his society, in which he became conscious of his own rational essence and of universal reason in its concreteness, and of their union through his participation in the on-going process of that society, integrating himself into it. This conception of human good as individual participation in society, illumined by a philosophical interpretation of history as a necessary process of development, is the pattern of marxist communism. The conception is repudiated by liberal thought, in so far as the historical development is held to be discernible and the future predictable, or at least rigorously determined. But liberalism shows a similar confidence that human good is an historical realization beyond the scope of human plans, in insisting that the perpetual twin social tasks of freedom and enlightenment, ineradicably rooted in human aspirations, are the sources of progress and of an achievement in which individual and social good are integrated.

This type of solution is essentially political. Of course, not all political thought is concerned with a total solution. Macchiavelli, one of the earliest liberals, was interested simply in studying the conditions of a stable and prosperous society, in which the activity and liberty of the citizens would be continuously promoted with their security. The modern democratic socialist may simply be concerned to organize basic welfare. Yet in both cases, and in others, there is the assumption that secular human good can be socially constructed and safeguarded, and that it is worth while. Macchiavelli cared more for Florence than for the salvation of his immortal soul. The modern social democrat may care supremely for social justice or for the achievement of a free and creative community. In such cases, the political solution is total, whether or not the theory says so.

III

The historical examples which have been used to describe the three typical attitudes are determined by historical conditions: Jewish quietism follows the destruction of the Jewish state, stoicism and epicureanism flourish in the centuries following the destruction of the Greek city-state, the society of medieval Christendom is heir to the Roman Empire, and so on. These attitudes made sense in the circumstances which prevailed, were responses to the historical situation. Further, as has been shown, they have profoundly influenced one another, the earlier historical experience and reflection upon it and response to it helping to inspire and shape later responses. Still further, the development of knowledge and the imperatives of temperament enter deeply into the determination of actual attitudes. The question is, how can the definition of abstract types have any validity or value when the facts are historical, non-recurrent, individual?

If there were not a core of recognizable identity at the centre of widely different historical and individual responses, a recurrent essence, there would of course be no type at all. The validity of the type is tested by asking whether or not it does reveal an identity in difference which is itself revealing, a clue, or whether it merely imposes an arbitrary abstraction on the historical complex of individual facts. Unless the type shows us a real identity, and unless the historical differences between the same attitudes help us to see the nature and the meaning of the attitudes, the type is a futile abstraction.

Take stoicism and existentialism as examples of the first type, and epicureanism and romanticism as examples of the second. One might easily pair stoicism with epicureanism and existentialism with romanticism. Both the stoic and the epicurean were out to gain self-sufficiency as the guarantee of tranquillity, and merely proposed different methods. Both the existentialist and the romantic are interested only in experience and keeping alive in the freshness of personal experience, even at the cost of suffering and tension, and will even promote and perpetuate suffering and tension for this purpose. On the other hand, the stoic is far from the existentialist in his reduction and elimination of the personal, by his invariable conformity making himself impersonal and universal, and in founding himself upon the principle of immanence, the immanence of divine reason, not upon the concrete individual and the transcendent. And the epicurean and romantic are, if possible, even more violently opposed, the one choosing in pleasure simply the avoidance of pain and disturbance of the mind, and finding sufficiency in little, the other refusing to be satisfied, were it with everything, and seeking only to be able to say at the end of a long, difficult, and stormy life, 'I have felt'. These differences and resemblances are profound and important and would wreck the classification proposed if it could not be shown that it is based on identities even more profound and important. Stoic and epicurean are only formally identified by their end. The stoic makes a global decision for the sake of an outright victory over himself and the world, whereas the epicurean seeks to build up a quiet enjoyment of life by picking and choosing and good management. The romantic by his ready adoption of any and every attitude for the sake of the experience bears resemblance to them all and is impossible to classify, but his indiscipline rules him out of kinship with the first and third types, and he is identified with the second by his individualistic pursuit of a chosen ideal constructed out of the materials of natural existence taken for their own quality and savour. And the existentialist, profoundly different from the stoic as he is by his rejection of immanence and his insistence on personality and on experience, is more essentially identified with him in his preoccupation with a world he is impelled both to reject and to accept in a total decision re-enacted every day, a world he desires only to transcend. The value of the identifications as a clue to the interpretation of each historical example could only be shown in detailed studies of individual exemplars.

On the assumption that a careful examination of historical attitudes would or could lead to the establishment of these three types, what permanent factors are there in the human situation or in human beings to explain it? There do seem to be two general factors which help to explain the nature and relations of these typical attitudes.

(1) All three are developed sophisticated attitudes that presuppose the vicissitudes of long historical experience and prolonged reflection upon it; they are complex theories and ideals of human life in the world shaped out of an accumulation of trial and error. Thus stoicism, epicureanism, and platonism are essentially, although not exclusively, three different solutions emerging out of reflection upon the breakdown of the Greek city-state. Within judaism, transcendental individualism and the priestly theocratic ideal were both reflective solutions of the problem posed by the destruction of Israel, and both reappeared inevitably in the Christian church. Although the third type is as much a reflective theory and ideal as the others are, it does conform more closely to the exigencies of society and to the actual pattern of a successful polity, and to that extent it is the norm which ideals of the other two types reject or modify. As types, all three are mutually exclusive, and historically they have been, although not altogether, independent solutions of the human problem. The conclusion would seem to be that they are related as permanent aspects of a total solution. Conjoined in such a solution, of course, the mutual modifications would make each of them unlike any of the historical manifestations in which they are dominant. A system of social good, individual venture and achievement, personal self-

transcendence: these may seem to be the normal and natural ingredients of a good life. So they may be, but the historical existence of these contrasted attitudes and typical ideals means the persistent tendency for one or another to be cultivated intensively and exclusively. The truth is that the total solution is exceedingly difficult.

(2) At bottom, there is the simple alternative of acceptance or rejection of human life in the world. This simplicity, however, is the result of a complex development, for it is hardly possible seriously to reach such a point of choice without a lot of experience and without being thrown back on oneself in reflection. Even then, acceptance or rejection is likely to be a reasonable description of a general attitude rather than actually a reasoned explicit decision. This anatomy of attitudes has not been an empirical analysis of prevailing psychological attitudes, but a dissection of abstract theories, which presuppose such attitudes but which as theories are developed and worked over by many generations. Any such theory, therefore, is likely to be more elaborate and complex than any such psychological attitude, and to be nearer the final simplicity of acceptance or rejection. Nevertheless, with all the room for diversity and complication which there is both in the theoretical attitudes and in actual attitudes, three primary attitudes seem to recur: rejection, leading to some form of effective withdrawal; acceptance, with the idea of exploitation, gaining for oneself some form of power, possessions, fame, pleasures; acceptance, with the idea of participation, taking part in some universal process or joining with others in the production and enjoyment of some common good. Looking again at the three developed types which have just been examined, one might apply these three primary attitudes and label the first, withdrawal, the second, exploitation, the third, participation. That would be too crude, for these primary attitudes are found in all disguises. Exploitation has characteristically been the ruin of systems of the third type, and also they have been attacked by existentialists for providing cover for almost universal withdrawal into the impersonal conventions which enable the individual to evade personal responsibility for the choice of life. Participation may even be practised by the romantic, the most shameless exploiter of all. These primary attitudes are entirely personal realizations and cannot be generalized nor objectified. Rather than say, even, that participation is the characteristic virtue of the third type, and that withdrawal is the characteristic vice of the first, and exploitation of the second, it would be

nearer the mark to say that they are all ideal types of participation, that the difference between them is partly a difference in assumptions about the character of human existence, and that the first two are in some cases, if not essentially, a recourse to which men are driven by the practical difficulties and historical failures of the third type, which promises the basis of the most powerful and complete participation that can be achieved.

Why is it supposed that participation is the 'right' attitude, the only appropriate attitude of such beings as we are to such a world as this is? Exploitation, as a general attitude, reduces all things to the measure of oneself, seeks to subdue everything to one's use and to bring everything to an end in oneself. Participation is not an obliteration of oneself, a sacrifice of oneself to the selfishness of others; it is to enter into a life beyond one's own which includes and consummates one's own. It is an attitude of expansion, of venture, of growth, of faith, as withdrawal and exploitation are at bottom both attitudes of despair, of *sauve qui peut*.

The general conclusion, then, would seem to be that personal participation in a universal system which is itself a form of participation in a universal life is the ideal to which history bears witness, either directly or by the light of the alternatives to which men are driven. It is fairly safe to say, however, that no historical realization, if ever so sweet and reasonable, could satisfy the romantic or the protestant. The one would always want to taste other possibilities. The other must gain transcendence by annihilation of the actual, through withdrawal, renunciation, or historical action. Since no historical realization is ever likely to deprive these attitudes of all justification, they will remain entitled to their share of truth and respect.

Chapter 15

HUMAN PROGRESS

I

I F the question of human progress is ever discussed at all today, and the topic is more embarrassing than fashionable, it is likely to be raised indirectly as the question of human survival, whether mankind can escape from the international jungle and from the malthusian coils which draw tighter. The heady idea of progress which made our fathers and grandfathers patronize the past is of course as clean gone as an exploded shell. For one thing, we see the vicious circle in which we move in virtue of the efficiency of our national organizations, the ironic logic of conflict in the state of nature which Hobbes described long enough ago and in which some contemporaries have rediscovered the doctrine of original sin. The beaten highway of linear advance does not get one out of a vicious circle. One can break out of it only by jumping into a new orbit. The attempt was made after the first world war in the League of Nations, which was going to provide the world with collective security. And the psychological opportunity was repeated with the end of the second world war, and the attempt renewed. It has not succeeded yet, and whether or not it can succeed is at issue. Quantitative change sometimes becomes qualitative change, and it may be that atomic power will introduce into the situation not only additional physical power but also a psychological difference which makes all the difference, creates a new situation which does in fact break the vicious circle, although the fact may not be recognized for a long time. If things were to turn out this way, the historical materialist would have no reason to be surprised: men forced by the momentum of material advance to make the progress their own wills had been impotent to achieve. There is nothing surprising in this even for

236

those who deny the thesis of historical materialism, for the undeniable close interdependence of voluntary and involuntary factors is the firm ground of both positions. For the historical materialist, the self-direction of humanity will come through the necessary destruction of the old owners of the means of production and rulers of the state who are inescapably caught in the contradictions of capitalism and unable to act save in defence of their class interests. For others, the self-direction of humanity is a difficult possibility, like the self-direction of a person, and a possibility which has come within human scope only with the techniques and creation that have gone to the making of one world. How may these inventions serve this purpose, and towards what end would human self-direction move?

Obviously, science is the fundamental human device that has made unification of the world possible, and has contributed enormously to man's consciousness of himself and his power to mould his environment. Obviously, if human self-direction is given all its dimensions it implies democratic principles and procedures dyed in the fabric of society. Science and democracy as historical achievements are the two wheels which make human progress and self-direction on a world scale practicable. Less obviously, but not less certainly, science and democracy were not inevitable historical achievements. There have been civilizations without them. They are therefore not indispensable to human existence in the future. On the other hand, there is nothing arbitrary about them; they are genuine discoveries and tested devices and they imply universal standards; that is to say, they may be abused and perverted. Thus they are not only practical means by which a universal civilization may be achieved but also criteria by which civilization may be judged. It would be unhistorical to judge past civilizations by their lack of science or democracy. The performance of the Roman Empire or of medieval Christendom is to be measured by its own characteristic ideals. It would be unhistorical not to judge modern civilization by reference to its own characteristic ideals, namely, science and democracy. If progress in the Roman Empire meant making the empire come true, making it more like itself, without reference to what went before or what was to follow, is there any sense at all in the idea of human self-direction towards human self-realization, is anything possible other than incommensurable phases of self-realization in historical modes differently conditioned? The question must be ballasted with some of the plain facts of historical human existence before it can be handled and brought to port.

The basic fact is that human existence sets mankind certain permanent problems, and that civilizations take shape with the solutions which men find for these problems as they have to deal with them concretely, employing the resources available to them. In solving these problems, examples are set and resources are developed by which later generations profit, and they profit also by the consciousness of themselves and of their tasks which they gain from comparison with other generations and their achievements. But the permanent problems remain, and have to be solved by each generation on the conditions set. What are these permanent problems?

II

(1) *The economic problem.* Economic needs are primary, and society is primarily organized for economic production, and to that extent its order is determined by the modes of production. There are well-marked stages in the development of economic production, but there is no final solution of the problem, since its conditions vary with population, raw materials, markets, productive techniques and organization, and many other factors. There is no solution which suits all conditions of the problem. To say that modern industry backed by science has solved the problem of production definitively is to ignore the extremely acute problems set by modern mass production. And policies associated with this large-scale development of science and industry have gravely aggravated the population problem, so that these conditions can all too easily result in greater net misery than was endured in more primitive and less productive economies. The improved techniques of production, bound up with an accelerating rate of improvement, set the modern conditions of the problem, rather than solve it out of hand. It is as idle to think that some form of industrial organization, say capitalism or communism, solves the problem as to think that in themselves the productive techniques of a machine economy solve them. The immensely increased productive capacity of modern industry is a prime condition of a relatively high standard of living and leisure all round (which may be considered as what is meant by solving the economic problem), but it is not a sufficient condition, for it creates severe and intractable problems, and unless they are

solved, earlier (irrecoverable) solutions will have been more successful.

(2) *The political problem.* The struggle for power for the sake of economic goods is a problem between groups in quite primitive conditions, and within groups as soon as they enjoy a settled existence with established property rights. The entire male population of a primitive group may engage exclusively in political action, in the form of war, instead of in economic production. Within the group, the ruling class may be a military caste whose domestic revenues are swelled by the plunder of war and empire. It is the nature of the political problem that it is regarded as solved by those who dispose of power securely, who can do injustice without having to suffer it; and for those who cannot do it and are obliged to suffer it the problem is urgent. The liberal solution of assuring equal security to all by treating the political problem as the problem of reconciling interests, instead of the question who shall kill whom, is universal in principle, and so is its analogue in international affairs, collective security, the principle that the sole justifiable use of force is to suppress the use of force; but the constitutional, institutional, or procedural checks and devices to give effect to the principle may be used in ways or for purposes which nullify the advantages they offer, and none of them can meet the intransigence of those who are determined to force the issue and to raise the ultimate question, and solve the political problem that way. Apart from this question of will, which is of the essence of the problem, there are practical difficulties and tendencies in working democratic institutions which threaten either to defeat democracy or to defeat effective government. Thus democracy, which in theory is the very type of final solution, founded on universal principle and an irreplaceable ideal, in practice is the very type of solution that is itself a hazardous problem.

(3) *The moral problem.* Traditionally and in principle the moral problem can hardly be separated from the political problem, for what ought to be done and aimed at by rational men, how they ought to behave towards one another and conduct their personal lives, is not a question which can be answered apart from established rights and expectations in an existing order of society. Metaphysical or religious notions of duty or right may be disguised revolutionary claims or justifications of the right to do injustice and not to suffer it; what is 'really' right and proper cannot be determined in abstrac-

tion from the actual order, for general principles which can be pronounced in abstraction are too general to have any content, and solve no problems. If the solution requires due weight to be given to social interests, individual interests, and rational norms, it is one that has continuously to be found in practice, but this is a morality that goes with democracy and is repudiated by authoritarian systems. The case for the 'open society' as morally superior to authoritarian systems has theoretical foundations, but essentially it is one that has to be made good in practice, so that to attempt to solve the moral problem on democratic assumptions is a venture of faith, an historical movement still in the making.

(4) *The problem of truth.* Rationality is in the end the distinctive characteristic and the rallying-point of humanity, however powerful irrational motives may be, and therefore the problem of truth is the most important of all the permanent problems of mankind. Scientific truth is triumphantly secure in its practical competence. Science raises two major problems which science cannot solve. The first is about the uses of science. Of course science can be used to save or to destroy, but that is not the radical problem; the radical problem here is how far man is to treat man scientifically. In a multitude of particular ways men apply scientific knowledge to men beneficially. Men may be treated scientifically in a total way. Science is drastic simplification that disregards individual cases. Man can be planned most simply and effectively by relying on certain cardinal generalizations and disregarding other possibilities. The rule of a priestly caste is superseded by the rule of a scientific *élite* or their managers. Such a regime produces a total solution of the whole complex of permanent problems. Marxist communism is only one early form of this type of solution. The respect for the individual in democracy, with the consequent untidiness, waste, indiscipline, and frustration of rational method, may be a source of irritation to the scientist. If science and democracy are the two wheels of progress, looked at on a world scale and not in the special conditions we are most familiar with, it does not seem likely that they will be easily yoked.

The other major problem is about the status of scientific knowledge. The question is whether there is any other source of knowledge or not. The claim of religions to non-scientific knowledge about the nature and destiny of man is in question. The final settlement of this question would make a great difference to the human future. But it is a question whether it can be settled beyond reasonable dispute. In any case that is a problem which science sets and cannot solve.

(5) *The religious problem.* Even if the question of truth were decided against the religions, there would remain the problem of reconciling man to his situation. There is the cosmic situation as well as the historical situation, and a satisfactory solution of all the historical problems does not necessarily imply a satisfactory solution of the cosmic problem of man's case. The solution is personal and therefore can never be definitive. Although personal to the end, it is always of the greatest social importance, a public concern.

(6) *The cultural problem.* Under this head can be comprehended a complex of related problems: the educational problem; the problem of maintaining and developing the arts and sciences; above all, the problem of the unity of culture and of the service of culture to life. Such problems are concerned with the delicate and all-important transmission of the human inheritance, dangerous both to the inheritance and to the spontaneous new life of another generation.

III

These permanent, complex, and interconnected problems, merely indicated above, have to be dealt with on the conditions on which they are concretely presented and with the means available, and to this extent different civilizations and different ages are incommensurable, in that it is not open to them to deal with the same problems in the same way. But the problems are permanently the same general problems, and there is continuity in dealing with them and an accumulation of reliable experience and of tested techniques. That is why progress would seem inevitable but for some dark perversity in human nature. Why should not human beings, steadily, sometimes rapidly, increasing in their knowledge of and power over themselves and their environment, solve their problems increasingly well, and ultimately with complete success? One major reason is, as indicated above, that each solution develops a train of consequential problems, some of them formidable, so that in practice the new and more resourceful or highly developed solution may be more exacting, make severer demands on human intelligence and character, than simpler solutions, and cause deterioration, more or less serious and perhaps catastrophic. It is absurd to think that the problems of production, of power, of truth, have been disposed of or definitively solved, respectively, by the machine and the resources of technology, representative government and free institutions, science; and it is equally absurd to think that these contributions to the solution are not revolutionary and, without catastrophe, irreversible, and do not raise human life to a higher power.

Although the permanent problems may be separated for the purpose of analysis and for other special purposes, they are vitally interconnected and call for an integral solution in society. They constitute one general problem. In Europe, Britain, and America, it is basically the problem of science and industry in a political democracy, or the problem of political democracy in an industrial and scientific society: the attempted solution of each problem conditions the others and requires a total solution of the whole complex. In the Soviet Union, and wherever that model is followed, the pattern of the integral solution is given as definitive, and all consequential problems are treated as local and dealt with by tactical manoeuvres.

Without exploring other vital differences between these two alternatives which divide the world, attention must be called again to the concepts of science and democracy which are characteristic and dominant interests in both and which were the key concepts in the idea of progress, for it was the liberal faith that by popular enlightenment and popular emancipation increasing prosperity and well-being would be achieved. Essential to both concepts in the Western mind is their sovereign universality. The phrase bourgeois science makes most Western scientists contemptuous. Equal laws and invariable public procedures in their making and enforcement claim as much objectivity and operational certainty as scientific methods. Yet Soviet science is both science and different from bourgeois science, and Soviet democracy both democracy and different from bourgeois democracy. In both regimes the two (science and democracy) are connected, historically and in principle. By science in the West is meant the pure research programme and its results which are, as it were, put on the market. No doubt the pure research programme exists also in the Soviet Union (in spite of Lysenko), but in organization and utilization science is yoked to a different democratic principle. The line which separates pure research from the applications of its results is real and of great importance, but in practice it is easily and frequently blurred and obliterated; and in the Soviet Union science means for the most part, though improperly, the application of science to democracy, and democracy is subject to the applications of science, for by democracy is meant basically economic production. Soviet science works within the frame of an ideology which is itself science applied to the nature and destiny of man. Such a science of man is a drastic simplification for the sake of bold treatment based on certain features: on certain scientific theses, man is planned (primarily) as an agent of economic production. In Western societies, the applications of science are still subject to democracy, understood as respect for the individual man. The Soviet economy applies engineering methods to man, treats man in the mass with the object of satisfying average wants under discipline. The Western economies attempt more complex satisfactions, and without a ruthless break with traditional interests and tastes and without direct compulsions. This exposes them to many risks: it carries along anomalies and inefficiencies; it allows indifference and hostility to science and its applications; middle-class luddites may exercise widespread sabotage of rational plans; employer-labour conflicts may become a serious strain; market fluctuations and dislocations may get out of control. The Soviet type of economy also has its strains and its problems, but its single-minded consideration of the mass, undisputed central control, and direct disposal of all resources simplify the problem. Moreover, it is a solution whose tested techniques are readily learned by a politically conscious *élite* and are readily applicable to the conditions of backward countries with dense populations.

The Soviet context of science and the Soviet conception of democracy as industrial development for the mass-production of goods and services for the masses, with hostility to every other interest, are likely to prevail for a long time to come in a large part of the world. This is far more a matter of history and local conditions than of the truth and merit of rival ideologies. In great part, communism is the response of backward peoples to the challenge of the industrial revolution in the West, it is their attempt to equip themselves in a hurry to survive in an industrialized world. Russia and China have suffered as the prey of their industrialized neighbours. The West can hold its own, and keep the initiative which was taken with the industrial revolution, not by propaganda offensives or offensives of any kind, nor by argument and conclusive refutations, nor by declarations of principles and ideals, nor by purges, but solely by solving the human problem with liberal democratic principles, that is to say, in spite of them and because of them. The Western demo-

R*   243

cratic nations are called to save themselves by their exertions and the world by their example. Any other course is but play-acting. For communism, in so far as it is not the conspiracy in the cave of Adullam, nor the despair of idealists, is the faith and discipline of people being industrialized in a hurry. Those in the Western democracies who solve the problem of communism by embracing the new faith or by retreating to old faiths, stampeded into either of the opposed camps, or by exploiting the heroics of despair in the moral isolation of no-man's-land, salve their own feelings but solve nothing and save nothing. The problem, as always, is not communism but the human problem, the complex of permanent problems, which have to be solved in the form in which they are set us, for the life and achievement of the generations of our time. Where communism is, for any reason, better equipped to solve them than the Western democracies, it will prevail. It is unhistorical and unphilosophical to see in the rivalry of the two ideologies a new period of religious wars for the sake of ideals and values. It is, rather, a period of consolidation and construction, consolidation of the revolution which undermined the basis of the old orthodoxy and the old legitimacy, construction of a new basis for world-wide collaboration in solving for all, though never for all time, the complex human problem. If the issue between the two rivals is allowed to develop as a religious war, the worst aspect of each will grow dominant and develop a common likeness. If it is turned to honest differences of approach to the common human problem, the best aspect of each can grow dominant and develop a common likeness. This is the supreme test of statesmanship in our time. The fact that science and democracy, in spite of sharp differences of interpretation, have world-wide authority as the dominant characters of contemporary society, emerges as a decisive contribution to a universal civilization, a common consciousness of the human problem, the possibility of communication, a unique standard of progress.

Appearances are to the contrary, and we are more exercised by the deep division, the break in communication, which is made by the difference in the conceptions of science and democracy than we are impressed by the meaning for the future of man of what they have in common. Attempts to bridge the gap in communication are less to the point than a sustained effort to solve the complex human problem on democratic terms, to achieve social integration by democratic methods, to become scientifically educated as a people. A self-disciplined, socially minded, scientifically educated people can in the long run defeat communism without fighting it. In any case, it cannot be destroyed by fighting.

Some people feel that it is democracy itself, the century of the common man, that eclipses the splendours of the human tradition and plunges mankind into a long night of mediocrity. On that view, it does not matter much whether the sleep is induced by communist violence or by slower and more complicated methods. Science, too, may be a refuge from thought and from life, and it may be employed solely for vulgar satisfactions. Progress, in these terms, is just a word for degeneration. These were the thoughts of Nietzsche, but they may stand for the opinions of a substantial minority. An answer might ramble over the entire earth, but one that is near at hand is quite conclusive: it is not open to this generation to live on the historical terms offered to the past, nor on imaginary and preferred terms; the live options are only to live well or ill upon the set terms. If it is the century of the common man, and nothing can make it otherwise, then that can be made a good thing or a bad thing. Every set of conditions on which the permanent problems are posed has characteristic tendencies and dangers, but they are not fixed and necessary characters. Science and democracy, taken as representing contemporary conditions of the human problem, have characteristic tendencies seen in communism and in political democracy and feared in Nietzsche's thoughts; but they have also other possibilities for the self-realization of man.

The set historical conditions, say, feudal Christendom or science and democracy, cannot be radically altered, but they are not merely given materials out of which to make something good or bad, perfected or botched, they are also, and primarily, phases of development. In the present phase of human development, as always, many possibilities of failure are open, failure to solve major problems on the conditions set, failures of mankind or of local groups; and there are possible solutions which might achieve grotesque success, in the applications of science to man, for example. The only success that would constitute progress would come through further development of science and democracy in continuity with the past and in application to the permanent problems as posed in the present, leading to a more subtle understanding and resourceful mastery of science and its uses and to a growth of the moral, psychological, and economic tissues of democracy and a quickening of its nisus to completion. This acquired mastery of the instruments of human development is necessary to the creation of a profounder experience of man and his possibilities. Progress has no meaning if it looks only forward and is contrasted with an obsolete past, for the past is one of its present dimensions. It is human development as a whole, with its interdependent material basis and conscious spirit; it is human self-discovery, which puts out one eye if it relinquishes the past. This human self-discovery which requires the past as well as the future, and which with growing awareness increasingly initiates and creates the future of man, has it an ideal term, a possible historical consummation?

IV

The question cannot be divorced from the permanent human problems from which mankind never can be freed. Even if the ultimate core of historical religion is not able to resist the corrosion of reason, if faith has laid up its treasures where moth and rust consume and where thieves break through and steal, and even if the other problems are successfully solved by any generation, and all consequential problems no less successfully dealt with, there would remain the human situation in its cosmic aspect; and although this is primarily and ultimately a personal problem, it also has an important social aspect; it is one of the problems that have to be taken into account in any estimate of progress. Birth and death, and the intermediate phases of human existence, aggression and trespass in the grain of human volition and action, chance and fate, the bitter uncertainty and fragility of things, the appalling ironies, the temporal structure of human existence and its entailed futilities: on the unchangeable cosmic fact is superimposed the social fact, and the relation between them has great consequences for human happiness and for the quality of life. The social fact may be so long-established, so intimate, full, and sweet, that it lies upon and obliterates the cosmic fact, and the canvas is not seen, not even the painted canvas, only the illusion, the picture: the domestic importance of every day, stretching back into the remembered past and forward into the proposed future, extinguishes in bright daylight the flickering of the brief candle; the comfort of common sense and flesh and blood is always there to chase into absurdity the moral nightmares of solitariness; if the recurrent pleasures and mild excitements of social intercourse suffice, there is none to think of storms, of violence and cruelty; from childhood to old age, the even flow of the diary is gently swelled by confessed emotions and related accidents that hardly disturb the surface of delighted uneventfulness from daylight to dark. The social fact, it has been said, is the foundation of English literature, in this sense of painting its illusion on the cosmic fact. On the other hand, the social fact may be weak, not yet established or in dissolution, as in the rough pioneer lands of yesterday or in Europe of today; and then the brute facts of our natural condition impose themselves on the naked and exposed human spirit. The later indigenous literature of America and contemporary European literature are founded on the uncovered cosmic fact, and existentialism has engaged in stripping off the social fact, even in the form of social religious assurances, in order to reveal personality to itself in its cosmic situation.

The existentialist attempt to awaken men from slumber under the social fact, and to get them to play their authentic part by taking in moral isolation individual life-making decisions, would atomize a problem that is basically social. (That the social solution must respect and include the cosmic problem was the fundamental insight of Plato and of Hegel, as it is of Paul Tillich.) Society is a human construction founded and maintained by solutions of the historical and cosmic problems which man's life is. If its solution of the historical problems ignores or distorts the cosmic problem, the house is built on sand. But how can society possibly solve the cosmic problem? Not by making human life violent and cruel, as though in conformity with nature; nor by making it all that spinster gentility would have it. Men, however, may in their social initiatives and through the structure of society respect the phasing of human life and meet and mitigate the hazards, the strife, the fatality, making use of the very conditions that threaten to undermine or to overwhelm human existence. For human life will always be in question, will always demand the skill and courage that can ride the whirlwind, will always buffet and defeat those who are passive and seek refuge, and this is first a social initiative beyond the scope of an individual's resources, but completed in personal life. In this sense a society may attempt to solve the religious problem, as the groundwork of personal life, by an integral solution of the complex of historical problems which respects and uses the cosmic conditions of human existence. This would be the supreme example of an economy, in which it would be false to see only the problems solved, and false to see only the life achieved. This is mankind in its maturity, and as a universal achievement it sets the goal and the standard of human progress.

INDEX

INDEX

Jesus, ethical teaching of, 174; imagination of, 54
Jews, dependence of upon God, 54, 57, 152, 175
Joubert, J., 188
Justice: confused with love, 175–9, 193–6; marxist view of, 103, 124; epicurean definition of, 92

Kant, Immanuel, 99
Kautsky, Karl, 141
Keynes, J. M., 108
Kierkegaard, S., 153, 185, 220

Latourette, K. S., 168
Law: universal, 37–8, 87; natural, 31, 36, 79; final, the object of Greek intellect, 7, 9, 43
Lenin, V.I.U., 99, 112–41 *passim*,
Leninism, 127–34, 141–2
Leonardo da Vinci, 28, 69
Liberalism, 226–8, 231
Locke, John, 32–7, 39, 40, 176
Love, confusion of with justice, 175–179, 193–6
Lukacs, Georges, 126

Machiavelli, Nicolo, 21, 231
Major, H. D. A., 161
Malthus, T. R., 46
Man: biblical conception, of, 181–4; predicament of, 186; situation of not determinate, 187
Mannheim, Karl, 189
Marcel, Gabriel, 160, 221
Maritain, Jacques, 161, 167, 168
Marx, Karl, 45, 100–42
Marxism: to be taken seriously, 97, 140; character of, 97; and philosophy, 98–9, 141–2; and the conception of history, 101–3; and the analysis of capitalism, 104–8; vision of, 109; strategy of, 110–14, 121–4, 129–35; contradictions of, 113–5, 117; and revolution, 115; and the social programme, 117; assumptions of, 135–6; appeal of, 136; general theory of, a

misconception, 137–40; fanaticism of, 142
Mediocrity, fear of, 50, 245
Milton, John, 26
Montaigne, Michel de, 21–3
Montesquieu, Baron de, 21, 42–3
Morality: ancient preoccupation with, 11, 13, 29, 41; simplicity of, 74; problem of, 239; knowledge of, 71–74, 84–7; naturalistic theories of, 75; customary, 76; and new claims, 77; and dues, 78–81; ideal of, 81–3; marxist idea of, 102–3, 129; error of platonic, 76; not the same as social order, 77; is self-sustaining, 78
Mussolini, Benito, 115

Neibuhr, Reinhold, 180–98
Niebuhr, Richard, 207
Nietzsche, F.W., 47, 50, 195, 222, 245

Occam, William of, 18
Organic theories, 227–31

Padua, 19
Participation, 152, 235
Pascal, Blaise, 68
Pater, Walter, 20, 48
Pattison, Mark, 199, 200
Peirce, C. S., 92
Pericles, 4, 8, 10
Plato, 6, 8, 16, 99, 101, 175, 247
Platonism, 16, 19, 26, 228; and Christianity, 15, 16, 19, 23, 26, 175, 229
Pomponazzi, Pietro, 19–20
Pragmatism, at Harvard, 46
Problems, the permanent, 116, 238–42
Progress, 47–8, 65, 188, 190, 191, 236–48; not a law, 241; distinguished from success, 245
Protestantism, 32, 152, 164, 219
Proudhon, P. J., 120, 142

Ramus, Peter, 19
Reason, 31, 34, 36, 37, 38, 52–3, 92, 240
Reformation, 24, 156, 182–4

251

INDEX

Religion: Greek, 4–7, 10; pagan, 57*n*; natural, 37–9, 87; problem of, 172, 241, 246–8

Renaissance, 18–25, 181–4, 224; an educational programme, 19; an archaeology, 20; a revival of platonism and stoicism, 24; consummation of in the eighteenth century, 38

Republic, The, 67, 152, 175, 228

Ricardo, David, 46, 106

Romanticism, 225–6, 232

Roman Empire, 9, 155, 237

Saint-Simon, Comte de, 120

Santayana, George, 99, 170, 226

Sartre, Jean-Paul, 48, 222

Scheler, Max, 49

Science: Greek, 6–9; in seventeenth century, 30, 37; in Soviet Union, 242–3; purpose of, 55; application and propagation of, 67; insufficiency of, 58; ideological elements in, 59–60; a source of morality, 81; a criterion of progress, 245; and truth, 240; and marxism, 111–17; and democracy, the fundamental historical achievements, 50, 237

Scott, Geoffrey, 19, 20

Self-interest, 40, 93, 94, 176, 178, 192–196

Sieyès, E. J., 42

Smith, Adam, 46, 104, 105

Socinianism, 19, 35

Sorel, Georges, 47

Sorokin, Pitirim, 177

Sparta, 8

Stalin, J., 112, 113, 114, 126–35

Stoicism, 7, 15, 23, 90, 219, 232

Theocracy, 27, 42, 229

Thomism, 16–17, 159–60

Thucydides, 4, 8

Tillich, Paul, 157–9, 164, 168, 247

Toleration, 13–14, 33–6, 170, 203–4, 212–13

Tolstoy, Leo, 177

Toynbee, Arnold, 11, 47, 153–6, 164–6

Tradition: common human, 50, 81, 153, 172, 209; humanist, uncertainty of, 3, source of, 4, the Enlightenment the great epoch of, 42, as the human tradition, 48, 153, 172, as the empirical tradition, 92; religious, and gospel, 159; Catholic, 15–17, 26, 159–61, 163–5; Protestant, 27, 157–9; liberal, 21, 33–7; culture a criticism of, 64; in art, 21

Truth, problem of, 240; humanist conception of, 189–91

Turgot, A. R. J., 47

Urquhart, W. S., 197

Venice, 19

Vico, Giovanni, 44

Voltaire, 28, 47

Whitehead, A. N., 52, 112

Williams, Roger, 34